Food and Beverage Service

D. R. Lillicrap M.H.C.I. M.A.

Senior Lecturer, School of Hotel Keeping and
Catering, Ealing College of Higher Education

Edward Arnold

© D. R. Lillicrap 1971
First Published 1971
by Edward Arnold (Publishers) Ltd.,
41 Bedford Square,
London WC1B 3DQ

Reprinted 1973, 1974, 1975, 1976, 1978
(twice), 1979

ISBN: 0 7131 1664 1

Printed and bound in Great Britain
at The Pitman Press, Bath

Contents

Preface

The contents of this book lead from the basic principles involved in food and beverage service to the more advanced food service techniques, banqueting organization and administration; basic drink service and the service of wines. These are followed by a brief survey of those other areas of food and beverage service that may interest the trainee and help him to decide which path he should take in his chosen career.

The book is suitable for the following courses, and is meant as a guide to the correct approach, procedures and techniques in all aspects of the work: Ordinary National Diploma in Hotel Keeping and Catering Operations; Higher National Diploma in Hotel Keeping and Catering Administration; 441 General Catering Diploma, Membership of the Hotel and Catering Institute, and the Food and Beverage Service courses offered by the City and Guilds of London Institute in conjunction with the Hotel and Catering Industry Training Board—the Food Service Certificate, Alcoholic Beverage Certificate and the Advanced Serving Techniques Certificate.

Acknowledgements

Most of the photographs were taken specially for the book at Ealing Technical College. We wish to thank the following for permission to reproduce other copyright photographs: p. 137 Allied Ironfounders Ltd.; p. 142 Marks & Spencers Ltd.; p. 147 GKN Sankey Ltd.; p. 151 Thomas A. Wilkie; p. 153 Watney Mann Ltd.; p. 155 Quantas; p. 159 Cunard; p. 162 Photo Coverage Ltd.; p. 164 Practical Press Ltd.; Grosvenor House p. 169.

Notes to the lecturer

From my experience it would appear that it depends very much on the lecturer whether or not his students find their subject interesting. A student can absorb only a certain amount of information over the limited period of one lesson. I have found it useful to break the lesson down into a series of steps, each one leading to the next and designed to hold the students interest so that he will be prompted to take part in the lesson by asking questions and through discussion. The series of steps might take the following pattern—Revision of previous material; introduction; development (new material); conclusion and questions.

Depending of the time available it is always a great help to commence a lesson by recapping on the previous one, and this should then act as a stepping stone for new information to be introduced. Where possible a lecture should include a visual demonstration. It is much easier to talk about something which can be seen.

Revision of the knowledge that has been acquired is vital and the direct question and answer method is of limited use as only one student can respond at a time and it becomes boring for the rest. I have developed a number of revision exercises which I have found catch the imagination of the student and hold his interest and Chapter 27 contains a selection. These ideas may be of some interest and use to other lecturers in Food and Beverage Service.

1 introduction

The aim of this book is to guide the trainee who has decided to enter the Hotel and Catering Industry as a profession through the basic stages of food and beverage service to the skilled work of the experienced operator. The trainee must be keen, ambitious, interested, and have initiative, a pleasant manner and the ability to accept change and be able to keep up with modern ideas as they affect his work.

Whereas formerly 'waiting' was regarded as a menial task, today the waiter is a member of a recognized profession. As an individual, the waiter or waitress, demonstrates his or her skill and technique at the table in front of the guest by giving a quick and efficient service. It is a profession for which there will always be a demand and which cannot be fully automated.

Management has many responsibilities which include the economics of costing the menu; portion control; wastage of food; customer-staff relations; labour shortages; staff training. If good relations exist between management and staff then problems are few and the atmosphere will be pleasing to the customer. The food service operators play an important part in the achievement of such good relations. Since they are in constant contact with the customer and with management their conduct influences the running of the establishment and the atmosphere created for the customer.

The opportunities for advancement in the profession are many, in such positions as restaurant manager; banqueting manager; station head waiter; wine waiter; catering officer, and so on depending on the type of establishment in which you finally decide to work. According to the individual and the type of catering in which he is most interested there is work in hotels and restaurants; catering organizations; hospital catering; welfare catering; clubs; industrial catering; residential catering; transport catering; and outdoor catering. Also there are many chances of seeing the world and travelling about the countries of your choice by land, sea and air, in such capacities as area or group manager; air stewardess; first class steward on the liners, or on public transport, and so on.

In this way a wealth of experience may be gathered by seeing the modern methods of food and beverage service in other countries. This book contains as much information as possible in order that the trainee may see what is involved in food and beverage service, and also to lay a sound foundation for his chosen career.

ATTRIBUTES

The waiter who wishes to progress must attain certain standards. It is most important that the service staff create a good impression on the customer, and the following points will assist him in achieving these standards.

Personal hygiene

This is of the utmost importance as the waiter is constantly handling food and working near the guest. Personal freshness is of great importance and he should be shaven, his hands immaculately clean with well trimmed, clean nails, and his hair must be short and well groomed. For waitresses, hair should be short or it should be tied up; no excessive make-up or jewellery worn. The waiter should not sneeze, cough or blow his nose near food whether in preparation or service.

A uniform must always be clean and well pressed especially trousers and jackets. Shoes should be well polished and black socks worn. Waitresses blouses and skirts or dresses, whatever type of uniform is required, as well as the appropriate aprons, should always be clean and smart. Being clean and smart in appearance gives one the confidence to work well.

Knowledge of food and drink

The waiter must have sufficient knowledge of all the items on the menu and wine list to advise and offer suggestions to the guest. He must know, how to serve correctly each dish on the menu, what its accompaniments are, the correct cover, the make-up of the dish and its appropriate garnish, and also how to serve various types of drink, in the correct glasses and at the right temperature.

Punctuality

Punctuality is all important. If the waiter is continually late on duty it shows lack of interest in his work and a lack of respect for management.

Local knowledge

In the interests of his guests the waiter should have a certain knowledge of the area in which he works so that he may be able to advise the guests on the various forms of entertainment offered; the best means of transport to places of interest and so on. This knowledge shows that the waiter is doing his utmost to give the guest satisfaction.

Personality

The waiter must be tactful, courteous, good humoured and of an even temper. He must converse with the customer in a pleasing and well spoken manner and the ability to smile at the right time pays dividends. With these attributes the waiter will help the management by becoming a good salesman.

Attitude to guests

The correct approach to the customer is of the utmost importance. The waiter must not be servile, but anticipate the guests needs and wishes. A careful watch should be kept on the guests at all times during the service without staring. Care should always be taken when dealing with the difficult customer. Never argue with the guest which will only aggravate the situation, but refer all complaints to someone in authority in the food service area, *i.e.* Restaurant manager or the Head waiter.

Memory

This is an essential asset to the waiter. It may help him in various ways in his work if he knows the likes and dis-likes of his guests, i.e. where they may like to sit in the food service area what are their favourite drinks and so on.

Honesty

This is all important to the waiter in his dealings with both the customer and the management. If there is trust and respect in the triangle of waiter/customer/management relationships, then there will be an atmosphere for work which encourages efficiency and a good team spirit amongst the food and beverage service operators.

OBLIGATIONS

TO MANAGEMENT

The waiter's obligations and loyalty are firstly to the establishment in which he is employed and its management. He should consider the following points:

Conduct

The waiter's conduct should be impeccable at all times, especially in front of the guest. The rules and regulations of an establishment must be followed, and respect shown to all senior members of the staff.

Punctuality

One of the waiter's assets is punctuality, which shows interest and keeness in one's work. The waiter should report on duty a few minutes before the service is due to commence so that he may check his station, sideboard and have a complete knowledge of the menu.

Appearance

The highest standards should always be maintained by the waiter. First impressions in the food service area go a long way towards creating a favourable image to the guest and attracting further custom.

Salesmanship

As has already been mentioned, the waiter works in the front of the house—the food service area—and he, to a large extent, reflects the image of the establishment. He is a salesman, and must therefore have a complete knowledge of all forms of food and drink and their correct service. Presentation of food and drink is all important and the work of a skilled chef should not be spoilt by the incompetence of the waiter, or there may be very quickly a loss of trade and good will.

Sense of urgency

So that the establishment has the maximum amount of business over the service period, with as high a net profit as possible, the waiter must develop a sense of urgency.

TO THE CUSTOMER
So that the waiter may give a complete service to the customer, he should observe the following points:

Customer satisfaction

The waiter must see that the guests have all they require and are completely satisfied. It is of great importance to anticipate a customer's needs. If he is comfortable in his surroundings then this is because of the warm and friendly atmosphere in the food service area, and the team spirit amongst the waiting staff.

Menu knowledge

The waiter must have sufficient knowledge of the menu; the make-up of the different dishes and their garnishes; the correct covers; accompaniments and service, in order that he may advise the guest in his choice.

Complaints

The waiter should have a pleasant manner, showing courtesy and tact, an even temper and good humour, and never displeasure even though at times things may be difficult. He should never argue with a guest, and if he cannot deal with the situation himself it should be referred immediately to a senior member of the team, who, because of his greater experience will be able to calm the guest and put right any fault. Remember loss of time in dealing with complaints only makes the situation worse.

THE RESPONSIBILITY OF THE SOMMELIER
The Sommelier or wine waiter must always bear in mind that a certain very profitable proportion of an establishment's turnover is in the sale of alcoholic and non-alcoholic beverages. He therefore holds a position of some importance within the food and beverage service team, and his efficiency may well determine, to a large extent, the financial position of an establishment. The Sommelier must have an extensive knowledge of all forms of drink and its correct service in order that he may advise his guests.

Management and the customer

Depending on the type of establishment and the area in which it is situated the Sommelier must abide by the licensing laws governing the establishment and also any rules and regulations that may be laid down by the management in connection with the license that they hold.

He must see that no alcoholic drinks are served in the food service area after the permitted hours; that all guests partaking of a meal are notified some ten minutes before the end of the permitted hours and any last orders taken. This achieves the maximum sale of drink for the establishment but he must then be sure that guests are aware that they have only half an hour for consumption after the end of the permitted hours. When this half hour is up then all tables will be cleared by the Sommelier or wine waiter.

It would be the responsibility of the Chef d'étage (Floor waiter), and the Lounge waiter to make certain that any alcoholic drink ordered after the permitted hours was paid for or signed for by the resident. From this it is clear that the Sommelier must have an extensive knowledge of the licensing laws and their operation in order to protect the establishment and maintain its reputation, and at the same time obtain maximum sales and customer satisfaction.

FOOD SERVICE AREAS

There are many different varieties of 'food service areas', each providing a service and aimed at attracting a certain sector of the community. Each is equally important in its own right, catering for the demands of the potential client who is drawn from the 'eating out public'. The basic factors to remember here would be the cost of the dishes offered in relation to the site of the establishment and the type of service offered, and the speed of turnover in relation to the customer time available.

In order to differentiate very simply between these various forms of 'food service areas' a brief description of each is given below.

First class or luxury hotel

This would normally have several restaurants open to both residents and non-residents; grill rooms; banqueting suites and private rooms. Each restaurant would have its own full brigade of waiters who would offer to the guests a choice of dishes from an extensive à la carte menu. Control of food served would be by means of the triplicate checking system (see page 94). On a number of evenings each week the main restaurant may offer a dinner-dance where a band would be playing and some light entertainment offered in the form of a cabaret.

The grill room would account for the majority of the non-resident trade and generally has a large turnover of custom. Here there would be no music but a very relaxed and pleasant atmosphere. All forms of alcoholic beverage offered would be from the dispense bars and cellar, and again a tight control would be kept. It follows that the luxury hotel would be fully licensed. The restaurant brigades would consist of full-time members of staff, whereas banqueting staff are normally engaged on a casual basis, as and when required. Depending upon the establishment the restaurant brigades would work either 'straight' or 'split' shifts in order to cover the service of all meals to the full.

Medium class licensed hotel

This would generally have only one restaurant catering for both residents and non-residents, and have a good turnover of trade depending upon where the establishment is sited. It would not carry such a complete restaurant brigade, there being a Head waiter in charge with a brigade of waiters under him. The menu offered would be an à la carte supported by a limited table d'hôte. Control, once again, would be by means of the triplicate checking system. There would be a seasonal banqueting trade, and the staff for this would be engaged on a casual basis.

An occasional supper or dinner dance would be offered by the establishment together with some form of cabaret in order that the establishment might promote sales and establish a reputation. Alcoholic beverages would be sold through the dispense bars, and a very tight control kept.

Unlicensed hotel

This would have only one restaurant to cope with residents and a very limited non-resident trade. The restaurant brigade would be made up of a Head waiter with a small staff under him, who would work on a 'split-shift' basis to cover the service of all meals. Afternoon teas would be covered by one member of the brigade on a rota basis. There would be no seasonable banqueting trade as such but only an occasional small luncheon or dinner party. The menu offered would be a three or four-course table d'hôte menu for lunch, and a four-course table d'hôte menu for dinner possibly supported in each case by one or two 'plats du jour'. Control here would be by either the triplicate or duplicate checking systems depending upon the requirements of the establishment and the information desired for management purposes.

First class licensed restaurant

This follows closely upon the first class or luxury hotel, offering an à la carte and table d'hôte menu; using the triplicate checking system; having a full brigade of waiters; being fully licensed; and if it has one or two private suites or rooms attached to the premises, then holding the occasional luncheon or dinner party.

Night club

Here a very extensive and expensive à la carte menu would be offered by a full brigade of waiters. The night club would be fully licensed, offering a full range of alcoholic beverages, and control would be executed through the triplicate checking system. There would be music, dancing and a cabaret every evening.

Buttery

This is sometimes the name given to a restaurant within a luxury hotel, therefore all those general points about the luxury hotel would apply here. In some instances the à la carte menu would be supported by a small table d'hôte menu and on occasions there are speciality dishes offered from a service point set up within the buttery. This may take the form of a shellfish bar. The turnover of custom would be mainly non-resident.

Department store

Here a team of waitresses would work under a restaurant manageress or supervisor. They normally work a straight shift from 9.0 am. to 5.0 pm. to cover the service of morning coffee, luncheons and afternoon and high teas. Many of the waitresses in this form of establishment work during the luncheon period only. Checking for control purposes would take the form of the duplicate checking system. The luncheon menu offered would be a three or four course table d'hôte menu, with choices within each course and at a set price, possibly with one or two 'plats du jour' or in conjunction with a very limited à la carte menu. Speed of service would be essential here to ensure maximum turnover of custom during the service period. If a high tea were offered this would include, apart from the normal afternoon tea menu of hot toasted tea-cakes or crumpets; assorted savoury sandwiches; different types of buttered bread and a choice of pastries or gateaux, some hot snacks generally on toast or grilled, shallow fried fish or meat pasties or pies of some sort. One of the main purposes of the departmental store restaurant is to draw people into the store, to encourage them to stay and to buy more. There would be a seasonal banqueting trade where a large number of evening functions may take place. The team of staff required on such occasions would be engaged on a casual basis.

Cafeteria

Here a form of self-service is in operation, although there may be a section within the cafeteria set aside for waitress service. The number of staff would be limited to those waitresses required for service plus some staff with trollies for clearing purposes and the counter service hands. The menu would normally be displayed near the entrance and all dishes priced individually. A good presentation and display of food is essential to assist the customer in his choice, and adequate service staff are required at the various service points to ensure maximum turnover in a minimum period of time. The cashier would be sited at the end of the service counter to collect payment for the meals served before the customers are seated. Where waitress service is in operation duplicate checking would be used.

Café

Here there is usually waitress service with control by means of duplicate checking. The menu offered would be a limited table d'hôte menu possibly supported by a variety of hot snacks each individually priced. The waitress would make out the bill, and payment may be to either the waitress concerned or a cashier. It would all be 'chance' trade.

Snack and milk bars

Here to ensure maximum income and turnover of custom all the equipment required for the service of the different dishes and beverages offered would be sited behind the main counter so that it may be operated by the minimum number of staff. This therefore cuts down on the labour costs. The customer orders at the counter, and receives his order over the counter. He may then seat himself at the table or on a bar stool at the main counter to consume the item ordered. Payment would be made at the conclusion of the meal to the operator behind the main counter; or possibly on receipt of the meal over the counter; or to a waitress generally employed for clearing purposes, relaying and to ensure the payment of all bills. It is a very quick and speedy form of service. A wide variety of cold and hot milk drinks would be offered.

2 the food and beverage service area staff

The employment of staff for this area of work is one of the catering industry's major problems. 'Waiting' is not regarded in this country as a profession worthy of a career as it is on the continent. It is looked upon, by many, as a menial task rather as a servant served his master in olden times. Look round next time you are 'eating' out and see how many of the full-time waiting staff are English.

There are other problems such as split-shifts, the necessity of tips to raise the basic wage to a living wage, staff meals and facilities such as changing rooms. It is recognised and accepted that to gain maximum efficiency and production from your staff they must be given pleasant surroundings in which to work and facilities for off-duty hours; good staff meals are a further asset. Industrial catering acknowledges these needs and very often provides excellent all round facilities for staff. Many hotels and restaurants are lagging behind in this respect. It will be appreciated that the staff requirements in various establishments differ according to the style of service and menu offered; the price range; speed of turnover and time available. Below are listed the staff that may be found in a first class establishment offering a full gueridon and silver service of dishes chosen from an extensive à la carte menu.

The Restaurant manager has overall responsibility for the organisation and administration of the food and beverage service areas. This includes the lounges, floors, grill rooms, restaurants and possibly some of the private banqueting suites. It is the Restaurant manager who sets the standards for service and he is responsible for any staff training that may have to be carried out on or off the job. With the assistance

of the Reception head waiter or Head waiter he may make out duty rotas, holiday lists, and hours on and off duty so that all the service areas run efficiently and smoothly. All staff would be engaged after interviews with the Personnel manager and the Restaurant manager.

The Reception head waiter is responsible for accepting any bookings and keeping the booking diary up to date. He will reserve tables and allocate these reservations to particular stations. He greets the guests upon arrival and will take them to the table and seat them, leaving them in the charge of the Station head waiter. The Reception head waiter should have a good knowledge of food and drink and be able to instruct trainees where necessary. He would relieve the Restaurant manager or Head waiter on their days off.

The Head waiter has overall charge of the staff team in the dining room and is responsible for seeing that all the duties necessary for the pre-preparation for service are well and efficiently carried out and nothing forgotten. He will aid the Reception head waiter during the service and possibly take some orders if the Station head waiter is very busy. He helps with the compilation of the duty rotas and holiday lists. Will relieve the Restaurant manager or the Reception head waiter on their day off. This is assuming there is no Assistant Restaurant manager.

The Station head waiter has the overall responsibility for the team of staff under him and serving a set number of tables, which could be anything from 4-8 in number, from one sideboard. The set of tables under the Station head waiter's control is called a **Station.** He must have a good knowledge of food and wine and its correct service, and be able to instruct those under him. He will take the order (usually from the host) and carry out all the service at the table with the help of his Chef de rang, who is the second in command of the station. This includes any gueridon work that may be necessary.

The Chef de rang must be able to carry out the same work as the Station head waiter and relieve him on his day off. He will normally have had less experience than the Station head waiter. Both he and the Station head waiter must work together as a team to provide efficient and speedy service.

The Demi-Chef de rang is a post which is usually found only on the continent. As the term implies he is next in seniority to the Chef de rang and aids him in his work.

The Commis de rang acts by instruction from the Chef de rang. He mainly fetches and carries, may do a little service of either vegetables, sauces, offering rolls, placing plates upon the table and so on. He will also help clear the tables after each course. During the pre-preparation period he would carry out some of the cleaning and preparatory tasks.

The Debarrasseur (Apprentice) is the 'learner', having just joined the food service staff, and possibly wishing to take up waiting as a career. During the service he will keep the sideboard well filled with equipment, and he may help to fetch and carry items as required. He would carry out certain of the cleaning tasks during the pre-preparation periods. The apprentice may be given the responsibility of looking after and serving hors d'oeuvre, cold sweets or assorted cheeses from the appropriate trollies.

The Carver (Trancheur) is responsible for the carving trolly and the carving of joints at the table as required. He will plate up each portion with the appropriate accompaniment. He has to be very skilled to get the maximum number of portions from each joint with as little wastage as possible.

The Chef d'étage (Floor waiter) is respon-

Sweet Trolly: used for the presentation of all varieties of cold sweets to be served at the table. The drawer holds the service spoons and forks, pastry slice and other equipment needed for the service. The plate holder allows the waiter two free hands when serving onto the guests' plate. The edging around the upper and lower shelf is to prevent dishes from slipping off when the trolly is pushed.

sible for the service of all meals in apartments and usually works from a floor pantry. When working in this position the waiter has to serve both food and drink and must therefore have a thorough knowledge of each and the correct service involved. The meals served by the Chef d'étage may include breakfast, luncheon, dinner, tea, private luncheon and dinner parties, cocktail parties, morning coffee and so on. He is responsible to the Restaurant manager.

Lounge waiters are responsible for the service of morning coffee, afternoon teas, aperitifs and liqueurs before and after both lunch and dinner and any coffee required after meals. The lounge duties are often given to each waiter on a rota basis, with an apprentice to help.

The Sommelier (Wine butler) is responsible for the service of all alcoholic drinks during the service of meals. He must have a thorough knowledge of all drink he has to serve; of the best wines to go with certain foods and of the licensing laws in respect of his particular establishment and area. He must be a salesman and sell as much liquor as possible as this is one of the main sources of income in an establishment.

The Cocktail barman must be a responsible person versed in the skills of shaking and stirring cocktails and should have a thorough knowledge of all alcoholic and non-alcoholic drinks, the ingredients necessary for the making of cocktails and of the licensing laws.

The Chef de buffet is in charge of the buffet in the room, its presentation, the carving and portioning of the food and its service. He would normally be a member of the kitchen team.

Banqueting staff

See *Banqueting*, p. 165.

The staff requirements in various establishments will differ for a number of reasons. The following is a guide to the food and beverage service staff which you are likely to find in five main types of establishment.

Medium Class Hotel
Hotel manager
   responsible for
   booking functions
Head waiter
Waitresses
Wine waiter
Sometimes a cashier

Department Store
Catering manager
Asst. catering
   manager
Supervisor
Asst. supervisors
Cashier
Dispense barman
Wine waitress
Waitresses

Industrial Concern
Catering manageress
Asst. catering
   manageress
Supervisors
Asst supervisors
Waitresses
Steward/Butler
Counter service hands

Popular Price
   Restaurant
Restaurant manager
Waitresses
Dispense barman

Cafeteria
Catering manager
Supervisor
Asst. supervisors
Counter service hands
Trolly hands
Cashier

Uniforms

The modern trend is to have the waiter wearing black trousers, white shirt, black bow tie and then a jacket made of a synthetic material such as nylon, the colour of which can tone in with the general decor. This could be orange, pale green, blue and so on. In the case of waitresses they would wear a nylon overall—made to measure—of the appropriate colour. The traditional uniform of the waitress is the black dress with white apron and sometimes white cuffs and white head piece. The alternative to this being a black skirt and white blouse with a black bow tie and a small white apron. The style of uniform to be worn is decided by the management. In speciality restaurants the uniform may be designed to blend with a particular speciality theme. However, in many first class hotels and restaurants the traditional waiter's uniform is still worn and will be for some time to come until some foresighted manufacturer produces a uniform which is smart in appearance, pleasant to wear and economic in price. As a guide, the traditional uniform worn may be as follows:

Restaurant manager. Morning suit consisting of pin-stripe trousers, black jacket and black waistcoat; silver/grey tie.
Head waiter. Tails, black waistcoat and black bow-tie during the day, and the same during the evening, except that a white waistcoat replaces the black one.
Station head waiter. Tails, black waistcoat and black bow-tie for all meals.
Chef de rang. Tails, black waistcoat and white bow-tie all day.
Commis de rang. Black jacket, white bow-tie and a long white apron.
Debarrasseur. White jacket, black bow-tie and a long white apron.

The Chefs de rang may sometimes wear white jackets for breakfast and lunch with epaulettes, and tails for dinner.

It is worth noting here that where a uniform is provided for staff by a particular establishment, it should be fitted, pleasant to wear for the person concerned and make him feel smart and proud of wearing it whilst going about his work. The appearance of the staff is most important and is another of the finer points which must be borne in mind in the overall appearance of the room.

Mise-en-place or Pre-service preparation

The duties to be carried out before the service commences are many and varied according to the particular food and beverage service area concerned. A list of the possible jobs is shown below, but it should be noted that not all of them are applicable to every situation and there may be some jobs not listed which are peculiar to a particular establishment. The term **mise-en-place** is the traditional term used for all the duties that have to be carried out in order to have the room ready for service. In other words 'preparation for service'. A duty rota showing the jobs to be completed before service, and which member of staff is responsible, is drawn up by the Reception head waiter or Head waiter of the waiting brigade or team. The term **brigade** is used to denote the 'team of staff' working together in the dining room and on the same shift. Important in the drawing up of the duty rota are the 'duties at the end of service' (see page 10), to be completed in order to leave the room in readiness for the service of the next meal.

Daily duties

The daily duties can be stated as follows:

1. *Head waiter*
a) Check the booking diary for reservations.
b) Make out the seating plan for the day and allocate guests accordingly.
c) Make out a plan of the various stations and show where the Chef and Commis will be working.
d) Go over menu with staff immediately before service is due to commence.
e) Check that all duties re the duty rota are covered and that a full team of staff is present.

2. *Restaurant cleaning.* To include the reception area.

Every day, hoover the carpet and brush surrounds. Clean and polish swing doors and glass. Empty waste bins.

a) Brush and dust tables and chairs — Monday.
b) Polish all sideboards, window ledges and cash desk. — Tuesday.
c) All brasses to be polished. Ash trays to be emptied. — Wednesday.
d) Clean and polish the reception area — Thursday.
e) Commence again as for Monday.

Each day on completion of all duties, line up tables and chairs for laying up.

3. *Linen.* Collect the clean linen from the House keeping department; check items against list; distribute to the various service points; lay table-cloths and fold serviettes. Spare linen to be folded neatly into the linen basket.

4. *Hotplate.* Switch on the hotplate. Ensure all the doors are closed. Items to be placed in the hotplate would be according to the menu offered e.g.:
Soup plates
Consommé cups
Fish plates
Joint plates
Sweet plates
Coffee cups
Set out the required kitchen silver on top of the hotplate, including cloches. Stock up after each service with clean and polished china in readiness for the next meal service.

5. *Silver.* To be cleaned daily:
a) Spirit and electric heaters
b) Flare lamps, spirit and gas
c) Ashtrays
d) Carving trolly
Additional cleaning of cutlery, flatware and hollow-ware as per the daily rota.
Monday: All round flats, all knives, large coffee pots and milk jugs.
Tuesday: 41 cm, 46 cm, 56 cm (16, 18, 22 inch) oval flats, all forks, small coffee pots and milk jugs.
Wednesday: Round vegetable dishes and lids, all spoons, large coffee pots and milk jugs.
Thursday: Oval vegetable dishes and lids, small items of special equipment, individual soup tureens.

Friday: Any other items that it may be necessary to clean on a regular rota basis in order to ensure that everything is cleaned at regular intervals and nothing missed. At the same time by using this method anything broken or that may be in need of re-plating can be noted and put on one side for repair.

Use the method of silver cleaning most suited to the silver to be cleaned. When using such machinery as the burnishing machine always ensure that you know how to handle the machine correctly and safely so that you may obtain the best results. Read the makers instructions carefully. When using a proprietary brand of silver cleaning material again always read the instructions carefully, especially Silver Dip.

6. *Accompaniments*. Write out a stores list of any dry goods required.

Polish and refill: cruets, oil and vinegar stands, sugar basins and dredgers, peppermills and cayenne pepper pots.

Prepare all accompaniments: tomato ketchup, French and English mustard, ground ginger, horseradish sauce, mint sauce, Worcestershire sauce, Parmesan cheese.

Distribute the cruets to the tables and the accompaniments to the sideboards. For the number of accompaniments and sets of cruets to prepare, check with the Head waiter the number of sideboards and tables that will be in use.

7. *Sideboards*. Items to be placed on the sideboard after ensuring it is polished and clothed up.
a) Assorted cutlery from right to left: service spoon and forks, dessert spoons and forks. soup, tea and coffee spoons, fish knives and forks, joint knives, side knives
b) Assorted china: joint plates, fish plates, side plates, sweet plates, coffee saucers, consomme saucers, etc.; according to the menu
c) Service plate and service salver
d) Soup and sauce ladles
e) Under-flats for vegetable and entrée dishes and for sauce boats
f) Spirit or electric heater after it has been cleaned
g) Roll basket
h) Check pads, service cloths, menu's
Gueridons may have to be laid up in conjunction with the sideboards according to the type of service offered.

8. *Dispense bar*. Clean bar; restock the bar with items sold the previous day; polish glasses; clean cocktail equipment and display on the bar counter; prepare lemon slices, cocktail cherries etc.; prepare stock control sheets, ensure the necessary wines have been chilled ready for service, and that an adequate supply of ice is available.

9. *Stillroom*. Make out an order for any dry goods required from the dry goods store; prepare melba toast and butter; pre-wrapped portions or curled portions made from fresh butter; coffee in still set or according to the method used in the particular establishment concerned; hot milk or cream according to the policy of the establishment; prepare butter dishes and the appropriate services for melba toast; coffee services to include coffee pot, milk or cream jug, sugar basins (white and brown sugar) on a service salver; any special requirements to be ready such as for lemon tea and so on.

10. *Miscellaneous*. Prepare and lay up the carving trolly; sweet trolly, and Hors d'Oeuvre trolly. Polish the sideplates and fish plates required for laying up.

As the necessary preparatory work is completed the staff are to report back to the Head waiter who must check that the work has been carried out in a satisfactory manner; then re-allocate the member of staff to work involving the laying up of the room.

Duties at the end of Service

The task numbers 1-10 relate to those under 'Daily Duties' page 9
  1. The Head Waiter to supervise all the clearing up and to see that it is done properly.
  2. Responsible for clearing the cold buffet to the larder; collect and wash all carving knives; to assist generally in clearing the restaurant.
  3. Collect all linen both clean and dirty. Check that the correct quantities of each item of linen is returned. The serviettes to be tied in bundles of ten. Place all linen in the linen basket and return with the linen list to the linen room.
  4. Switch off the hotplate. Clear away any service silver remaining. Restock with clean china.
  5. Return all the silver together with the cutlery trollies to the silver store. You are respon-

sible for the neat arrangement and putting away of silver as shown by the shelf lables.

6. Collect all cruets and accompaniments. Return to their correct storage place. Where appropriate return sauces etc. to their original containers.

7. Check all the sideboards are completely empty. Hotplates are switched off and the dirty linen compartment is empty.

8. Clear down the bar top; put all the equipment away. Wash and polish used glasses. Put them away in their correct storage places. Remove all empty bottles etc. Complete consumption and stock sheets. Lock up.

9. Put away all equipment that has been used. Empty all coffee pots and milk jugs. Wash and put away. Put all perishable materials in their correct storage places. Empty still set and milk urns and wash out. Leave standing with cold water in them.

10. Empty and clean all trollies and return to their appropriate places. Any unused food

items from the trollies should be returned to the necessary department. Any silver used on the trollies to be cleaned and returned to the silver room.

Duty rota

The following diagram is a suggested duty rota showing the pre-service duties previously mentioned and how they may be allocated to a team of waiters. The exact nature of the duty rota varies with every establishment according to the duties to be performed, the number of staff, time off, and whether a split/straight shift is worked.

The object of a duty rota is to ensure that all the necessary duties are covered in order that efficient service may be carried out. At the same time it allows every member of staff to have a chance to carry out each duty in turn. This relieves the boredom of some of the more monotonous tasks.

Duty Rota Waiter	1-6-72	2-6-72	3	4	5	6	7	8	9	10	11	12	13	14-6-72	TASK No.
A	1	11	10	9	8	7		6	5	4	3	2	1		1. Head Waiter
B	2	1	11	10	9	8		7	6	5	4	3	2		2. Restaurant cleaning
C	3	2	1	11	10	9		8	7	6	5	4	3		3. Linen
D	4	3	2	1	11	10	A	9	8	7	6	5	4	A	4. Hotplate
E	5	4	3	2	1	11	W	10	9	8	7	6	5	W	5. Silver
F	6	5	4	3	2	1	A	11	10	9	8	7	6	R	6. Accompaniments
G	7	6	5	4	3	2	O	1	11	10	9	8	7	O	7. Sideboard
H	8	7	6	5	4	3	L	2	1	11	10	9	8	L	8. Dispense Bar
I	9	8	7	6	5	4	U	3	2	1	11	10	9	U	9. Stillroom
J	10	9	8	7	6	5		4	3	2	1	11	10		10. Miscellaneous
K	11	10	9	8	7	6		5	4	3	2	1	11		11. Day - off

Cleaning Sequence

So that the duties may be carried out efficiently they should proceed in a certain order. It goes without saying that the dusting would not be done after the tables are laid, or the tables and chairs all put in place before the hoovering is completed. Therefore the suggested order of work according to the duties shown on the duty rota would be as follows:

a) Dusting
b) Stacking chairs on the tables
c) Hoovering
d) Polishing
e) Arrange tables and chairs according to the table plan
f) Linen
g) Accompaniments
h) Hotplate
i) Stillroom
j) Sideboards
k) Silver cleaning
l) Miscellaneous: trollies

Some of these jobs will be carried out at the same time, and the Head waiter must ensure they are completed efficiently. We must again remember that the overall impression of the room is a very important factor, and efficient pre-service preparation will ensure this.

3 restaurant presentation and equipment

In any establishment a client's first impressions on entering the dining room are of great importance. A customer may be gained or lost on these impressions alone. The creation of atmosphere by the right choice of furnishings and equipment is therefore a contributing factor to the success of the restaurant. The choice of furniture and its placing; linen, tableware; small equipment and glassware will be determined by considering:

1. The type of clientele expected
2. The site or location
3. The layout of the food and beverage service area
4. The type of service offered
5. The funds available

Décor

Modern designs tend towards a versatile system of lighting by which a food and beverage service area may have bright lighting at lunchtime and a more diffused form of lighting in the evening. It is also an advantage to be able to change the colours of the lights for special functions, cabarets, etc. The caterer must find a colour and lighting scheme which will attract and please as many people as possible.

There is a definite association between colour and food which must not be overlooked. The following colours are regarded as most acceptable: pinks, peach, pale yellow, clear green, beige, blue and turquoise. These colours reflect the natural colours found in good and well presented foodstuffs. Bright illumination may be found in bars with light colours on the walls, but food service areas are better with dimmer illumination and warmly coloured walls, giving

a more relaxed and welcoming atmosphere. Colour should also contribute to a feeling of cleanliness. Just as colour and light play an important role so will table accessories need careful choice; slip cloths, serviettes and place mats will help to make the environment more attractive.

Furniture

Furniture must be chosen according to the needs of the establishment. Very often by using different materials, designs and finishes and by careful arrangement one can change the atmosphere and appearance of the food service area to suit different occasions.

Wood is the most commonly used material in dining-room furniture. There are various types of wood and wood grain finishes, each suitable to blend with a particular décor. Wood is strong and rigid and resists wear and stains. It is found as the principal material in chairs and tables in use in all food and beverage service areas with the exception of canteens, some staff dining-rooms or cafeterias.

Although wood predominates it must be noted that more metals, mainly aluminium and aluminium plated steel or brass are gradually being introduced into dining-room furniture. Aluminium is lightweight, hardwearing, has a variety of finishes, is easily cleaned and the costs are reasonable. One very often finds now the wooden topped table with a metal base, or the frame of a chair being light weight metal with a plastic finish for the seat and back.

Formica or plastic coated table tops may be found in many cafeterias or staff dining-rooms. These are easily cleaned, hard wearing and eliminate the use of linen. The table tops come in a variety of colours and designs suitable for all situations. If desired, place-mats may take the place of linen.

Plastics and fibreglass are now being used extensively to produce dining-room chairs. These materials are easily moulded into a single piece seat and back to fit the body contours; the legs are usually made of metal. The advantages are that these are durable, easily cleaned, light-weight, may be stacked, are available in a large range of colours and designs, and are relatively inexpensive. They are more frequently found in bars, lounges and staff dining-rooms at the moment rather than in the first class hotel or restaurant.

The general points which must be considered when purchasing equipment for a food and beverage service area are as follows:
 1. Flexibility of use
 2. Type of service to be offered
 3. Type of customer
 4. Design
 5. Colour
 6. Durability
 7. Ease of maintenance
 8. Stackability
 9. Cost, funds available
10. Availability in the future
11. Storage
12. Rate of breakage, i.e. China.

Chairs come in an enormous range of designs, materials and colours to suit all situations and occasions. Because of the wide range of styles the chairs vary in height and width, but it is sufficient to say that, as a guide, a chair seat is 46 cm (18 in) from the ground, the height from the ground to the top of the back is one metre (3 ft), and the depth from the front edge of the seat to the back of the chair is 46 cm (18 in). Points to note in purchasing are as above.

Tables come in three accepted shapes: round, square and rectangular. An establishment may have a mixture of shapes, to give variety, or tables of all one shape according to the shape of the room and the style of service to be offered. These tables will seat 2 or 4 people, and two tables may be pushed together to seat larger parties, or extensions may be provided in order to cope with special parties, luncheons, dinners, weddings, etc. By using these extensions correctly a variety of shapes may be obtained allowing full use of the room, and getting the maximum number of covers in the minimum space. In many instances the tabletop may be found to have a plasticised foam back or green baize covering which is heat resistant, non-slip, so the tablecloth will not slide about as it would on a polished wooden top table, and deadens the sound of china and cutlery being laid. As a guide tables may be said to be approximately the following sizes:

Square
76 cm (2 ft 6 in) square to seat 2 people, 1 m (3 ft) square to seat 4 people
Round
1 m (3 ft) in diameter to seat 4 people 1.52 m (5 ft) in diameter to seat 8 people
Rectangular
137 cm × 76 cm (4 ft 6 in) × (2 ft 6 in) to seat 4 people
to which extensions would be added for larger parties.

Sideboards. The style and design of a sideboard varies from establishment to establishment. It is dependent upon:
 1. The style of service and the menu offered.
 2. The number of waiters or waitresses working from one sideboard.
 3. The number of tables to be served from one sideboard.
 4. The amount of equipment it is expected to hold.

It is essential that the sideboard is of minimum size and portable so that it may be moved easily if necessary. If the sideboard is too large for its purpose it is then taking up space which could be used to seat more customers. The top should be of a heat resistant material which can be easily washed down. If a hotplate is to be used then it should be inserted in the top so that it is level with the working top. After service the sideboard is either completely emptied out or restocked for the next service. In some establishments the waiters or waitresses are responsible for their own equipment on their station. After service they restock their sideboard and it is then locked. Where this system is carried out the sideboard also carries its own stock of linen. In other words everything necessary to equip a particular waiters station or set of tables. The material used in the make-up of the sideboard should blend with the rest of the décor.

The Sideboard is used to hold all the equipment required by a waiter during the service of a meal. The design of sideboard varies from one establishment to another. The welled compartment holds a hotplate. Ensuring it will be the same level as the rest of the working surface is an important safety consideration. The cutlery drawers should hold, from right to left

Service spoons and forks
Dessert spoons and forks
Soup, tea and coffee spoons
Fish knives and forks
Meat Knives
Side Knives

(This is only a suggested order. The order used in your establishment should always be maintained for efficiency and speed of service.)

The lower compartment is used for dirty linen; the hole in the back of the sideboard above the welled hotplate area is for an electric flex to be passed through; and on the right-hand side is a tray rack. The sideboard may have fitted castors for easy moving.

The actual lay-up of a sideboard depends firstly on its construction—the number of shelves and drawers for cutlery etc.—and secondly, on the type of menu and service offered. Therefore the lay-up in every establishment could vary slightly, each being suited to its own needs and style of service and presentation. It is suggested, however, that in each particular establishment the sideboards would be laid up in the same fashion. If this is done the waiters get used to looking for a certain item in a certain place and this facilitates speedy service which is essential. The items to be found in a sideboard are shown in the photograph on page 15. These would be required if the service was a full silver service from a large table d'hôte menu running in conjunction with a limited à la carte menu. The items required would be adjusted according to the style of service to be given.

Linen

This is perhaps one of the more costly items in the overheads; therefore its control is of the utmost importance. The generally recognised routine in the majority of establishments is an exchange of one for one. In other words one clean item is issued for one dirty item handed in. The original stock of clean linen is issued upon the receipt of a requisition form written in duplicate and signed by a responsible person from the food service department. The top copy of the requisition form goes to the housekeeping department or linen room and the duplicate copy remains in the requisition book held in the food and beverage service area. This is one of the more important jobs in the preparation and is usually undertaken by one of the Chefs de rang. A surplus linen stock is usually held in the food service area in case of emergency.

At the end of each **service** the dirty linen should be noted and sent to the housekeeping department to be exchanged for clean. Because of the high cost of laundering such linen, where a tablecloth is perhaps only a little grubby a slip cloth would be placed over it for the succeeding service. This is not so expensive to have re-laundered as a tablecloth would be. Dirty serviettes when being exchanged for clean ones should be tied in bundles of ten. It is as well to mention here the wide range of disposable serviettes, place mats and tablecloths available in varying colours and qualities. A good example would be the *Calypso* range introduced to the

trade in 1969. There are also now reversible tablecloths with a thin polythene sheet running through the centre, preventing any spillages from penetrating from one side to the other. Although the expense may seem high there are many advantages, and comparable laundry charges may well be higher.

Linen should be stored on paper-lined shelves, the correct sizes together, and with the inverted fold facing outwards, which facilitates counting and control. If the linen is not stored in a cupboard it should be covered to avoid dust settling on it. There are many qualities of linen in present day use, from the finest Irish linen and cotton to the synthetic materials such as nylon and rayon. The type of linen used would depend on the class of establishment, type of clientele, the cost involved, and the style of menu and service to be offered. The main items of linen normally to be found are:

1. *Tablecloths:* 137 cm × 137 cm (54 in × 54 in) to fit a table 76 cm (2 ft 6 in) square, or a round table 1 m (3 ft) in diameter.
   183 cm × 183 cm (72 in × 72 in) to fit a table 1 m (3 ft) square.
   183 cm × 244 cm (72 in × 96 in) to fit rectangular shaped tables
   183 cm × 137 cm (72 in × 54 in) to fit rectangular shaped tables.
2. *Slipcloths:* 1 m × 1 m (36 in × 36 in) used to cover a 'grubby' tablecloth.
3. *Serviette:* 46/50 cm (18/20 in) square if linen.
   Serviette: 36/42 cm (14-17 in) square if paper.
4. *Buffet Cloths:* 2 m × 4 m (6 ft × 12 ft) this is the minimum size and where there are longer tables there may be longer cloths.
5. *Trolly Cloths and Sideboard Cloths:* are usually made from tablecloths well worn and not suitable for use on tables, mended by the housekeeping department and folded to fit a sideboard or trolly.
6. *Waiters Cloths or Service Cloths:* used by every waiter as protection against heat and to keep uniforms clean.
7. *Tea and Glass Cloths:* the best are made of linen or cotton.

China

This is an important aspect in the presentation of the table. The china must blend in with the rest of the items on the table and also with the general décor of the establishment.

More and more people are eating out and they like to see china which is cheerful and colourful in design and pattern similar to that used in their own homes. An establishment generally uses one design and pattern of china, but when an establishment has a number of different food service areas it is easier from the control point of view to have a different design in each service area. This may not at first seem practical, but nowadays forward thinking manufacturers are producing a range of perhaps ten patterns, and will guarantee a supply for a period of ten years to replace breakages, etc.

Very few caterers can afford to buy high quality china for normal day to day use, because of the high initial capital outlay and replacement costs. The caterer therefore has to turn to what is termed 'earthenware'. This has been vastly imporved over the last few years both in appearance and durability. Badged china at the present time is not so popular and patterned china is the more acceptable. When purchasing china the points previously mentioned should be borne in mind. Other factors to consider here are:

1. Every item of earthenware should have a complete cover of glaze to ensure a reasonable length of life.
2. China should have a rolled edge which will give added reinforcement at the edge, which if well done means that chipping will only occur on the under edge which is not visible to the customer. One word of caution here is that hygiene is most important and if not carefully watched the chips could harbour germs.
3. Check whether the pattern is underneath or on top of the glaze. To be satisfactory it should be under the glaze. This demands additional glaze and firing. Patterns on top of the glaze will wear and discolour very quickly. Therefore china with the pattern under the glaze is more expensive but its life will be longer.

Very often earthenware produced for catering purposes is given a trade name by the manufacturer to indicate its strength. Some examples of these are:

a) Vitreous
b) Vitrock
c) Vitrex
d) Vitresso
e) Ironstone
f) Vitrified

Of these vitrified ware is recognised to be the strongest, but this does not always mean that every caterer buys vitrified hotelware as other factors apart from strength and economy have to be taken into account. Two newer forms of crockery recently on the market are known as 'Steelite' and 'Micratex'. Steelite is advertised as Vitreous china and has a high chip resistance. A range of 'Steelite' is to be found on the new Cunard liner the *Queen Elisabeth 2*. Micratex is a form of crockery where the body strength of the china has been re-inforced by a technique employed in grinding the clay. This is to make the article stronger without adding to the weight.

There are various classifications of catering china. Very briefly these are as follows:

Bone China.
This is a very fine and hard china and is very expensive. The decorations are to be found under the glaze only. It can if necessary be made to thicker specifications, if requested, for hotel use. The price of bone china puts it out of reach of the majority of everyday caterers, and only a few of the top class hotels and restaurants would use it. Obviously a price of a meal in these establishments is high in order to cover this aspect of the overheads. The range of design, pattern and colour is very wide, and there is something to suit all occasions and situations.

Hotel Earthenware.
This is the normal earthenware which as we have seen (a-e above) can be made stronger than that designed for domestic use. It is not however guaranteed to the British standard 4034 as is *Vitrified* Hotelware (f above). The specification for BS. 4034. demands that vitrified tableware be non-porous which is also a guarantee of its strength. This form of tableware is cheaper than bone china. There is a standard range of designs and patterns in varying colours. As it is the only type of Hotel Earthenware to come up to BS. 4034 specifications it is dearer than the other classifications of hotel earthenware.

Vitrified earthenware is particularly economical where it is in continuous use 24 hours a day, has heavy handling with a high turnover and where hygiene is particularly important for example motorway cafetarias and hospitals.

A domestic weight earthenware is also available but this is lighter and thinner than the hotel earthenware or vitrified hotelware

A range of china, some or all of which may be in use in a service area depending on the type of meals served.

Platter	Soup plate
Meat plate	Soup bowl
Fish plate	Breakfast cup and saucer
Sweet plate	Tea cup and saucer
Sideplate	Coffee cup and saucer

previously mentioned. Because of its short life, lack of strength and possible high breakage rate it is not regarded as suitable for the average caterer, except perhaps the seaside boarding house. It should be noted when purchasing china that some manufacturers stamp the date/month/year on the base. From this, the life of the china under normal usage, can be determined more accurately.

China should be stored on shelves in piles of approximately two dozen. Any higher may result in them toppling down. They should be stored at a convenient height for placing on, and removing from, the shelves without any fear of accidents occuring. If possible keep covered to prevent dust and germs settling on the china. There is a wide range of items available and their exact sizes vary according to the manufacturer and the design he produces. As a guide they are as follows:

	diameter
Sideplate	15 cm (6 in)
Sweet plate	18 cm (7 in)
Fish plate	20 cm (8 in)
Soup plate	20 cm (8 in)
Joint plate	25 cm (10 in)
Cereal/Sweet plate	13 cm (5 in)
Salad Crescent	
Breakfast Cup and Saucer	23-28 cl (8-10 fluid oz)
Tea Cup and Saucer	18.93 cl (6²/₃ fluid oz)
Coffee Cup (Demi-tasse) Saucer	9.47 cl (3¹/₃ fluid oz – ¹/₆ pint)
Consommé Cup and Saucer	

Teapot   28.40/56.80/85.20/113.60 centilitres
                              or
0.284/0.568/0.852/1.136 litres (^{1}/$_2$/1/1^1/$_2$/2 pint
                                        capacity).

Hot Water Jugs
Milk Jugs
Cream Jugs
Coffee Pots
Hot Milk Jugs
Sugar Basin
Slop Basin
Butter Dishes
Ashtrays
Egg Cup
Soup Bowl/Cup
Platter

Tableware (Flatware, Cutlery, and Hollow-ware)

We shall now consider tableware:

1. *Flatware:* in the catering trade denotes all forms of spoons and forks.
2. *Cutlery:* this refers to knives and other cutting implements.
3. *Hollow-ware:* consists of any items made from silver apart from flatware and cutlery, e.g. teapots, milk jugs, sugar basins, oval flats.

Manufacturers are producing varied patterns of flatware, hollow-ware and cutlery in a range of prices to suit all demands. One new pattern of flatware and cutlery is scaled down to three-quarters the normal size specifically for tray service. This demonstrates the manufacturer's desire to keep in touch with the caterer's needs. The majority of food service areas use either plated silverware or stainless steel. Once again the points mentioned previously concerning purchasing should be borne in mind. In addition, when purchasing flatware and cultery consider:

1. The type of menu and service offered.
2. The maximum and average seating capacity.
3. Rush hour turn-over.
4. Washing-up facilities and its turn-over.

The manufacturers will often quote 20, 25, 30 year plate. This denotes the length of life a manufacturer may claim for his plate, subject to fair or normal usage. The length of life of silver also depends upon the weight of silver deposited. The term A1 often heard in connection with silver plate has no significance whatsoever. There is no standard laid down and the quality of A1 plate differs with every manufacturer. There are three standard grades of silver plate—full standard plate, triple plate, and quadruple plate.

The Hallmark on silver tells two things. The two symbols represent the standard of silver used and the Assay office responsible. The two letters are the maker's mark and the date letter.

Plain cutlery and flatware is more popular than pattern for the simple reason that it is cheaper and easier to keep clean. Handles are an important factor in cutlery. The best investment are knives with hard soldered silver plated, nickel or good stainless steel handles. Plastic materials are much cheaper and usually satisfactory. The 'Sanenwood' handled stainless steel is very good. This is a material which is impervious to boiling water and will not crack or chip.

Stainless steel flatware and cutlery is available in a variety of grades. The higher priced designs usually have incorporated in them alloys of chronium which makes the metal stainless, and nickel which gives a fine grain and lustre. Good British-made flatware and cutlery is made of 18/8 stainless steel. This is 18% chromium and 8% nickel. Stainless steel is finished by different degrees of polishing:

1. High polish finish
2. Dull polished finish
3. A light grey matt, non reflective finish

It is worth noting that stainless steel resists scratching far more than other metals and may therefore be said to be more hygienic. At the same time it neither tarnishes nor stains.

Careful storage of cutlery and flatware is most important. The ideal place would be boxes or drawers for each specific item, each box or drawer being lined with baize to prevent the items concerned sliding about and becoming scratched and marked. Other items of hollow-ware should be stored on shelves which are labelled showing where the different items go. They must be stored at a convenient height for placing on and removing from the shelves. Ideally all flatware, cutlery and hollow-ware should be stored in a room or cupboard which can be locked since they constitute a large part of the capital of the restaurant. Cutlery and flatware may be stored in cutlery trollies of which there are a number now on the market to suit all purposes.

There is an almost unlimited range of flatware, cutlery and hollow-ware in use in the catering industry today. These items are those necessary to give efficient service of any form

Special Equipment

Top row — from left to right

Asparagus tongs	Caviare knife
Gateaux slice	Dessert fork
Oyster fork	Dessert knife
Pastry knife/ fork	Nut crackers
Corn-on-cob holders	Grape scissors
Lobster pick	Lemon press
Butter knife	

Bottom row — from left to right

Grapefruit spoon	Snail dish
Ice cream spoon	Snail fork
Sundae spoon	Cheese knife
Snail tongs	Skewer (Kebabs)

of meal at any time of the day. Everyone is familiar with the knife, fork, spoon, flats, vegetable dishes and lids, entrée dishes and lids, soup tureens, teapot, hot water jugs, sugar basins and so on that we see in every day use. Over and above these however there are a number of specialist items of equipment provided for use with specific dishes. Some of these more common items of specialist equipment are listed below together with a brief note of the dish which they may be used for.

EQUIPMENT	DISH
1. Oyster fork	1. Shellfish cocktail/oysters
2. Grapefruit spoon	2. Grapefruit halves
3. Steak knife	3. Grilled meats.
4. Corn-on-the-cob holders	4. Corn-on-the-cob. One to pierce each end of the cob.
5. Cheese knife	5. Cheese board
6. Fruit knife and fork	6. Dessert—fruit basket
7. Pastry slice	7. Sweet trolly—serving portions of gateaux
8. Grape scissors and	8. To cut and hold a portion of grapes
9. Nutcrackers	9. Dessert—fruit basket
10. Jam spoon	10. Preserves
11. Sundae spoon	11. Ice-cream sweet in a tall glass
12. Lobster crackers	12. To break the shell to gain access to meat
13. Lobster pick	13. To extract the flesh from the claw
14. Finger bowl	14. Part of the make up of a cover to certain dishes, i.e. oysters, dessert, globe artichoke, etc.
15. Caviar knife	15. Has a short broad blade used for spreading the caviar
16. Snail tongs	16. To hold the snail shell.
17. Snail fork	17. To extract the snail from its shell.
18. Snail dish	18. Round with two ears. Has 6 indentations to hold a portion (6) of snails.
19. Silver skewers	19. For attractive presentation of a Kebab.
20. Pastry knife and fork	20. Used in the service of afternoon teas.
21. Shellfish cocktail holder	21. In which a shellfish cocktail would be presented.

Glassware

Glass also contributes to the appearance of the table and the overall attraction of the room. There are many standard patterns available to the caterer. Most manufacturers now supply hotel glassware in standard sizes for convenience of ordering, availability and quick delivery. Glasses are measured in terms of capacity by 'fluid ounces' or 'out' or (centilitres). The term a '3 out' sherry glass denotes that one is able to get three glasses from one gill or a quarter of a pint (14.20 centilitres). A 6⅔ ounce (18.93 centilitres) goblet denotes that this particular goblet holds 6⅔ fluid ounces (18.93 centilitres), or one third of a pint.

Except in certain speciality restaurants or high class establishments, where either coloured glassware or cut glassware may be used, hotel glassware is usually plain. The one exception sometimes found is Hock glasses with brown stems—the same colour as the Hock bottle—and Moselle glasses with green stems,—the same colour as the Moselle bottle. However many establishments now use a clear stemmed glass for both Hock and Moselle wines, there is a saving in the quantity to be purchased since the same glass may be used for the service of both wines, and therefore a saving in both storage space and cost. The tulip shaped glass for champagne is more usual now than the traditional 'saucer' shape, because it retains the sparkle and effervesence.

A good wine glass should be plain and clear so that the colour and brilliance of a wine can be clearly seen; it should have a stem for holding the wine glass so that the heat of ones hand does not affect the wine on tasting; there should be a slightly incurving lip to help to hold the aroma and it should be large enough to hold the particular wine being tasted.

The glasses are normally stored in the glass pantry, and should be placed in single rows on paper lined shelves and upside down to prevent dust settling in them. An alternative to this is to have plastic coated wire racks made specifically for the purpose of stacking and storing

A range of glasses that may be found in the Dispense Bar. From left to right

Liqueur glass
Cocktail glass
Brandy glass
Port glass

Club shaped spirit glass
Saucer Champagne glass
Tulip Champagne glass
Elgin Sherry glass
Copeta (tasting glass)
5 oz Paris goblet

6²/₃ oz Paris goblet
8 oz Paris goblet
Hock/Moselle glass
  (clear stem)
Lager glass

the glasses. Such racks are also a convenient method of transporting glassware from one point to another, and cuts down on breakages.

Tumblers should not be stacked inside one another as this may result in heavy breakages and cause accidents to staff.

When carrying tumblers and lager glasses during the pre-preparation period they may be carried upside down on a service salver—round silver salver with a serviette on it—to prevent dust getting into them. If wine glasses—goblets —are being carried, they may be transported by hand, the stems between the fingers, and the bases flat against the palm of the hand. During a service period however all glassware should be carried on a service salver. When placed on the table all glasses should be put at the top right hand corner of the cover.

There is a variety of glasses in use, some of which are as follows, with their approximate sizes:

1. Wine goblets — 5/6⅔/8. fluid oz. (14.20/18.93/22.72 cl)
2. Hock, Moselle — 6/8 fluid oz. (18-23 cl)
3. Tulip Champagne — 6/8 fluid oz. (18-23 cl)
4. Saucer Champagne — 6/8 fluid oz. (18-23 cl)
5. Cocktail glasses — 2/3 fluid oz. (4-7 cl)
6. Sherry/Port — 3 out (4.735 cl)
7. Highball — 8/10 fluid oz. (23-28 cl)
8. Stemmed Beer glass — 10/12 fluid oz. (28-34 cl)
9. Lager glass — 10/12 fluid oz. (28-34 cl)
10. Brandy baloon — 8/10 fluid oz. (23-28 cl)
11. Liqueur glass — '6 out.' (2.367 cl)
12. Tumblers — ½ pint. (28.40 cl)
13. Beer tankards — ½/1 pint. (25 and 50 cl)

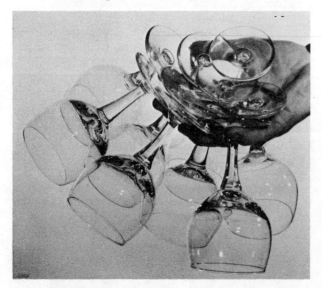

Goblets may be carried this way during the pre-preparation period. This enables the waiter to carry a large number of goblets safely in one hand, having the other hand free in case of accident. The base of the goblets should overlap one another, thus helping them to remain firmly in position when being carried.

4 procedure for the service of a meal

A cover

One of the technical terms very often used in the catering industry is **a cover.** What does this mean? There are two definitions according to the context.

1. When discussing how many guests a restaurant or dining room will seat, or how many guests will be attending a certain cocktail party, we refer to the total number of guests concerned as so many 'covers'. For example:
   A restaurant or dining room will seat a maximum of 85 covers (guests) *or*
   There will be 250 covers (guests) at a certain cocktail party *or*
   This table will seat a party of six covers (guests).
2. When laying a table in readiness for service there is a variety of place-settings which may be laid according to the type of meal and service being offered. We refer to this place-setting as a certain type of cover being laid. In other words a cover denotes all the necessary cutlery, flatware, crockery, glassware and linen necessary to lay a certain type of place-setting for a special meal.
   For example:
   To lay an à la carte cover for first class silver service.
   To lay a table d'hôte cover for luncheon service in a department store.
   To lay a full English breakfast cover in readiness for breakfast service.

An à la carte cover

This is the place-setting normally laid in a good class restaurant, dining room or hotel in readiness for service of either luncheon or dinner.

It would consist of the following:
1. Fish plate
2. Serviette
3. Fish knife
4. Fish fork
5. Side plate
6. Side knife
7. Wine glass

A table d'hôte cover

This is a place-setting normally laid in a good class restaurant, dining room, hotel, medium-sized hotel, department store, etc. in readiness for service of either luncheon or dinner. It would consist of the following:
1. Serviette
2. Soup spoon
3. Fish knife
4. Fish fork
5. Joint knife
6. Joint fork
7. Dessert spoon
8. Dessert fork
9. Sideplate
10. Sideknife
11. Wine glass

Table accompaniments

The table accompaniments required to complete the table lay-up are the same whether an à la carte or table d'hôte cover has been laid. These would be as follows:
1. Cruet: salt, pepper, mustard and mustard spoon
2. Ashtray
3. Table number
4. Vase of flowers

A table d'hôte cover

These are the basic items required to complete the table lay-up. In some establishments certain extra items will be placed on the table to complete its lay-up. These may be as follows:

1. Roll basket
2. Melba toast
3. Gristicks
4. Cayenne pepper
5. Peppermill
6. Butter pats

If some or all of the extra items (1-6) are placed on the table this would be peculiar to a particular establishment. It is worth noting however that in first class service the rolls, melba toast and gristicks will not be placed on the table beforehand but offered to the assembled guests once they are seated. Butter would not be placed on the table until the guests are all seated at the table—the reason for this is that if placed on the table too soon before the guests are seated it becomes warm and begins to melt, losing some of its flavour. Cayenne pepper and a peppermill are accompaniments with particular dishes and should not be placed on the table unless these dishes are being served.

It is generally recognised that where an à la carte cover has been laid that the cutlery and flatware required by the guest, for the dishes he has chosen, will be laid course by course. In other words there should not, at any time during the meal, be any more cutlery and flatware on the table than is required by the guest at that specific time.

Where a table d'hôte cover has been laid the waiter will remove, after the order has been taken, any unnecessary cutlery and flatware and re-lay any extra items that may be required. This then means that before the guest commences his meal he should have all the necessary cutlery and flatware required, for the dishes he has chosen, set out as his place-setting or cover. If this is done correctly then once the meal is finished the items making up the cover should all have been removed.

The service salver

A service salver consists of a round silver salver with a serviette set on it. It may be used in a number of ways during the actual meal service:

1. Carrying clean glasses and removing dirty glasses from a table
2. Removing clean cutlery, flatware from the table
3. Placing clean cutlery, flatware on the table
4. Clearing side plates and side knives
5. Placing coffee services on the table

An à la carte cover

1. When carrying clean glasses they should be placed upside down on the service salver. This reduces the risk of dust etc., getting in the glasses. When being placed on the table the waiter should hold the stem and place the glass at the top right hand corner of the cover and the correct way up. This ensures that the bowl of the wine glass is not touched, which is most important when a wine is being served.

2/3. When removing from or placing clean

Carrying glasses to the table.

cutlery and flatware on a table the cutlery and flatware should be carried on a service salver. The blades of the knives to be placed under the 'arch' in the middle of the forks, and if carrying dessert spoons and forks the prongs of the fork to go under the 'arch' in the middle of the spoon. The reason for this is to help to hold the items steady on the service salver, bearing in mind that the handles of cutlery and flatware are generally the heaviest part and this method prevents them sliding about too much.

4. When clearing dirty side plates and side knives after the main course has been consumed, by taking a service salver to the table the waiter has a larger area on which to stack these small items. The side plates may be stacked one upon another with all the debris in a separate pile and the side knives laid flat upon the service salver. This is a much safer and speedier method especially when large numbers are involved.

5. When taking coffee services to a table the side plates may be stacked in one pile on the service salver, the coffee saucers in another, all the demi-tasse together and all the coffee spoons laid flat on the service salver. When the waiter is at the table he places the coffee service down from the right hand side having first set a coffee saucer on a side plate, a demi-tasse on the saucer with a coffee spoon on the coffee saucer and to the right of the demi-tasse. He goes to the right hand side of each guest, and completes this simple operation.

It is a speedier and safer method especially when slightly larger numbers are involved, than putting the coffee services up at your sideboard and then carrying as many as you can to the table. The reason for putting the coffee service down from the right and placing it on the right hand side of the cover is that the coffee will be served from the right. This then means you do not have to stretch right across the front of the guest when laying the coffee service or serving the coffee. A small technical point which helps towards giving a first class service.

Service plate

is a joint plate with a serviette upon it. It has a number of uses during the meal service:

1. Removing clean cutlery and flatware from the table.
2. Placing clean cutlery and flatware on the table.

3. **Crumbing down** after the main course, or any other stage of the meal if necessary.

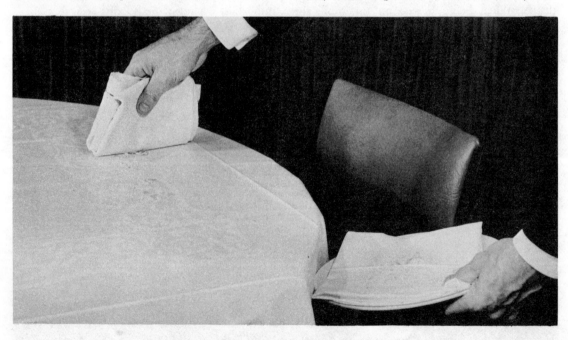

The service plate and service cloth as they should be used when 'crumbing down'. Note the neatly folded service cloth.

4. To clear accompaniments from the table as and when necessary.

1/2 See notes 2/3 under heading 'Service Salver'.

3. **Crumbing down** is a procedure generally carried out by the waiter after the main course has been consumed and all the dirty items of equipment cleared from the table. The waiter then brushes any crumbs and other debris lying on the tablecloth on to his service plate with the aid of either his folded service cloth or a small brush used for this particular purpose. This is another of the finer points of good service.

4. The service plate would be used to clear such items as the cruet, cayenne pepper, pepper mill or other accompaniments which are not already set on an underplate.

Serviette folds

There are many forms of serviette fold to be found in use in food and beverage service areas. Some are intricate in their detail whilst others are more simple. The simpler folds are used in everyday service and some of the more complex and difficult folds may be used on special occasions such as luncheons, dinners, weddings. There are three main reasons why the more simple folds are better than the more complex ones. First the serviette, if folded correctly, can look well and add to the general appearance of the room whether it be a simple or difficult fold. Secondly, and perhaps more importantly, is the question of hygiene. The more complex fold involves greater handling to complete the fold, and its appearance, when unfolded to spread over the guest's lap, is poor, as it has many more creases in it. Finally there is the question of time. The complex fold takes much more time to complete properly than does a very simple fold. The majority of serviette folds have special names, the photograph below shows six folds, which would be suitable for everyday service or special occasions.

1. Cone
2. Bishop's Mitre
3. Rose
4. Prince of Wales Feather
5. Cock's Comb
6. Triple wave

The **rose** fold of serviette is one in which rolls or melba toast may be presented at the table. The **triple wave** is an attractive fold which may be used for a special function to hold the menu and a name card.

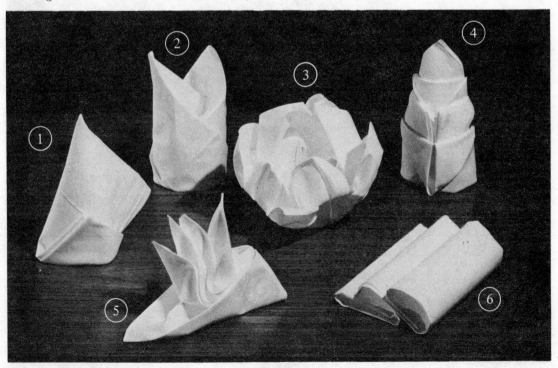

Laying the tablecloth

Before laying the tablecloth the waiter must ensure that the table and chairs are in their correct position. Secondly he must see that the table top is clean, thirdly that the table is level and finally see that it does not wobble. If the table wobbles slightly then a small wedge or an old menu folded up will correct the fault.

Next the waiter must collect the correct size of tablecloth for the table to be clothed up. Most tablecloths are folded in what is known as a screen fold. The waiter must stand in the correct position to lay the tablecloth properly, that is between the legs of the table. This is to ensure that the corners of the tablecloth cover the legs of the table and do not fall between the table legs. The tablecloth folded in the screen fold has one inverted fold and two single folds and should be opened out across the table in front of the waiter with the inverted and two single folds facing him and with the inverted fold

on top. The tablecloth should then be laid in the correct manner. The points which should be noted if the tablecloth is laid correctly are as follows:

1. Corners of the tablecloth should cover the legs of the table.

2. The overlap should be even all round the table: 30/45 cm (12-18 in).

3. The creases of the tablecloths should all run the same way in the room.

4. If two tablecloths are necessary to cover a table for a larger party then the overlap of the two tablecloths should face away from the entrance to the room. This is for presentation purposes of both the room and the table.

Nothing is more attractive in the room than tables clothed-up with clean, crisp and well-starched linen tablecloths. The tablecloth should be handled as little as possible and this will be ensured by laying the tablecloth in the correct manner.

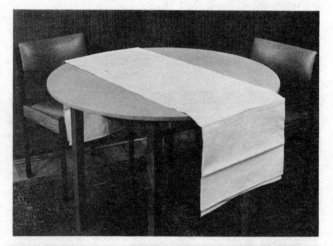

The tablecloth opened out across the table. Note that the fall of the cloth over the edge of the table lies between the table leg. It should not fall over the legs of the table. The inverted and two single folds should be facing the waiter.

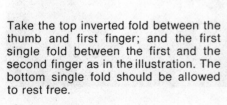

Take the top inverted fold between the thumb and first finger; and the first single fold between the first and the second finger as in the illustration. The bottom single fold should be allowed to rest free.

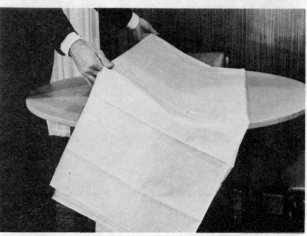

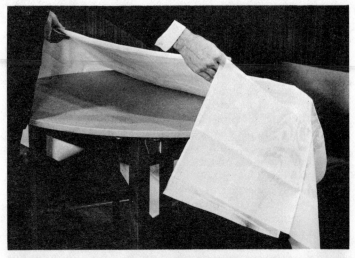

Lift the tablecloth and throw the bottom free single fold over the far edge of the table. Judge the amount of overlap necessary from the creases running across the tablecloth and parallel to the waiter.

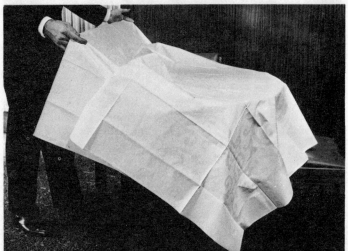

Release the inverted fold held between the thumb and first finger, and draw the first single fold, held between the first and second finger, slowly towards you.

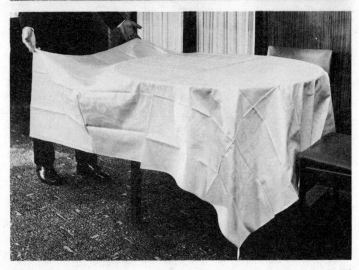

Shake the cloth gently as you draw it towards you and this will allow it to unfold more easily. Ensure the corners of the tablecloth cover the legs of the table.

Laying the table

Once the table is clothed-up it would be laid in readiness for service. If the cover being laid is an à la carte cover then the first item set on the table is the fish plate in the centre of each cover. If it was a table d'hôte cover being laid then the first item to be set on the table would be the serviette or sideplate in the centre of each cover. If the sideplate was laid in the centre of each cover it would be moved to the left hand side of the cover once all the cutlery and flatware had been laid. The purpose of initially placing something in the centre of the cover is to ensure the covers are exactly opposite one another and that the cutlery and flatware of each cover are the same distance apart. Cutlery and flatware should be laid from a service salver or service plate. An alternative to this is to use a service cloth and hold the items being laid in the service cloth, giving a final polish before setting the item on the table. In some instances a cutlery trolley is used for storing the cutlery and this would be pushed around the tables and then the cutlery and flatware laid after a final polish with the waiter's cloth. When laying a table d'hôte cover the cutlery and flatware should be laid from the inside to the outside of the cover. The purpose of this is that it ensures even spacing of the cover and normally lessens the chances of having to handle the items laid more than necessary. In other words the order of laying should be:

1. Joint knife
2. Fish knife
3. Soup spoon

1. Joint fork
2. Fish fork

1. Dessert fork
2. Dessert spoon

The waiter must ensure that where applicable all cutlery and flatware is laid 1.25 cm ($\frac{1}{2}$ inch) from the edge of the table and badged crockery with the badge at the head or top of the cover. The glass after polishing would be placed upside down at top right hand corner of the cover. Once the covers have been laid the table accompaniments would be placed on the table according to the fashion of the establishment.

Re-laying of tables

It is very often the case in a busy restaurant or dining room that a number of the tables have to be relaid in order to cope with the inflow of customers. Where this is the case the table should first of all be completely cleared of all items of equipment. It would then be crumbed down. At this stage if the tablecloth is a little soiled or grubby a slip cloth should be placed over it. It will then be relaid in the approved manner. It is essential that this procedure is carried out as quickly as possible to ensure maximum turnover of guests in the limited amount of time available for service. This will then allow for maximum sales which in a well run establishment will mean more profit.

Removal of the spare cover

In many instances tables are reserved for parties of guests. Where this happens the party sometimes turn up with one guest less in the party than was quoted when the original booking had been made. The waiter must then remove the spare cover laid on the table. He must use his judgement as to which cover he removes, a lot depending on the actual position of the table. It should be noted here however that all guests where possible should look into the room. The cover would be removed in the correct manner using a service plate or a service salver. When this has been done the position of the other covers should be adjusted if necessary and the table accompaniments re-positioned. The spare chair would have been removed.

Staff on duty early

The reasons for the food and beverage service staff coming on duty a few minutes before the service is due to commence are:

1. To check the sideboards have all equipment necessary for service
2. To check the tables are laid correctly
3. To check the menu and have a full understanding of the dishes, methods of cooking, garnishes, the correct covers, accompaniments and mode of service
4. The allocation of 'stations' if this is not already known and other duties
5. For the head waiter to check all his staff are dressed correctly in a clean and well presented uniform of the establishment

Reception of guests

The social skills shown by the food and beverage staff go a long way towards selling an establishment and making a guest feel at home in a friendly and relaxed atmosphere. This aspect of service is very often neglected and all employers should impress upon their staff at regular intervals the great importance attached to *customer contact* (Chapter 5). It must be remembered that a pleasant welcome to a guest can gain a sale, a poor welcome will lose a sale. It is always first impressions that count.

Procedure for service of a meal

The procedure for service to a guest from the moment he enters the establishment until he leaves will be listed in point form to make it easier to follow. This is a suggested order and it should be noted that this order may change and vary according to the establishment, the type of menu and service offered and the time available.

1. Guest enters. Greeted by reception head waiter. Check if have a reservation. If not see if a table is available.

2. Reception head waiter to ask if the guests would like an aperitif in the lounge or reception area or have one at the table.

3. Take guests to table. Hand over to the station head waiter who will pass the time of day with guests and help to seat them.

4. Unfold serviette and place over guest's lap.

5. Sommelier comes to table to offer wine list for choice of aperitif. Takes order.

6. Rolls and melba toast are offered. Butter placed on the table.

7. Menus presented to host and his guests. Allow a few minutes for party to make their choice.

8. **Recognition** of the **host** is most important.

9. Station head waiter takes order of party through host. Stands to left of host and should be ready to offer suggestions and advice on the menu, or translate any items if necessary.

10. Sommelier comes to tables to see if any wine is required with meal. Takes order through host. Should be able to advise suitable wines to accompany certain dishes.

11. Waiters change covers where necessary for the service of the first course. Place accompaniment on the table.

12. Lay plates and service of first course.

13. Clear first course in approved fashion.

14. Lay covers for the fish course. Place any accompaniment required on the table.

15. If wine is to be served with fish course the correct glass would be placed on the table.

16. Wine presented to host and opened. Taste to host. Serve guests, ladies first. Serve host last. It is as well to remember here that one can get approximately 3 glasses of wine from a half bottle and 6 glasses of wine from a bottle. White wines served chilled and red wines served at room temperature.

17. Lay fish plates and serve fish course.

18. Clear fish course.

19. Lay covers for main course. Place any accompaniments required on the table.

20. If a wine is also to accompany the main course the correct glasses would be placed on the table. Clear dirty wine glasses.

21. Wine presented to host and opened. Taste to host. Serve guests, ladies first. Serve host last.

22. Lay joint plates and serve main course. The Station head waiter must ensure he has everything he requires on his sideboard before he commences service of this course. Otherwise this can disrupt his service and may mean some of the guests food is getting cold whilst he is waiting for it all to be served. All cold dishes should be served before hot.

23. Underflats should be used under vegetables dishes and sauce boats. All hot food being served should be piping hot and served onto hot joint plates. The meat will be served first and placed on that part of the plate nearest the guest or at the bottom of the cover. This will be followed by the potatoes, vegetables and any hot sauces and accompaniments that have to be offered.

24. Sommelier to top-up the wine glasses when necessary. Station head waiter to offer more rolls, melba toast and butter as required.

25. Clear main course to include sideplates and side knives, cruets, butter dish, gristicks, accompaniments. Everything should be cleared in the approved manner.

26. Crumb down.

27. Change ashtrays if necessary.

28. Offer menu for guests to choose a sweet dish. Take order.

29. Lay sweet covers and accompaniments.

30. Sommelier to clear wine glasses and wine bottle.

31. Serve sweet course. Cold dishes served before hot dishes.

32. Clear sweet course.

Silver service of vegetables
Note:
1. The use of an underflat under the vegetable dishes
2. Serving a variety of vegetables at one time by using a larger underflat

33. Take coffee order.

34. Sommelier to present liqueur trolly. Serve liqueurs as required.

35. Coffee service placed on the table. Service of coffee. Offer more coffee at the appropriate time.

36. Presentation of the bill. Payment to waiter who has bill receipted by cashier and it is then returned with any change to host.

37. Station head waiter see guests out of restaurant.

38. Clear down table. Relay if necessary.

Procedure for taking bookings

1. When the telephone rings, lift receiver and say: 'Good morning, [the Cathedral Room Restaurant,] can I help you'.

2. When taking a booking the essential information required is as follows:

3. Use of service cloth for protection and to prevent the underflat from slipping
4. Correct handling of the service spoon and fork
5. A separate service spoon and fork for each variety of vegetable served
6. Service from the left

   a) Day
   b) Date
   c) Name
   d) No. of covers
   e) Time
   f) Any special requests

3. When you have received this information from the prospective client it is advisable to repeat it all over the telephone as confirmation to the client.

4. If a cancellation is being received then again confirm the cancellation with the client, by repeating his request to him over the telephone and then ask if you can take a booking for any other occasion in place of the cancellation.

5. At the end of a telephone call for a booking one should say: 'Thank you for your booking, good morning'.

5   social skills

We have already mentioned that the 'social skills' of the food and beverage service team are most important in their dealings with the guest, that is **customer contact**. It is the way each and every member of the team copes with the day to day incidents which may arise and for which there is really no stereotyped answer, each incident being settled in a way best suited to the situation. The staff, if they are carrying out their job correctly, are there to satisfy and supply the demands of the customer. When an unforeseen incident arises it must be coped with promptly and efficiently without causing any more disturbance than is necessary to any of the other guests. Quick action will very often soothe the irate customer and ensure a return visit to your establishment. It is worth remembering at this stage that in case of complaints, whatever their nature, they should be referred to the Head waiter or someone in a responsible position immediately. Delay can only cause confusion and very often the wrong interpretation may be put on a situation if left to be dealt with later. In the case of accidents, whether of a minor nature or serious, a report of the incident must be kept and signed by those involved.

Listed below are a few of those incidents which might occur and the suggested steps that should be taken in order to put right any fault.

Accident procedure

1   It is possible that during the service of a course a few drops of sauce or roast gravy may have fallen on the tablecloth. The following steps should be taken:

1. Check immediately that none has fallen on the guest being served. Apologise to the guest.

2. If some has fallen on the guests' clothing allow the guest to rub over the dirtied' area with a clean damp cloth. This will remove the worst of the spillage.
3. If it is necessary for the guest to retire to the cloakroom to remove the spillage then his meal should be placed in the hotplate until his return.
4. Depending on the nature of the spillage the establishment may offer to have the garment concerned cleaned.
5. If the spillage has gone on the tablecloth then the waiter should first of all remove any items of equipment that may be dirtied or in his way.
6. Then he will mop or scrape up the spillage with either a clean damp cloth or a knife.
7. An old menu card will then be placed on top of the table but under the tablecloth over the damaged area.
8. A second menu will be placed on the tablecloth over the damaged area.
9. A clean rolled serviette is then brought to the table and rolled completely over the damaged area. The menu will prevent any damp from soaking into the clean serviette.
10. Any items of equipment removed should be returned to their correct position on the table top.
11. Any meals taken to the hotplate should be returned and fresh covers put down where necessary.
12. Again apologise to guests for any inconvenience caused.

B)   A glass of water knocked over accidently by a guest. The following steps should be taken.

1. Ensure none has gone on the guest.

33

2. If some of the water has fallen on the guests clothing then follow *A)* 2 and 3.

3. Where possible, as this form of accident usually involves changing the tablecloth, the party of guests should be seated at another table and allowed to continue their meal without delay.

4. If they cannot be moved to another table then they should be seated slightly back from the table so that the waiter can carry out the necessary procedures to rectify the fault speedily and efficiently.

5. The guests meals should be placed in the hotplate to keep warm.

6. All dirty items should be removed on a tray to the waiters sideboard ready to go to the wash-up area.

7. All clean items should be removed and kept on the waiters sideboard for relaying.

8. The table cloth should be mopped with a clean absorbent cloth to remove as much of the liquid as is possible.

9. A number of old menu's should be placed on the table top but underneath the table-cloth.

10. A clean tablecloth of the correct size should be brought to the table. It will be opened out and held in the correct manner as if one were laying a tablecloth during the pre-service preparation period. The table will then be clothed up in the usual manner except that when the clean cloth is being drawn across the table towards the waiter he is at the same time taking off the soiled tablecloth. The soiled tablecloth is removed at the same time as the clean tablecloth is being laid so that none of the tabletop can be seen by the guests at any time. The old menu's will prevent any dampness penetrating to the clean tablecloth.

11. When the table has its clean tablecloth on then it must be relaid as quickly as possible.

12. The guests re-seated at the table and the meals returned to them from the hotplate.

C) A guest suggests that the fish dish served to him is 'off'. The following steps should be taken:

1. Apologise to guest.

2. Remove dish to sideboard to be returned to Aboyeur at hotplate.

3. Offer the menu to guest and ask if he would like another portion of the same dish or choose something else as an alternative.

4. Write out a special check for the new order.

T. No	No. of Covers
	'Retour'
	Fish dish + Price
	'En place'
	Alternative dish + Price
Date	Signed.

This shows the dish being returned and what the guest is having in its place.

5. Lay fresh cover.

6. Collect the new dish as soon as possible from the hotplate.

7. Serve to guest.

8. Apologise for any inconvenience caused.

9. The waiter must ensure that the Aboyeur receives the dish being returned and checks it immediately, because it may mean that the particular dish concerned has to be taken off the menu to prevent the chance of any food poisoning.

10. The policy of the establishment would dictate whether or not the guest is to be charged for the alternative dish.

D) A waiter finds a wallet under a chair, recently vacated by one of his clients. The following steps should be taken:

1. Check immediately whether the guest has left the service area. If he is still in the area the wallet may be returned to him.

2. If he has left the service area the waiter should hand the wallet to the Head waiter or supervisor in charge.

3. The supervisor or Head waiter can check with reception and Hall-porter to see if the guest has left the building.

4. If the guest concerned was a resident, then reception may ring his room and let him know his wallet has been found and ask him to collect it at a convenient time.

5. If the guest was a regular customer then it is possible that the Head waiter or Head porter may know where to contact him and he will be asked to call in for his wallet.

6. If the guest is a regular customer but cannot be contacted then his wallet will be kept in the lost property office until his next visit.

7. If the owner has not been found or contacted immediately then the Head waiter or Supervisor must list the items contained in the wallet with the waiter who found the wallet. This list will be signed by both the

Head waiter or Supervisor and the finder (waiter). The list must be dated and also show where the article was found, and the time.

8. A copy of this list goes with the wallet to the Lost Property Office who double checks the contents of the wallet against the list before accepting it. The details of the find are then entered in a Lost Property Register.

9. Another copy of the list goes to the Hall porter in case he receives any inquiries concerning a wallet. Anyone claiming Lost Property should be passed on to the Lost Property Office.

10. Before the Lost Property Office hand over any lost property they should ask for a description of the article concerned and its contents to ensure as far as possible that it is being returned to the genuine owner. The Office should also see proof of identity of the person claiming ownership.

11. In the case of all lost property the above mentioned steps should be carried out as quickly as possible as this is in the best interests of the establishment and causes the guest minimum inconvenience. On receipt of his lost property the guest should be asked to sign for the article concerned, also giving his address.

12. Any lost property unclaimed after three months may become the property of the finder who would claim it through his Head waiter or supervisor.

E) A guest falls ill in your establishment. The following steps to should be taken:

1. As soon as it is noticed that a guest is feeling unwell whilst in your dining room or restaurant a person in authority should be immediately called to the spot.

2. The person in authority must enquire of the guest if he can be of any assistance. At the same time he must try to judge for himself whether the illness is of a serious nature or not.

3. It is often advisable in cases such as this to take the guest to another room to see if they are able to recover in a few minutes.

4. If this happens his meal will be placed in the hotplate until his return.

5. If the illness appears to be of a serious nature, a doctor, nurse or someone qualified in first-aid should be immediately called for.

6. The guest should not be moved until after a doctor has seen him.

7. If necessary screen off the area.

8. Although this is a difficult situation to deal with in front of the general public the minimum fuss should be made, and service to the rest of the guests carried on normally.

9. It will be realised now why it is best, if at all possible, to have the guest who has fallen ill immediately moved to another room where he may rest out of the heat of the eating area. This causes minimum fuss in the restaurant or dining room itself.

10. The doctor should advise whether an ambulance should be called.

11. If the guest falling ill is a woman then a woman member of staff should attend her.

12. The guest may have had a sudden stomach upset and wish to leave without finishing his meal. Then a taxi should be called to take the guest home.

13. It would be left to the good judgment of the staff concerned whether the guest should be accompanied or not.

14. Payment for that part of the meal consumed, and the taxi fare would be according to the policy of the establishment.

15. It is most important that for all accidents, minor or serious, that *all* details should be recorded in an accident book. This is in case of a claim against the establishment at a later date.

16. If after a short period of time the guest returns and continues with his meal, then a fresh cover will be laid and his meal returned from the hotplate.

F) If a guest is suspected of having too much to drink the following steps should be taken:

1. If a prospective client asks for a table and the staff believe he is possibly under the influence of drink they may refuse him a table, even though there may be one available.

2. It is not always possible however, to recognise a guest who may prove objectionable later on.

3. If difficulty is found in handling this type of person then assistance in removing him from the eating area may come from the members of staff or the Hall porter.

4. If a guest is suspected of being drunk this must first of all be ascertained by the Head waiter or supervisor.

5. The guest will then be asked to leave rather

than let him become objectionable to other guests later on.

6. If the guest has already consumed part of his meal but is not being objectionable then the remainder of his meal will be served to him in the normal fashion, but the Head waiter or Supervisor must ensure he receives no more alcoholic beverage.

7. On finishing his meal the guest will leave and he should be watched until he has left the premises.

8. It is always advisable to make out a report of all such incidents, and they should be brought to the immediate attention of the restaurant manager in case of any claim at a later date concerning a particular incident.

G) A customer's appearance is not satisfactory. The following steps should be taken:

1. If a guest's appearance is likely to give offence to others then he may be asked to correct his dress to the approved fashion or asked to leave the establishment.

2. If a guest's braces are showing, or he has no coat on, then he will be requested by the Head waiter or Supervisor that he correct his dress as appropriate.

3. He may go to the cloakroom to adjust his dress if necessary.

4. If the guest will not comply with the request then he should be asked to leave.

5. If he has partly consumed a meal then whether he will be charged or not depends on the policy of the house and the discretion of the Head waiter and Supervisor.

6. A report of this incident must be made and signed by the people concerned.

It is advisable that when any incident occurs a report is made out immediately. The basic information that should be found in the report is as follows:

1. Place.
2. Date.
3. Time.
4. Nature of incident.
5. Individual reports from those concerned and signed.
6. Action taken.
7. Name, address and phone number of the guest involved, and also of the staff involved.

All reports will be kept in case similar incidents occur at a later date.

6 types and styles of service

The service of a meal may be carried out in many ways depending on a number of factors.

a) The type of catering establishment
b) The type of customer to be served
c) The time available for the meal
d) The turnover of custom expected
e) The type of menu presented
f) The cost of the meal served
g) The site of the establishment

One cannot always determine the style of service offered by the type of establishment. One assumes that the first class establishment will offer a first-class service, namely **gueridon** or **full silver** service. The trend today however is towards what we widely refer to as **popular catering**. This type of service may be found in many of the smaller, good class establishments where their position demands a quick turnover of custom, and which are served by a minimum of staff, with all costs cut to the lowest level possible. The 'popular catering' theme may be offered in a wide variety of ways, each with its own particular speciality or gimmick, all of which are aimed at a certain section of the public. The potential customer has to be attracted towards an establishment, and this may be done in many ways—the type of menu and its presentation; the name of the establishment; the atmosphere in the food service area—a combination of decor, furniture, fittings, lighting, together with a good brigade of waiters or waitresses who work well together as a team; the social skills of the food service staff; the good **salesmanship** of the food service staff; type of wine list offered and the price range of the various dishes and wines offered. One catering establishment may only offer one type of food service depending on the demand. The trend today however seems to be towards the multi-restaurant, offering various forms of food service. This means that under one roof may be found a bar serving draught beer and sherry together with snacks such as sandwiches and pies; a 'doubles bar' with drink at slightly reduced prices and hot snacks, and a waitress service restaurant with an à la carte menu including specialities such as a **platter** meal.

This type of establishment must be sited in a fairly heavily populated area as it is aimed at more than one section of the public or type of customer. A motorway cafeteria is another form of establishment offering varied types of service aimed at certain sections of the public. Many industrial and institutional establishments offer more than one form of food service: such as counter-cafeteria service where the turnover rate is high in a limited time, and where more than one sitting is necessary; waitress service in a dining room for senior staff or full silver service in a director's dining room. The various forms of service are each discussed briefly below.

Gueridon service: This is a meal served to a guest by the waiter from a trolly or sidetable. It is the most advanced form of food service and demands dexterity and skill on the part of the waiter who in turn must be a showman and have good organisational ability. This is because he has to carry out such procedures as fileting, carving, flambéing, and preparing and cooking speciality dishes at the table. The menu presented where this type of service is offered is what we term an à la carte menu, with all the dishes individually priced. This type of menu gives more scope to the professional waiter to display his flair and skills than does the limited table d'hôte menu. It is often found however that an

37

establishment will offer in conjunction with a table d'hôte menu a list of 'Specialities of the House' which are all individually priced and enable the waiter to complete the dish at the table.

Full silver service: This is a form of table service where the waiter brings the meal to the guest who is seated at the table. The menu presented here may be either a table d'hôte or à la carte menu or a combination of both. The waiter receives the food from the Aboyeur at the hotplate. He takes it to his sideboard and deposits the food on his hotplate on the sideboard. For presentation purposes all the food is dressed-up on silver flats or entrée dishes and in vegetable dishes, with the appropriate sauces and accompaniments in silver sauce-boats. The waiter now works from his sideboard, placing the plate in front of the guest and then presenting the main meat dish before serving it onto the guest's plate. This is then followed by the service of the potato and vegetable dishes and the necessary sauces and other accompaniments. The waiter must ensure that the food is served on to the guest's plate in an attractive and presentable manner. This form of service demands skill on the part of the waiter in handling and manipulating a service spoon and fork, and in organising his service so that all the meals are served quickly and efficiently.

Plate/silver service: This is a combination of two forms of table service. Where this form of service is offered the menu presented to the guest is most likely to be a table d'hôte menu, the meal being charged at a set price, or as sometimes happens in department stores the price of the meal served is shown against the main dish chosen from the menu. In this form of service the main meat/fish dish chosen is plated by the kitchen and the potato, vegetables, sauces and other accompaniments dressed up in silver. Therefore in serving the meal the main dish is served to the guest plated and the rest of the meal silver served. The same skills are demanded of the waiter for this form of service as in silver service.

Plate service: This is another form of table service, where the menu presented would be table d'hôte. This form of service is very often offered where there is a rapid turnover of custom and speedy service is necessary. It also demands

less equipment for the service of the meal and therefore is labour saving as far as washing-up is concerned. This all helps an establishment to keep the cost of a meal down to a minimum. The waiter receives the meal all ready plated from the service hotplate and only has to place it in front of the guest ensuring at the same time that the correct cover is laid and the necessary accompaniments are on the table.

Family service: When speaking of 'Family Service' we may well think of an old Victorian family seated in a large dining room with the Head or Master of the House carving the joint and plating it, and the butler serving it to the members of the family. The accompanying potatoes, vegetables, sauces and other accompaniments are placed on the table for the family to help themselves. In many Clubs today a type of 'Family Service' is still carried out. Here the main dish may be either plate or silver served by the waiter. All the accompanying potato and vegetable dishes together with the sauces and other accompaniments are placed on the table for the members to help themselves. This form of service may also be carried out at functions where a large number of covers are being catered for and only a minimum of staff are available. Because there is less actual service for the waiter to do it enables him to serve an extra one or two tables, depending on size. A further variation is for the main dish to be placed on a small hotplate on the table near the host together with the necessary hot plates. The host then plates the main dish and passes it to the guests at his table. The guests in turn help themselves to the potatoes, vegetables, sauces and other accompaniments.

Counter or Cafeteria service: This is a form of service whereby the customer collects a tray from the beginning of the service counter, moves along the counter selecting his meal, pays cash and then collects the appropriate cutlery for his meal. The type of establishment carrying out this form of service would have a high customer turnover rate. The speed of customer turnover depends on the efficient organisation of the service counter and the rapid replenishing of all dishes as and when necessary. One would find this type of service in large industrial catering concerns; institutions; large department stores and various sections of the popular catering field. The menu offered would show a wide range

38

of dishes from simple hot and cold snacks and beverages all individually priced, to a limited table d'hôte menu with the set price of the meal being shown against the main course dishes offered.

At the entrance to the cafeteria or food service area the menu should be prominently displayed so that all customers may decide as far as possible what meal they will purchase before they arrive at the service points. This will save time at the service points and ensure that the customer turn-over is as quick as possible. At the beginning of the service counter will be a tray stand and each customer will collect his tray before pro-ceeding along the service counter. The layout of the counter is most important and it generally follows that the dishes are found in the order in which they appear on the menu. This could be as follows: Hors d'œuvre, fruit juices, fruit cock-tails, cold meats and salads, bread, rolls, butter, soups, hot fish dishes, hot meat dishes, hot vege-tables, hot sweets, cold sweets, ice-cream, assorted sandwiches, cakes and pastries, beverages and cold drinks. This makes it more convenient for the customer as the food items are in a logical order. An important aspect of the service coun-ter is the presentation of the cold items to be sold. These must be well and attractively dis-played, under cover for hygiene reasons and at the correct temperature. Those dishes put on show will act as a selling aid and bearing this in mind the responsibility rests with the person in charge of the kitchen and his or her staff.

With this form of service the meal may either be completely pre-plated or just have the main meat/fish dish plated and the potatoes, vege-tables, sauces and other accompaniments added according to the customer's choice. If the former is carried out this then ensures a quicker turn-over of custom through the various service points and requires less service top space. If the latter is the type of service offered then the turn-over of customer is much slower as the necessary potato, vegetables, sauces and accompaniments have to be added on request from the customer. Also more service top space is required for the vegetable and potato dishes and sauces and accompaniments to be kept hot in readiness for service. In this instance more staff will be required for service and this in turn could increase the cost of the meal. However, with this latter form of service wastage is cut to a minimum as the customer is able to choose exactly what he requires. The length of counter will generally be determined by the size of menu offered, but should not be too long as it would then restrict the speed of service. At the end of the counter would be sited the cashier who would charge for the meals chosen by the customers before they passed on to the seating area. The cutlery stands would be placed after the cashiers. They are placed here so that if a customer initially forgets to collect his cutlery he may go back for it with-out interrupting the queue of customers.

Where this form of service is being carried out cost is most important. To this end certain portion control equipment is used to ensure standardisation of the size of portion served. Such equipment would include scoops, ladles, bowls, milk dispensers, cold beverage dispensers, etc. At the same time great use is often made of pre-portioned foods such as butter, sugars, jams, cream, cheeses, biscuits, etc. All this is done to control the cost of the meal served and obtain the required profit.

Where the customer turnover rate is particular-ly high in a very limited period of time then a variation on the Cafeteria/Counter type service would operate with a number of separate service points. Each of these service points would offer a different main course dish together with the appropriate potato and vegetable dishes, and sauces and accompaniments. Other service points would offer hot and cold sweets, bever-ages, sandwiches, pastries, confectionery items and miscellaneous foods. In this way the customer on entering the food service area, checks the menu to see what he requires and then goes immediately to the appropriate service point. Thus, someone requiring just a sandwich and a hot drink is not held up by those selecting a full meal. This method will speed up the service so long as each of the service points are organised and staffed properly and with no delay when food needs replenishing.

The seating arrangements will depend on:
a) Size and shape of the food service area
b) Design of tables and chairs used
c) The allowance made for gangways and clearing trollies
d) Type of establishment.

As a guide, an allowance of $2\frac{1}{2}$-4 sq. m (10-12 sq. ft) per person is sufficient, this takes into account seating, table space, gangways and access to counters. The type of furniture used here must be pleasant to look at, hard-wearing, durable and easy to clean. The chairs used are usually of the stacking variety as this takes up less storage space when the food service area is being used for other types of functions and for cleaning. The tables themselves should be a variety of shapes, thus breaking the monotony of the lay-out of the room. The tops are usually of formica which facilitates cleaning. The edges and corners of the tables must be reinforced to avoid chipping and cracks when knocked by trollies, trays, etc. The formica top may come in a variety of colours and should tone in with the décor.

Care should be taken when planning a cafeteria that the customers waiting for a meal from the various service points do not interrupt the flow of customers around the tables, or going out through the main entrance. If this is not carefully watched then the flow and speed of service will be slowed quite considerably. At the same time stands should be placed in convenient positions for trays as they are finished with by the customer. Clearing staff should be moving around all the time with trollies clearing the dirties from the table, wiping down the table tops and emptying ashtrays. The dirties will then be deposited in the wash-up area, which should be sited as near the food service area as possible. Then when clean plates and cutlery are required they are immediately to hand. All dirties should be removed as quickly and quietly, with as little disturbance to the customer as is possible.

Snack Bar service: This again is a form of popular catering and there are many variations on this particular theme. For this form of service a number of customers are seated at the actual service counter itself. The menu can offer a wide range of dishes which should come within the popular price range. A very quick turnover is necessary for this form of service and labour costs are reduced to a minimum because as many customers as possible are seated at the service counter. Therefore the counter hand can take the order, prepare and plate up the dish required, and serve it. In order to do this effi-ciently and quickly and to keep the number of staff employed down to a minimum as much labour-saving equipment as possible should be used. This would include tea/coffee making machines; salamander, grill, cooling unit, refrigerators, deep frying unit, bain marie, hotplate and ovens, steam heat injectors and mixers. There may be a number of tables sited round the service counter and if this is the case a waiter or waitress would be needed to take the orders of customers seated at the tables, serve the dishes requested, receive the cash for the meal served and keep all the tables clear. Most snack bars are unlicensed unless incorporated within a larger concern as in railway catering.

Service à la française (French style): The main principle here is that the guests are able to help themselves to the dishes offered. It is very similar to the 'Family Service' already described. For a true **French service** the plates are placed at each cover and then the food items are presented to each guest in turn in order that they may help themselves.

Service à la russe (Russian style): This form of service is almost non-existent today. The principle involved was to have whole joints, poultry, game, and fish elaborately dressed-up and garnished which would be presented to the guests who would help themselves. Display and presentation was a great part of this form of service. Today it may still be seen to some extent in the form of the now popular **cold buffet.** The other aspect still seen is when gueridon service is involved and whole chickens, ducks, game, and fish are presented to the guest and then carved or filetted on the gueridon.

From what has been discussed one can see there are many forms of service, each with many variations, all of which are adapted to meet the demands of a particular situation.

7 food hygiene regulations

In every catering establishment hygiene is of the utmost importance. We have already talked about atmosphere and what helps to bring it about, and the social skills necessary in welcoming the guest and providing him with efficient service. This however will all be wasted if staff are not aware of the importance of:
1. Personal hygiene
2. Hygiene in the service and handling of food.

All food and beverage service staff must have a pride in their job. This shows in the clean and efficient way their work is carried out. Members of staff who are careless in their work, who have dirty habits and a slovenly manner very often lack the knowledge of how disease may be spread through the handling and service of food.

Food poisoning is caused by bacteria. Many of these bacteria are unable to move and their movement from one place to another may be effected by the human body, insects, animals and the wind. Food poisoning due to bacteria is classified into three main groups:

1. Staphylococcal food poisoning.
Staphylococci are found in infected cuts, burns, pimpels and boils. The infected area is usually the starting point of an outbreak, and generally human beings are the sources of infection in outbreaks of food poisoning due to this organism. Food handlers and service staff may carry this germ on their hands or in their nose and food is generally infected in its preparation or service. This is why great care must be taken when a member of staff receives a cut or burn or has a cold. They should receive immediate attention in order to prevent as far as possible any outbreak of food poisoning. Symptoms of this type of food poisoning are nausea, sickness, stomach cramp and diarrhoea, 2-4 hours after eating the contaminated food.

2. Salmonella food poisoning.
The source of infection here is sometimes the excreta of infected persons. Spread of this disease is caused by the food handler not washing his hands after using the toilets, and thereby contaminating food in its preparation and service. Symptoms of this type of food poisoning may not appear for up to 3 days after consuming the contaminated food, and are more severe than Staphylococcal food poisoning. Prevention may be effected by good personal hygiene in food handlers. It is useful as a reminder to post notices in prominent places to say 'Please wash your hands on leaving the toilet'.

3. Organisms other than Staphylococci or Salmonella.
Outbreaks of food poisoning here are usually caused by organisms which are not toxic to man in small numbers and are found in the mouth, skin and bowels. The foods usually affected are gravy, made-up dishes, trifles and custards. Symptoms usually appear 12-18 hours after consuming the contaminated food.

Very simply therefore we may say that food poisoning is mainly due to lack of personal cleanliness and not protecting food adequately against insects and vermin. Personal hygiene is of great importance as is the correct storage of all foods.

Personal Hygiene: Personal hygiene reduces the possibility of infection. The main points to note are:
1. Regular washing of the skin improves personal freshness removing perspiration.

2. Well groomed hair. Neatly cut. Covered where necessary.
3. Clean hands and nails. No nicotine stains. Washbasins, soap, towels, nailbrushes, hot water, must be provided.
4. Neat in appearance. Uniform smart, clean, and well starched. The employer must provide lockers for out-door clothing.
5. Clean and comfortable shoes are essential as staff are on their feet most of the day.
6. Coughing and sneezing over or near foods must be discouraged as this spreads infection.
7. Wash hands after leaving the toilets. Notices should be displayed to this effect.
8. Adequate provision should be made for drying hands. To avoid the possibility of cross-infection hot air dryers and disposable paper towels should be used wherever possible.
9. All cuts and burns should be treated (covered) immediately to avoid infection. First aid boxes must be kept near or in the food and beverage service areas.
10. All staff with colds, stomach upsets etc., should immediately report to the Doctor for a check-up before continuing work.
11. No smoking allowed whilst preparing or handling food.
12. No one is allowed to sleep in a food preparation room.

Hygiene in the service and handling of food

The main purpose of hygiene is to reduce the possibility of infection to a minimum. Points to note are:

1. All equipment used such as glasses, silver, china must be properly washed, rinsed and polished before being brought into use, and must not be used if chipped or cracked in any way. Adequate drying-up materials must be provided.
2. All storage space for such equipment must be scrupulously clean.
3. Refrigerators and other such storage space should be given special attention as this can become a breeding area for insects and bacteria.
4. The correct items of equipment should be used for the service of food and never the hands.
5. All equipment should be checked for cleanliness before use.
6. Where counter service is in operation appearance and personal hygiene is most important.
7. All services and equipment used must be thoroughly cleaned after the service is finished.
8. Any left over foods should be stored in the correct manner.
9. A proper refuse area must be provided so that debris does not collect in the service areas.
10. All areas used for the preparation, handling and service of food must be well ventilated and lit, so as to avoid accidents.
11. The employer is obliged to ensure that all toilets are kept clean and sufficient hand wash-basins with adequate materials are available at all times.

It is essential that all staff are aware of the points previously mentioned in order that their hygiene standards are as high as possible. This boosts their morale and will show in their work. It is advisable for an employer to have regular sessions with his food preparation and service staff to emphasise how important this is in catering and show how detrimental it can be without proper attention. How the employer puts this over is a matter of judgment for the individual, but it may be by means of films, specialist lectures, a basic training programme or an informal discussion between employer and employees. The Food Hygiene Regulations list all those points previously mentioned and elaborates on many of them. It must be remembered that both the employer and employee working in food premises are guilty of an offence and liable to a fine not exceeding £100 or to a term of imprisonment not exceeding 3 months if either fail to comply with the requirements of the *Food Hygiene Regulations 1960*, as applied to catering establishments.

8 the service area

The **service area** is usually between the kitchen and the food service areas. It is an important unit in the make-up of a catering establishment acting as the link between kitchen or food preparation unit and the restaurants or food service units. It is a meeting point for staff of various departments as they carry out their duties, and therefore there must be close liaison between these various members of staff and the departments under whose jurisdiction they come. The service area itself is one of the busiest units of a catering establishment especially over the service periods. Because of this it is most important that department heads ensure that all staff know exactly what their duties are and how to carry them out efficiently and quickly. A pride in the job and in doing it well means that the staff will co-operate with one another to give a complete and efficient service to the customer. The service area is made up of five sections as follows:

1. Stillroom
2. Silver or Plate room
3. Wash up
4. Hotplate
5. Spare linen store

The layout of these sections, in the service area, is most important to ensure an even flow of work by the various members of staff. The layout itself may vary with different catering establishments according to their needs. We will now deal, in turn, with each of the sections making up the service area.

1. THE STILLROOM

The main function of the Stillroom is to provide items of food and equipment required for the service of a meal and not catered for by the other major departments in a hotel, such as kitchen, larder and pantry.

The duties performed in the Stillroom will vary according to the type of meals offered and the size of the establishment concerned.

Staff

In a large first class establishment a Head still-room man or maid is in charge of the stillroom. Depending on its size and the duties to be performed he or she may have a number of staff under their control. The person in charge would be responsible for the compilation of work rotas for all the Stillroom staff so that all duties are covered and that it is fully manned from first thing in the morning till last thing at night. A further responsibility of the Head stillroom man or maid would be the ordering of supplies from the main dry goods store and the effective control of these items when issued to various departments.

When ordering goods from the main dry goods store all requirements should be written out on a requisition sheet in duplicate. The top copy goes to the store to be retained by the storekeeper after issuing the goods and the duplicate remains in the requisition book as a means of checking the receipt of goods from the store by a member of the Stillroom staff. No goods should be issued by the Storekeeper unless the requisition has been signed by the Head stillroom man or maid. Because of the number of hours that the Stillroom has to remain open and running efficiently the staff will normally work on a straight shift basis doing an early shift one week and a late shift the next. They are responsible for washing up all their own equipment.

Equipment

Because the requirements of most Stillrooms are basically the same, it follows that the equipment in all Stillrooms is of a similar nature. A wide range of food items are offered and therefore to ensure their correct storage, preparation and presentation a considerable amount of equipment is used. The following are the more essential items needed:

a) *Refrigerator:* for storage of milk, cream, butter, fruit juices etc.
b) *Butter Machine:* for portion control purposes.
c) *A Coffee Machine:* generally of the Still-Set type. Contained within this would be facilities for the provision of hot milk and hot water. Other forms of coffee machines which may be used would possibly be of the portable type and used and operated in the food service area itself. Depending on the type of establishment and its requirements the type of machine used here may be one of the following: Cory coffee machine, Cona coffee machine, Melitta automatic coffee machine etc.
d) *Large double sink and draining boards:* for washing up purposes and a *washing up machine* of a size suitable to a particular Stillroom.
e) *Tea Dispenser* for portion control purposes. This would always be kept locked and the key held by the Head stillroom man or maid.
f) *Salamander:* for the preparation of breakfast or melba toast.
g) *Bread Slicing machine*
h) *Hot Cupboard:* for plates, cups etc.
i) *Working top table* and cutting board.
j) The necessary storage space for all the *small equipment* such as china, glassware and silverware that is in everyday use.
k) *A storage cupboard* for all dry goods held in stock, and for such miscellaneous items as doilys, kitchen papers, paper serviettes, etc.
l) *A double gas ring* for preparation of porridge and boiled eggs.
m) *Coffee Grinding Machine.*

Provisions

As a basic guide the following food items would normally be dispensed from the Stillroom.

1. All beverages such as: coffee, tea, chocolate, Horlicks and other food drinks.
2. Assorted fruit juices: orange, pineapple, tomato, grapefruit.
3. Milk and cream
4. Sugars: loaf, pre-wrapped portions, brown coffee crystals.
5. Preserves: marmalade, cherry, plum, raspberry, strawberry, honey. For the purpose of control and saving with regard to wastage many establishments now offer pre-portioned jars or pots of jam at breakfast and for afternoon tea, rather than the preserve dish in which, if the preserve is unused it will very often be thrown away.
6. Butter: either passed through a butter pat machine, curled or pre-wrapped portions. Once prepared it is best kept in bowls of iced water.
7. Sliced and buttered brown, white and malt bread.
8. Rolls, brioche, croissant may be issued from here.
9. Melba toast: made by toasting a slice of bread, on both sides. Trim three sides and then cut through the slice horizontally on to the remaining crust. The crust acts as a guard against accidents. Remove the remaining crust. Remove any surplus dough on the untoasted side of the now two slices. Toast the untoasted sides to a golden brown colour. Each slice being so thin will curl slightly all round the edges. The melba toast would be served cold in a rose shaped serviette on a doily on an underflat. It is generally offered to the guest in place of rolls or gristicks at the beginning of the meal, either lunch or dinner.
10. Breakfast toast: This is thick sliced bread, toasted both sides, the crusts removed, cut into two triangles and placed in a toastrack.
11. Gristicks and starch reduced rolls.
12. Dry cracker and water biscuits and digestive for service with the Cheese Board. Sweet biscuits for service with early morning/afternoon teas.
13. Assorted breakfast cereals: cornflakes, weetabix, shredded wheat, rice crispies etc., In many establishments one now finds cereals of all types offered in a pre-wrapped, portion controlled packet. This again is a form of control and prevents the rapid deterioration of the cereal that one finds when a larger size packet is used. This deterioration occurs

when the cereal is left unwrapped and open to the air.

14. Toasted scones and tea-cakes: prepared to order and generally served with afternoon tea.

15. In a large establishment the pastries and gâteaux for afternoon tea will come from the Pastry department and the assorted savoury sandwiches from the larder. In a smaller establishment the pastries and gateaux would be bought from an outside firm but issued from the Stillroom, and sandwiches would be made and issued from the Stillroom. Also in the small establishment the Stillroom often provides both porridge and boiled eggs.

If the Stillroom prepare the sandwiches it is useful to know that an ordinary loaf contains 25 slices and that a quarten contains 50. This then makes 12 and 25 rounds respectively. Once prepared the sandwiches should be kept covered with a moist cloth, and the crusts removed only immediately before serving.

Control

A very careful and precise check must be kept on everything issued from the Stillroom.

There are two main ways of checking for goods to be issued, namely:

1. By issuing items in bulk on receipt of a requisition received from a food service area. The requisition must be signed by someone in authority. This would include such food items as butter, preserves, sugar etc.,

2. By issuing tea, coffee or any other beverage required in the necessary portions on receipt of a waiters check.

Morning coffee and afternoon tea are controlled in this way, the pastries, gateaux, toasted tea-cakes, sandwiches, bread and butter and preserves being issued on receipt of a waiters check, either in portions with the beverage, or in bulk by the sale or return method.

2. SILVER ROOM OR PLATE ROOM

In the larger more luxurious, establishments the Silver room, or Plate room as it is sometimes known, is a separate unit on its own. In the smaller establishment it is more often than not combined with the Pantry wash-up.

The Silver room should hold the complete stock of silver required for the service of all meals, together with a slight surplus stock in case of emergency. It will often be found that the silver for banqueting service is of different design and kept specifically for that purpose. The storage of silver is most important. The large silver such as flats, salvers, soup tureens, cloches etc., will be stored on shelves, with all the flats of one size together, and so on. All shelves would be labelled showing where each different item will go. This makes it easier for control purposes and for stacking. It should be remembered when stacking silver that the heavier items should go on the shelves lower down and the smaller and lighter items on the shelves higher up. This in itself will help to prevent accidents. All cutlery, and flatware together with the smaller items of silver such as ashtrays, cruets, butter dishes, special equipment, table numbers, menu holders, etc., are best stored in drawers lined with green baize. This helps to prevent noise and stops the cutlery sliding about the drawer when it is opened and closed and becoming scratched and marked.

All the service silver should be cleaned and burnished on a rota basis. It is the duty of the **Head plate man** to ensure that this is carried out and that all silver is cleaned regularly. Obviously those items in constant use will require more attention. He will also put on one side any articles of silver broken or that require buffing-up or replating, so that they may be sent to the manufacturers for any faults to be corrected.

The Head plate man may have a number of staff under him depending on the size of the establishment, whereas in the smaller medium class establishment where the Plate room is possibly combined with the Pantry wash-up it would be the duty of either the washing-up staff or the waiting staff to ensure that all the service silver is kept clean.

The cleanliness of all service silver is most important. There are various methods of silver cleaning, and the method used generally depends on the size and class of establishment. The larger establishments use a burnishing machine which would be in constant use all through the day, whereas the smaller establishment, which possibly could not afford a burnishing machine, would use 'silver dip' which is a much speedier method. The main methods used are as follows:

a) *Burnishing machine*

This is a revolving drum with a safety shield. It may be plumbed into the mains or remain portable with the water being poured in by means of a hose from a tap. Depending on the size of burnishing machine in use it may be divided into compartments to hold specific sizes of silver, and have a rod through the centre of the drum from one end to the other. This rod is removable and is passed through the handles of tea-pots, coffee pots, milk jugs, sugar basins etc., to hold them in position whilst the drum is revolving.

In order for the burnishing machine to run effectively and efficiently it is approximately half-full of ball-bearings. To these a certain amount of soap powder is added according to the makers instructions. The silver would be placed in and then the lid clamped down tightly. The main water supply is then turned on to ensure a constant flow of water. If the machine is not plumbed in then it should have water poured into the drum until the ball-bearings are covered, before the lid is clamped down. Then switch on. As the drum revolves the mixture of the water and soap powder acts as a lubricant between the silver and the ball-bearings. Thus any tarnish is removed but the silver is not scratched. On being removed from the burnishing machine the silver should be rinsed in hot water and dried with a clean tea cloth. This method of silver cleaning keeps the silver in good condition with minimum effort, and gives a lasting polish. The ball-bearings must always be kept covered with water, otherwise they rust very easily.

b) *Polivit*

A polivit is an aluminium metal sheet with holes in it. It is best used in an enamel or galvanised iron bowl. The polivit is placed in the bowl together with some soda. The silver to be cleaned is then put in the bowl making sure that at least one piece of silver has contact with the polivit. Sufficient boiling water is poured into the bowl to cover the silver being cleaned. A chemical reaction takes place between the polivit, soda, boiling water and silver, which causes the tarnish to be lifted. After 3-4 minutes the silver should be removed from the bowl and placed into a second bowl of boiling water and rinsed. Remove from the second bowl. Drain and then polish with a clean, dry teacloth. This method produces good results but is a little time consuming. It is

not a method found in many establishments at the present time.

c) *Plate powder*

This is a pink powder which has to be mixed with a little methylated spirit to a smooth paste. The reason for using methylated spirit to mix the powder with is that when the paste is rubbed on the article the spirit evaporates much more quickly than water would and the silver is therefore ready for polishing much quicker. If however methylated spirit is not available then water may be used, the cleaning process then taking a little longer. The smooth paste once prepared is rubbed onto the article being cleaned with a clean piece of cloth. The paste must be rubbed well in to remove all tarnish. The article is then left until the paste has dried, and the paste is then rubbed off with a clean cloth. It is advisable to rinse the article in very hot water and give a final polish with a clean dry teacloth. Where silver is cleaned which has a design or engravings on it a small toothbrush may be used to brush the paste into the design, and a clean one used to remove it. This method is both time consuming and messy but produces very good results. This method is not widely used.

d) *Silver Dip*

This is a pink coloured liquid which must be used in a plastic bowl. The silver to be cleaned is placed into a wire basket and dipped into the plastic bowl containing the Silver Dip. All the silver articles being cleaned should be covered by the liquid. The silver should be left in the bowl only a very short while and then lifted out and drained. After draining place in warm water and rinse. Polish with a clean dry teacloth. This method is very quick and produces good results, but it is harder on the silver than other methods because of the chemical reaction between the liquid and the silver. However this method is popular in the medium-sized establishment because staffing does not allow for a permanent Plate man and because it is quicker than other methods.

e) *Other forms of silver cleaning*

There are many other proprietory brands of silver cleaning material on the market. These take the form of pastes, powders or cloths impregnated with silver cleaning properties. Very few, if any, of these would be used in a catering establishment as most of them are on the market for domestic purposes.

3. THE WASH-UP

The Wash-Up is a most important part of the service area, and must be sited correctly so that the brigade can work speedily and efficiently when passing from the food service areas to the kitchens. The waiter should stack his trays of dirties correctly at his sideboard, with all the correct sized plates together, and cutlery stacked on one of the plates with the blades of the knives running under the arch in the middle of the fork. All glassware should be stacked on a separate tray and taken to a separate wash-up point. On entering the service area from the food service area the waiter should immediately meet the wash-up where he will deposit all his dirty plates, stacking them correctly and placing all the cutlery in a special wire basket or container in readiness for washing. The waiter must place any debris into the bin or bowl provided. All used paper serviettes, doilies or kitchen paper will be placed in a separate bin. The china itself may be washed by one of two main methods.

a) *Tank method*
The dirty china will be placed into a tank of hot water containing a soap detergent. After washing, the plates are placed into wire racks and dipped into a second sterilising tank containing clean hot water at a temperature of approximately 75° C (170° F). The racks would be left for two minutes and then lifted out and the china left to drain. If sterilised in water at this temperature the china will dry by itself without the use of drying-up cloths. This is therefore more hygenic. After drying, the china is stacked into piles of the correct size and placed onto shelves until required for further use.

b) *Machine method*
Many of the larger establishments have washing-up machines. These are necessary because of the high turnover rate of china. The instructions for use of a washing-up machine are generally supplied by the manufacturer together with details of detergent to be used, and in what quantity. These directions should be strictly adhered to. The china itself has any debris removed and is then placed into either wooden or wire racks. The racks are then passed through the machine, the china being washed, rinsed, and then sterilised in turn. Having passed through the machine the china is left to drain for 2-3 minutes and it is then stacked and placed

on shelves until required for further use. As with the tank method the plates do not require drying with teacloths.

4. THE HOT PLATE

The hotplate may be regarded as the meeting point between the food service staff and the food preparation staff. It is most essential that there is active co-operation and a good relationship between the staff of these two service area's. This helps a great deal to ensure that the customer receives an efficient and quick service of his meal, from a polite and courteous waiter who has not been 'roused' because of bad service at the hot plate. This co-operation will also ensure that all the dishes served are well and attractively presented. At the same time all orders written by the waiters must be legible to the Aboyeur so that there is no delay in 'calling-up' a particular dish Also the food service staff should, queue at the hotplate in order and not cause confusion by jumping the queue.

The Aboyeur (or Barker) is in charge, and controls the hotplate over the service period. As an aid to the food service staff the Aboyeur would control the 'Off Board', which tells the waiter/ess immediately any dish is 'off'. It should be sited in a prominent position for all to see. The hotplate itself should be stocked up with all the china necessary for the service of a meal. This would include some or all of the following items: soup plates, fish plates, joint plates, sweet plates, consommé cups, platters, soup cups and demi-tasse. The silver required for service is often placed on the top of the hot-plate and used as required. The hotplate is usually gas or electrically operated and should be lit well in advance of the service to ensure all the necessary china and silver is sufficiently heated.

The Aboyeur who controls the hotplate over the service period will initially receive the food check from the waiter. He checks that it is legible to him and that none of the dishes ordered are 'off' the menu. He then calls up the order from the various corners of the kitchen as each particular dish is required. It is important that if a dish required has to be prepared and cooked to order that the Aboyeur orders this to be done before the waiter comes to the hotplate to collect it. Then there will be no major delay by the waiter who is going to serve the dish, or by the customer who is waiting for the next course to be served. When a food check is finished with it is placed into a control box. This 'box' is kept locked and can only be opened by a member of staff from the 'control department' who for control purposes marries up the copy of the food check from the kitchen with the copy the cashier has and the duplicate copy of the bill.

To ensure there is no delay in any food dish reaching the hotplate the Aboyeur should call them up allowing time for preparation cooking and presentation. To this end special kitchen terms are used to warn the food preparation staff working in the various corners to get ready certain dishes.

These terms are as follows:

i. General warning to kitchen that the service is about to commence.
   '*Le service va commencer*'.
ii. An indication to the kitchen of the number of covers.
   '*Ca marche trois couverts*'
iii. Inform the '*partie*' concerned of the order required.
   '*Poissonier faites marche trois sole veronique*'.
iv. When the order is required at the hotplate by the waiter the Aboyeur calls it up from the appropriate '*partie*'.
   '*Poissonier envoyez les trois sole veronique*'.
v. Each '*chef de partie*' must reply to the order

called out by the Aboyeur. The reply being: '*Oui*'.
vi. Where an extra special order is required the term called out by the Aboyeur before the actual order is: *Bien soigné!*
vii. To hurry up an order use the word: *Dépêchez-vous*.
viii. To cancel an order use the term: *Arréter*
ix. Foods requiring special degrees of cooking are given the following terms:
   Omelette: *Baveuse*, soft inside.
   Steak Grille: *à bleu* (rare), surfaces well browned, inside raw
   saignant, underdone
   à point, medium
   bien cuit, cooked right through. Well done.

All food service staff should be familiar with these terms in order to appreciate exactly what is going on at the hotplate and how the particular 'kitchen french' terms help to ensure quick and efficient service.

5. SPARE LINEN STORE

Generally within the service area is found a spare linen cupboard. This is normally the responsibility of a senior member of the food service staff. It is kept locked for control purposes. This spare linen stock is held near the food service area in case of emergency. The linen is changed when necessary on a basis of 'one clean' for 'one dirty'.

9 beverages

The word beverage means simply a drink. When the word beverage is used with reference to the Stillroom it means tea or coffee no matter in what form it may be served. Tea is regarded as the Englishman's national beverage, although nowadays in many spheres of the catering trade, especially in industrial catering, coffee is becoming the most popular beverage. There has been an increased consumption of both tea and coffee over the past few years, and this, together with the gain in popularity of coffee, is perhaps largely due to the boom in vending machines. This is emphasised by the fact that the sale of goods, including coffee, from machines totalled over £2 million in 1966, an increase of 35% on 1965, and a 23% growth was forecast for 1967/68.

The provision of a well-made and piping hot beverage is of the utmost importance in concluding a good dinner, or putting the guest in the right frame of mind at breakfast and throughout the day, or in giving the member of staff more zest for his job. A good beverage is said to be regarded as a factor contributing towards job continuity, minimising absenteeism and increasing production. The importance of the Stillroom and its staff cannot, therefore, be underestimated as it is from here that the majority of beverages are made and despatched via the commis-waiter to the restaurant; the lounge waiter to the lounge, and sometimes the floor-waiter or chambermaids to various apartments and suites. The staff in the Stillroom must have a first hand knowledge of the various methods of making and service of both tea and coffee. The Stillroom itself is generally situated within the service area, that is between the kitchen and food service areas as this is most convenient for the food and beverage service staff. For other information on the Stillroom or service area see the section on the Service Area, page 43.

TEA

Most teas used in the Stillroom are blended teas sold under proprietary brands or names. All teas are fermented during the process of manufacture which gives them their black colour. The one exception is China tea which is classed as a green tea. Although the tea used in the Stillroom may be requisitioned daily from the dry goods store, tea is an expensive commodity, even when bought in bulk (chest), and bad storage may cause loss of money to the establishment concerned.

Points to note with regard to storage are as follows:
a) Dry, clean and covered container.
b) Well ventilated Stillroom.
c) Away from excess moisture.
d) Must not be kept near any strong smelling foods as tea very quickly absorbs strong odours.

If the above points are noted by the Stillroom staff the quality of the tea in use will remain first class. The type of tea used will of course depend on the customers' choice and cost, but most Stillrooms carry a varied stock of Indian, Ceylon and China tea. The quantities of dry tea used per pot or per gallon may vary slightly with the type of tea used but as an approximate guide the following may be adhered to:
42.5-56.7 grammes ($1\frac{1}{2}$-2 oz) dry tea per 4.546 litres (1 gallon).
$\frac{1}{2}$ litre (1 pt) of milk will be sufficient for 20/24 cups.
$\frac{1}{2}$ kilogramme (1 lb) loaf sugar for approximately 80 cups.

When brewing smaller amounts in the Still-room, such as a pot for one or two, it is often advisable to install a measure. This then ensures standardisation of brew and control on the commodity in use. Other means of pre-portioning tea may be used, such as tea-bags. When making tea in bulk and calculating quantities of tea required for a party, allow approximately 1/6 of a litre (1/3 of a pint) per cup or 24 cups per 4.546 litres (1 gallon). If breakfast cups are used, capacity approximately $\frac{1}{4}$ litre ($\frac{1}{2}$ pint), then allow only 16 cups to 4.546 litres (1 gallon)

Because tea is an infusion and therefore the maximum flavour is required from the brew, a few simple rules carefully observed will obtain satisfactory results. These are:

1. Heat the pot before putting the dry tea in, so that the maximum heat can be obtained from the boiling water.
2. Measure the dry tea and water exactly.
3. Use freshly boiled water.
4. Make sure the water is boiling on entering the pot.
5. Allow to brew for 3-4 minutes to obtain maximum strength from the brew.
6. Remove the tea leaves at the end of this period if making in multipot insulated urns.
7. Ensure all equipment used is scrupulously clean.

The type of tea served should always govern the style of service.

Indian or Ceylon

Indian or Ceylon tea may be made in either china or metal tea-pots, remembering that the simple rules mentioned above must always be adhered to. Usually both are offered with milk in this country. Sugar would be offered separately.

China tea

This is made from a special blend of tea which is more delicate in flavour and perfume than any other tea, but lacks 'body'. Less dry tea is required than for making Indian or Ceylon tea.

It is made in the normal way and is best served in a china pot. China tea is normally drunk on its own, but may be improved, according to taste, by the addition of a slice of lemon. Slices of lemon would be offered on a doily on a sideplate with a small (dessert) fork. China tea is rarely served with milk. Sugar may be offered.

Russian or Lemon tea

This may be brewed from a special blend similar to China tea, but more often than not is made from either Indian or Ceylon tea. It is made in the normal way, and is usually served with a slice of lemon. The tea is served in $^1/_4$ litre (half-pint) glasses, which stand in a silver holder with a handle, and on a doily on a sideplate with a teaspoon. A slice of lemon may be placed in the glass, and a few slices of lemon served separately on a doily on a sideplate with a small (dessert) fork. Sugar would be served separately.

Iced tea

Make strong tea and chill well. This iced tea may then be strained and stored chilled until required. It should be served in a tumbler, on a doily, on a sideplate, and with a teaspoon. A slice of lemon may be placed in the glass and some lemon should be served separately as for Russian tea.

Herb teas

These are an infusion of certain herbs and grasses and used for medicinal purposes. Also, they do not contain caffein, which is a stimulant. Such teas are Camomile, Mint, Senna. They should always be made in china pots in order to preserve the delicate flavour, and served without milk or any other additions.

COFFEE

Coffee, like tea, may be made in many different ways and will be served from the Stillroom, or appropriate service point, according to the waiter's check received. As coffee is also an infusion, and the maximum flavour and strength is required, similar rules should be observed in its making as those for tea. The rising popularity of coffee over the past few years may be attributed to the fact that nowadays more and more people spend their holidays on the Continent. Coffee is the Continent's most popular drink and therefore is one of the first habits that tourists pick up abroad. The coffee bar, relatively new in catering, is now here to stay and has become the informal meeting place for many of the younger generation where they can obtain a good cup of coffee at a reasonable price. Methods of brewing can vary, ranging from instant coffee brewed by the cup, through 1$\frac{1}{2}$-3 litre (3-6 pints) units and up to machines that may cope with large functions. It must be remembered that it is very important to choose a method of coffee making suitable to ones particular catering requirements. Coffee beans may themselves be purchased either roasted or unroasted and may then be ground according to requirements. The beans should not be ground until immediately before they are required and this will ensure the maximum flavour and strength from the oils within the coffee bean. If ground coffee is purchased it normally comes in vacuum packed packets in order to maintain it in first class condition until use. These packets contain set quantities to make 4.5 litres, (1 gallon) and 9 litres (2 gallons) and so on. As for tea it must be noted that coffee is an expensive commodity and therefore the utmost care must be taken in its storage. Points to note with regard to storage are as follows:

1. well ventilated storeroom
2. air-tight container for ground coffee to ensure that the oils do not evaporate, causing loss of flavour and strength
3. away from excess moisture
4. must not be stored near any strong smelling foods, as coffee will absorb their odour

When making coffee in bulk for a special party, in order to work out their requirements with regard to the beverage it should be noted that 283.5-340 g (10/12 oz) of ground coffee are sufficient to make 4.5 litres (1 gallon) of black coffee. Assuming that tea-cups with a capacity of 1/6 of a litre (1/3 of a pint), will be used then 283.5-340 grammes (10/12 oz) of ground coffee is sufficient to provide 24 cups of black coffee or 48 cups if serving half coffee and half milk. When breakfast cups are used then 16 cups of black coffee or 32 cups of half coffee and half milk will be available. Capacity, at a dinner where demi-tasse, 1/12 of a litre (1/6 of a pint), are used is 48 cups of black coffee or 96 cups of half black coffee and half milk are available.

The rules to be observed when making coffee are as follows:

1. Use freshly roasted and ground coffee.
2. Buy the correct grind for type of machine you may have in use.
3. Ensure all your equipment is clean before use.
4. Use a set measure of coffee to water: 283.5-340 grammes per 4.5 litres (10/12 oz p. gallon).
5. Add boiling water to the coffee and allow to infuse. The infusion time must be controlled according to type of coffee being used and the method of making.

6. Control temperature as to boil coffee is to spoil coffee. The coffee develops a bitter taste.
7. Strain and serve.
8. Add milk or cream separately.
9. The best serving temperatures are, for coffee 82°C (180°F); and for milk 68°C (155°F).

Reasons why bad coffee is produced:

Weak Coffee
1. Water has not reached boiling point.
2. Insufficient coffee
3. Infusion time too short
4. Stale or old coffee used
5. Incorrect grind of coffee used for equipment in operation

Flat Coffee
1. All points for weak coffee
2. Coffee left in urn to long before use, or kept at wrong temperature
3. Dirty urn or equipment
4. Water not fresh, or boiled too long
5. Coffee reheated

Bitter Coffee
1. Too much coffee used
2. Infusion time too long
3. Coffee not roasted correctly
4. Sediment remaining in storage or serving compartment
5. Infusion at too high a temperature
6. Coffee may have been left in urn too long before use.

Service of coffee
Coffee may be made in many ways and the service depends on the method used. The Still-room staff must again have a full knowledge of the methods of making and serving coffee in order to ensure it reaches the guest in peak condition with maximum flavour and strength, piping hot, correct accompaniments and served in the right type of container.

The following are ways in which coffee may be made and served.

Instant coffee
This may be made in individual coffee or tea-cups or in large quantities. It is the mixing of soluble coffee solids with boiling water. When making instant coffee in bulk allow approximately 71 grammes (2½ oz) to each gallon of water. This form of coffee may be made very

quickly, immediately before it is required, by pouring freshly boiled water onto a measured quantity of coffee powder. Stir well. Hot or cold milk, cream and sugar may be added to taste.

Saucepan or jug method

This is an American method of making coffee more often used in the home than in a catering establishment. A set measure of ground coffee is placed in a saucepan or jug and the required quantity of freshly boiled water is poured onto the coffee grounds. This should then be allowed to stand for a few minutes to extract the full flavour and strength from the ground coffee. Then strain and serve. Hot or cold milk, cream and sugar may be added as desired.

Percolator method

This method is again used more in the home than commercially. A set quantity of coffee grounds are placed in the percolator, which is then filled with freshly drawn water. The water upon reaching boiling point rises up through a tube and percolates the coffee grounds extracting to the full, flavour, colour and strength, Upon reducing the heat to the percolator the liquid no longer infuses with the coffee grounds and falls back into the percolator as coffee ready to serve. Hot or cold milk, cream and sugar may be added to taste.

Cona coffee

This method of making coffee has considerable eye appeal in the restaurant, and has the advantage of the coffee served always being fresh as only limited quantities are made at one time. It also avoids making too much coffee and therefore avoids wasting or serving old, flat, bitter coffee during another food service period. Many appliances are electrically operated or heated by means of a methylated spirit lamp. Banks of these machines may be used for varying requirements, housing two, three, four or five containers at one time. They are compact and portable and very easy to keep clean. The method of making the coffee is fairly simple in itself, but is best supervised to ensure obtaining the best results and a constant standard. The filters in this vacuum-type equipment are sometimes of glass, but more often than not they are made of plastic or metal and held in place by a spring. This in itself is a saving as breakages are not so frequent. This also applies when the Cory type coffee

making machine is used, as here the upper bowl or both upper and lower bowls may be made of aluminium. This detracts to some extent from eye appeal in the room, but is again a saving in breakages and it produces a cup of coffee of equivalent quality.

The method of making coffee here is similar to the percolator method. Fill the lower bowl with cold water, or to speed up the operation, freshly heated but not boiled water, up to the water level. Place the filter in place in the upper bowl ensuring it is securely fixed, and then put in the required quantity of ground coffee according to the amount of water being used. Now set the upper bowl in the lower bowl making sure it is securely in place, and proceed to heat the water. As the water reaches boiling point it rises up the tube into the upper bowl mixing with the ground coffee. As it rises in the upper bowl it is very often best to stir the mixture gently to ensure that all coffee grounds infuse with the liquid, as sometimes the grounds are inclined to form a cap on top of the liquid and therefore do not fully infuse. At the same time beware you do not knock the filter as this may cause grains to pass into the lower bowl. On reducing the heat the coffee liquid, as it now is, passes back into the lower bowl leaving the grounds in the upper bowl. Remove the upper bowl and filter and wash them ready for re-use. The coffee in the lower bowl is now ready for use and should be served at a temperature of approximately 82° C (180° F). The coffee may be served with hot or cold milk or cream, with sugar to taste.

Filter coffee (Café filtre)

This is a method largely used in France and which reverses the processes for making Cona coffee. The filter method produces excellent coffee. Fresh boiled water is poured into a container with a very finely meshed bottom which stands on a cup. Within the container is the required amount of ground coffee. The infusion takes place and the coffee liquid falls into the cup. Filter papers may be used to avoid the grounds passing into the lower cup, but this may depend on how fine or coarse is the ground coffee that is being used.

By means of this method coffee may be made individually by the cup or in bulk for a party. One must ensure before starting to make coffee by this method that all equipment is hot otherwise the resulting coffee is cold. This is also an excellent method for the 'bar top' in a public house where coffee may be served in conjunction with hot or cold snacks, or where it may be offered at the end of a meal. For this purpose, when one is unsure of the quantity required, the automatic 'melitta' may fill the gap. It makes 2-8 cups of coffee in about 5 minutes and may be set up on either the bar top or any small space available. This is a fully automatic coffee machine.

A further alternative is the disposable, individual filter, bought with the required amount of coffee already sealed in the base of the filter. This is sufficient for one cup and after use the whole filter may be thrown away. The advantage of this method is that every cup may be made to order, and appeals to the customer as he sees that he is receiving entirely fresh coffee as well as it having a certain novelty value.

When making a cup of coffee by this method freshly boiled water should be poured into the filter up to the required level. The boiling water causes the seal to break and the coffee liquid then falls into the cup. A lid should be placed over the water in the filter to help retain the temperature. Time of making is approximately 3-4 minutes.

Espresso coffee

This method, Italian in origin, came to Britain in the 1950's. The machines used in making this form of coffee can provide cups of coffee individually in a matter of seconds, some machines being capable of making 300/400 cups of coffee per hour. With this type of machine the coffee used must be finely ground. The method involves passing steam through the finely ground coffee and infusing under pressure. The advantage is that each cup is made freshly for the customer. Served black the coffee is known as 'Espresso' and is served in a small glass cup. If milk is required it is heated for each cup, by a high pressure steam injector, and transforms a cup of black coffee into 'Cappuccino'. As an approximate guide, from $\frac{1}{2}$ kg (1 lb) of coffee used, 80 cups of good strength coffee may be produced. The general rules for making coffee apply here, but with this special and delicate type of equipment extra care should be taken in following any instructions.

Still-set coffee

This is perhaps the most widely used method in all Stillrooms. It normally consists of a small central container into which the correct sized filter paper is placed with the ground coffee on top, and an urn on either side of varying capacities according to requirements. The urns may be $4\frac{1}{2}$, 9, 13 or 18 litres (1-2-3-4 gallons) in size. These still-sets are easy to operate but must at all times be kept very clean and regularly serviced. The urns should be rinsed before and after each brew until water runs clear. This removes the thin layer of cold coffee which clings to the side of an urn and, if left, will spoil the flavour and aroma of the next brew. Boiling water is passed through the grounds and the coffee passes into the urns at the side. Infusion should be complete in 6-8 minutes for $4\frac{1}{2}$ litres (1 gallon) of coffee, using medium ground coffee. The milk is heated in a steam jacket container. It should be held at a constant temperature of 65.5° C because if held at too high a temperature, or boiled, or heated too soon, on coming into contact with the coffee it will destroy its flavour and taste. At the same time the milk itself becomes discoloured. The coffee and milk should now be held separately, at their correct temperatures ready for serving.

De-caffeinised coffee

Coffee beans contain caffein which is a stimulant. De-caffeinised coffee is made from beans after the caffein has been extracted. This coffee is sold in Europe under the trade name of *Café Hag*, whilst in America it is known as *Sanka coffee*.

Iced coffee

Make strong black coffee in the normal way. Strain and chill well until required. It may be served mixed with an equal quantity of cold milk for a smooth beverage, or with cream. It is served in a tall glass, with ice cubes added and with straws. The glass should stand on a doily on a sideplate with a teaspoon and where necessary some cream served separately.

Irish coffee

Heat a 18.93 cl (6⅔ oz) paris goblet, and place in it the coffee sugar required by the guest. (A certain amount of sugar is always required when serving this form of coffee as it is an aid to floating the double cream on the surface of the hot coffee. The waiter must ensure the guest realises this.) Placing a teaspoon in the goblet to conduct the heat and avoid cracking the goblet, pour in the strong black coffee. Stir well to dissolve the

sugar. Now add one measure of Irish Whiskey. The liquid should now be within $2\frac{1}{2}$ cm (1 in) of the top of the goblet. Using double cream, pour it slowly over the back of a teaspoon on to the surface of the coffee until approximately 1.9 cm or ($\frac{3}{4}$ in) thick. Do not stir: the best flavour is obtained by drinking the coffee and whiskey through the cream. This method of making coffee may be carried out at the table and has eye appeal. As the fat content of cream is much higher than that of milk less may be used, and it should not be heated. When the Irish coffee has been prepared the goblet will be put on a doily on a sideplate and placed in front of the guest. If brandy is used

A tray laid for the service of Irish coffee.
Irish coffee is normally served by the waiter at the table. He requires the following equipment:
Silver salver
Serviette
18.93 cl ($6^2/_3$ oz) Paris goblet on a doily on an underplate
Teaspoon
Jug of double cream
'6 out' measure
Coffee pot
Sugar basin of coffee sugar with a teaspoon
Bottle of Irish whiskey

instead of whiskey the coffee is known as Café Royale.

Turkish or Egyptian coffee

This is made from darkly roasted Mocha beans which are ground to a fine powder. The coffee is made in special copper pots which are placed on top of a stove or lamp and the water is then allowed to boil. The sugar should be put in at this stage to sweeten the coffee as it is never stirred once poured out. The finely ground coffee may be stirred in or the boiling water poured onto the grounds. The amount of coffee used is approximately one heaped teaspoonful per person. Once the coffee has been stirred in, the copper pot is taken off the direct heat and the cooling causes the grounds to settle. It is brought to the boil and allowed to settle twice more and is then sprinkled with a little cold water to settle any remaining grains. The coffee is then served in small cups. While making the coffee it may be further flavoured with vanilla pods but this is optional.

From the various methods shown for making and serving tea and coffee it is obvious that the thorough training and supervision of Stillroom staff is all important for producing first quality tea or coffee.

A new fuel which may be used for heating jugs of coffee in the room is the 'Instaheat' a non-melting jelly like fuel, which ignites readily and which may be extinguished and relit as many times as desired. Other beverages may be offered from the Stillroom such as cocoa, drinking chocolate, Horlicks and Bovril, and these should be readily available. They should be prepared and served according to the makers instructions.

Equipment required for the service of a tea and coffee tray

Tea tray

1. Tray or salver
2. Tray cloth
3. Tea pot
4. Hot water jug
5. Jug of cold milk
6. Slop basin
7. Tea strainer
8. Stands for tea pot and hot water jug
9. Sugar basin and tongs
10. Tea cup and saucer
11. Tea spoon

Coffee tray

1. Tray or salver
2. Tray cloth
3. Tea cup and saucer
4. Teaspoon
5. Sugar basin & tongs or a teaspoon according to the type of sugar offered.
6. Coffee pot
7. Jug of hot milk or cream
8. Stands for the coffee pot and hot milk jug

Variations of the above basic equipment will depend on the type of tea or coffee offered. Points to note in laying up a tea or coffee tray:

a) Positioning of the items to ensure an evenly balanced tray for carrying.
b) Positioning of the items for convenience of the guest: beverage on the right with handles facing the guest for ease of pouring.
c) Ensure the beverage is placed on the tray at the last moment so that it is served piping hot.

Note: When serving coffee the waiter must remember to ask the guest if he would prefer black coffee or coffee with milk or cream. Not 'black coffee' or 'white coffee'. There is no such thing as white coffee.

10 the duties of the floor waiter and lounge waiter

The lounge waiter and floor waiter are members of the food and beverage team who work outside the main area of service, namely the restaurant/dining room or grill room. Each have their own specific duties to carry out according to the type of establishment in which they work. The Chef d'étage, or Floor waiter as he is known, is generally responsible for a complete floor in an establishment; or depending on the size of the establishment, a number of rooms and suites on one floor. Floor service of all meals throughout the day is normally only offered by a first class establishment where the charge for such a service is quite high. In medium class establishments floor service is usually limited to early morning teas and breakfasts. As the name suggests, Floor service (also known as room service) means the service of a meal of some sort to a guest in his room. Where a full floor service is in operation the staff would consist of a Head floor waiter with a number of floor waiters working under him.

The Lounge waiter may deal with Lounge service as a specific duty only in a first class establishment. In a smaller establishment it is usual for a member of the food and beverage service team to take over the duties of a lounge waiter on a rota basis. The lounge waiter and the floor waiter may be the first to greet potential customers and show the standards of service set by the establishment. They must be, therefore, smart in appearance, have a good overall knowledge of food and beverage service, and be attentive and efficient in their service to the guest.

Chef d'étage (Floor waiter)

The Floor waiter operates his service from a floor pantry: there may be one on each floor of an establishment or one sited to service two or three floors. An alternative system is where all food and beverages come from a central kitchen and would be sent to the appropriate floor by lift and then taken to the rooms in a hot trolly.

It is appreciated that the Floor waiters must have considerable experience as they have to deal with the service of all types of meals. They also have to deal with the service of all alcoholic beverages and so must have a good knowledge of the licensing laws. The Floor waiters work on a shift system as a service has to be provided virtually 24 hours a day, from first thing in the morning until last thing at night.

The guest may call for the Floor waiter by pressing a button which lights up a series of coloured lights in the corridor, or alternatively lights up a panel in the floor pantry which is divided into numbered sections denoting the rooms. The guest may telephone direct to the floor pantry, or telephone his request to reception or the restaurant or dining room where a note is made of it and immediately passed on to the necessary floor pantry so that the service may be organised.

It is essential that a strict control is kept for service given on all the floors. A food or wine check must be made out for all requests from the guests, or in the event of special luncheon or dinner parties a bill will be made out and presented to the host who will sign it to show he has received the services listed. It is most important that a signature is obtained in case of any query or complaint when the bill is presented to a guest on leaving an establishment. All checks once signed by the guest should be passed immediately to reception or control so that the services rendered may be charged to his account. All orders are taken in triplicate, the top copy

The **hot trolly** or **cabinet** is used by the Floor waiter (Chef d'étage) to transport hot meals from the kitchen or floor pantry to the host's suite. The trolly may be plugged in and switched on until the meal is required. The heating of the trolly may be thermostatically controlled. The Floor waiter should ensure that the trolly is sufficiently heated before any hot food is placed in it.

going to the department supplying the food or beverage required, a duplicate going to control or reception after being signed by the guest and the third copy kept by the Floor waiter as a means of reference.

This suggested method of control varies slightly according to the establishment. In many establishments it should be noted that the guest is rarely asked to sign for service given in his room or suite. Where this is the case and any queries arise on the presentation of the bill then it could cause some difficulty and embarrassment to both the establishment and the guest, and possible result in the loss of a future customer.

The floor pantry from which the Floor waiter operates holds all the equipment required for the service of any meal. This equipment would include:

1. Sink unit
2. Hotplate
3. Refrigerator
4. Lift to central kitchen
5. Salamander
6. Open gas rings
7. Small still set or other coffee making machine
8. Cutting boards
9. Knives

10. Storage space-shelves and cupboards for
11. China
12. Silverplate, hollow-ware
13. Cutlery, flatware
14. Glassware
15. Cruets, Worcestershire sauce, sugars etc.,
16. Linen
17. Gueridon trollies
18. Chaffing lamps and Suzette pans
19. Wine service equipment, wine buckets, stands, baskets etc.,
20. Trays etc.,

Sufficient equipment must be available so that efficient service can be given at all times and a high standard maintained. The Floor waiter carries out all his own pre-service preparation (mise-en place) before the service of a meal. This would include the checking and refilling of cruets and other accompaniments, laying up of breakfast trays, changing of linen, laying up of tables, washing and polishing glasses, cleaning trays etc. A strict control of all equipment is essential and to this end it should be noted that some establishments provide a different style and design of china, etc., for the service of meals on the floors. This is an aid to control and although possibly a little extravagant this charge is included in the price charged for floor service. Regular stock-taking should be carried out.

Finally it is sufficient to say that the Floor waiter must co-operate with other staff within the establishment. In this instance it would be with the House keeping staff. The Floor waiter would ensure that all rooms are cleared as soon as meals are finished so as not to be in the way when rooms are being cleaned.

Lounge waiter

In a first class establishment a Lounge waiter may possibly operate from his own service pantry, although in most instances the lounge waiter works and liases with the Stillroom or one of the dispense bars for the service of all types of beverage required, alcoholic or non-alcoholic. The Lounge waiter generally has a small service cupboard, of which only he has the key, and which holds a basic stock of items that he may need in case of emergency. These items may be as follows:
1. Small linen stock
2. Ashtrays
3. Salvers

4. Glasses: assorted
5. Cups, saucers for the service of hot beverages
6. Basic alcoholic drink stock for use when bars are closed and he has to serve guests in the Lounge, to include:
   Spirits
   Aperitifs
   Brandies
   Liqueurs
   Minerals
7. Coctail snacks:
   olives
   cocktail onions
   cocktail cherries
   gherkins
   salted peanuts
   cheese sticks, etc.
8. Beverages: Horlicks, Ovaltine, Coffee, Bovril, Cocoa, Chocolate
9. Dry goods: coffee, loaf and granulated sugar
10. Check pads, bill pads, stock sheets for alcoholic drink

The Lounge waiter must be prepared for the service of the following in the Lounge:
1. Morning coffee and biscuits
2. Aperitifs and cocktails before luncheon
3. Coffee, liqueurs and brandy after luncheon
4. Afternoon tea
5. Aperitifs and cocktails before dinner
6. Coffee, liqueurs and brandy after dinner
7. Service of late night beverages both alcoholic and non-alcoholic.

A tight control must be kept on all items served. It is normal for a chance customer to pay cash for a service rendered, but a resident may not wish to pay cash and the Lounge waiter must then ensure that the guest signs the check to confirm the services received. The amount outstanding will then be charged to his account which will be paid when he leaves the establishment at the end of his visit. All checking will be in triplicate, the top copy going to the supplying department, i.e. Stillroom or Dispense bar. A duplicate will either stay with the Lounge waiter if he has to make out a bill for a chance customer, or go to reception, or control, and the resident's account will be charged accordingly. The 'flimsy' or third copy will remain with the Lounge waiter as a means of reference. Stocktaking should be held at regular intervals with the occasional spot check on certain items. Stocksheets should be completed daily and may be in the form of a Daily consumption sheet showing the daily sales and the cash received, and this may be checked against the checks showing the orders taken.

The Lounge waiter commences his preparation in the morning ensuring all the lounge is clean. The carpets must be hoovered, coffee tables polished, ashtrays emptied and clean, tables in position, brasses polished and everything ready for service. In a busy establishment once the service commences in the morning it may be almost continuous throughout the day, and therefore it should be one of the Lounge waiters duties to keep the lounge presentable at all times, the table tops clean, ashtrays emptied and all 'dirties' removed.

Before luncheon and dinner he would place cocktail snacks on the coffee table and after lunch he would prepare the tables for the service of afternoon tea. Finally it should be noted that the Lounge is very often the front window of the establishment and there the standards of service should be high, reflecting the overall standards. This responsibility rests with the Lounge waiter and he must therefore be of smart appearance, efficient and attentive to the guests. He should have a good knowledge of food and beverage service and especially the licensing laws and his obligations to both guest and management.

11 the menu

Origin of the menu

In olden times the 'Bill of fare' as it is termed in English, or '*menu*' in French, was not presented at the table. The banquet consisted of only two courses, each made up of a variety of dishes, anything from 10-40 in number. The first 10-40 dishes were placed on the table before the diners entered—hence the word *entrée*—these, when consumed, were removed or relieved by 10-40 other dishes—hence the words *relevés* and *removes*.

It is said that in the year 1541, Duke Henry of Brunswick was seen to refer to a long slip of paper. On being asked what he was looking at he said it was a form of programme of the dishes, and by reference to it he could see what was coming and reserve his appetite accordingly. Thus we may presume that the menu developed from some such an event.

The Bill of fare was very large and was placed at the end of the table for everyone to read. As time progressed the Menu became smaller and increased in quantity allowing a number of copies per table. Depending on the establishment and the occasion the menu may be plain or artistic in its presentation.

The menu is the most important part of the caterer's work and its compilation is regarded as an art only acquired through experience and study. The menu may be likened to a bridge linking the establishment to the customer and in part determining the volume of turnover. Thus this important link—the menu—should be compiled by a number of people in liaison with one another, namely the Chef de cuisine, Maître d'hotel and the Manager. In this way the menu should list a well balanced, appetising meal.

Points to consider when compiling a menu

There are a number of considerations to bear in mind when compiling a menu:

Type
a) Assess the type of meal required.
b) Assess the type of kitchen and staff available in relation to equipment and skills.
c) Assess the type of food service area and its number capacity in relation to the china, silver and glassware available, the skills of food service area staff and the number of courses to be served.

Supplies
a) Seasonal supplies.
b) Local availability of supplies.

Balance
a) Light to heavy and back to light.
b) Vary the sequence of preparation of each course.
c) Change the seasoning, flavouring and presentation.
d) Ensure that garnishes are in harmony with the main dishes.

Food Value
a) Use commodities and methods of cooking which will preserve the natural nutritive properties of the raw materials.

Colour
a) Avoid either clashes of colour or repetition of similar colour.

Language
a) The menu should be written either all in

French or English and be easily understood by the customer expected.

b) Ensure proper spelling, correct terms and the correct sequence within courses.

Classes of menu

Although there are many types of functions carried out at different times in various forms of establishments, there are only two basic classes of menu, namely,

1. Table d'hôte.
2. À la carte.

1. The definition of a table d'hôte menu is covered by the following points:

a) The menu has a fixed number of courses.
b) There is a choice within each course.
c) The selling price of the menu is fixed.
d) The dishes provided will all be ready at a set time.

This type of menu may be offered by itself or in conjunction with an à la carte or carte du jour menu. It is the more popular and simpler form of menu, being easier to control and operate and giving less wastage of food. The set price of the table d'hôte menu is charged whether or not the full menu is consumed.

Example of a table d'hôte menu:

[*Name of the Establishment*]

Price: 65 p, incl.   Monday, 17 September

Salade de tomates

ou

Consommé Celestine

ou

Purée St. Germain

Omelette fines herbes

ou

Spaghetti Napolitaine

Rognons grillés vert pré

ou

Caneton rôti à l'Anglaise

Pommes nouvelles ou fondantes

Petits pois à la française ou navets glacées

Flan aux cerises

ou

Crêpes au citron

Café

2. The term à la carte may be translated as 'from the card'. An à la carte menu may be defined by the following points:

a) It gives a full list of all the dishes that may be prepared by the establishment.

b) Each dish is priced separately.

c) A certain waiting time has to be allowed for each dish as

d) it is cooked to order.

This type of menu may be offered on its own in a first class establishment, or in conjunction with a form of table d'hôte or carte du jour menu in a smaller catering establishment.

The dishes on an à la carte menu may be changed according to season—oysters, melon, asparagus, game—but each item will remain individually priced.

Another form of à la carte menu is the **plat du jour** or 'speciality of the house'. This consists of dishes individually priced which may be changed from day to day or remain for a certain period of time. The dishes concerned here are normally main courses. Usually the 'plats du jour' supports or is supported by a table d'hôte menu, and in some cases a limited à la carte menu. This form of à la carte menu will normally be offered in a medium size establishment.

The carte du jour menu

Many large hotels and restaurants carry this form of menu which is printed daily, one for lunch and one for dinner. This form of menu combines the table d'hôte, à la carte and plat du jour menu, each being priced according to its type.

Smaller establishments for economy reasons may offer this form of menu or just an à la carte menu for a number of weeks until the seasons change. Where only a table d'hôte menu is offered it will normally be altered day by day.

Courses in an à la carte menu

The number of courses on an à la carte menu, and dishes within each course, depends on the size and class of the establishment. In an establishment where full food preparation and service brigades are in operation a full menu may be offered. In this case the courses or sections of the menu may be divided as follows:

1. Hors d'oeuvre	7. Grillades
2. Potages	8. Rôties
3. Farineux	9. Légumes
4. Oeufs	10. Salades
5. Poisson	11. Buffet Froid
6. Entrées	12. Entremets

13. Glaces   16. Dessert
14. Savoury   17. Beverages
15. Fromages

Any new dishes that one may wish to introduce on the menu should first of all be added in the form of a plat du jour or 'speciality of the house'. The dish would then be recommended by the food and beverage service operator to the guest and if it proves to be a success it would be placed in its appropriate section on the menu.

Approximate waiting times for dishes on an à la carte menu

Special Hors d'oeuvre: 10 mins.
Soup: 5 mins.
Egg: 10 mins.
Fish (fried or grilled) 10 mins.
Liver: 15 mins.
Rump/Fillet steaks: according to order.
Châteaubriand: 15 mins.
Roast Chicken: 25 mins.
Lamb cutlets: 10 mins.
       chops: 15 mins.
Omelettes: 10 mins.
Soufflés: 30 mins.

Examples of dishes that may appear on an à la carte menu

Hors d'oeuvre and Substitutes

Hors d'oeuvre variés
Caviar
Shellfish cocktail
Melon
Saumon fumé
Truite fumée
Pâté Maison
Huîtres
Escargots
Moules marinière
Cocktail Florida

Oeufs

Omelette Espagnole
Omelette aux tomates;
Omelette aux champignons;
Omelette fines herbes
Oeufs en cocotte à la crème
Oeuf sur le plat Bercy
Oeuf poché Florentine
Oeuf brouillé au lard

Poisson

Sole meunière
Sole Colbert
Filets de sole véronique;
       bonne femme;
       cubat
Filets de plie frites, sauce Tartare
Tronçon de turbot poché, sauce Hollandaise
Darne de saumon grillée, sauce Bearnaise
Truite au bleu
Blanchailles diablées
Scampi frit, sauce Tartare
Homard Newburg

Potages

Tortue claire
Consommé Julienne;
       Celestine;
       en gelée
Petite marmite
Bisque de homard
Crème de tomates
Soupe à l'oignon
Bortsch
Potage Germiny

Entrées

Poulet sauté chasseur
Suprême de volaille sous cloche
Emincée de volaille à la king
Foie de veau au lard
Noisette d'agneau mascotte
Kebab Orientale
Pilaff de foies de volaille
Entrecôte bordelaise
Côtelettes d'agneau réforme
Steak Diane
Rognons sautés turbigo

Farinaceous

Spaghetti Napolitaine;
       Bolognaise
Raviolis
Gnocchi Romaine
Cannelloni

Grills

Rump steak
Filet steak
Chop d'agneau

Mixed grill
Châteaubriand
Chop de porc
Porterhouse steak

Rôties

Poulet
Caneton
Perdreau
Grouse

Légumes

Pomme purée
    persillées
    sautées
    lyonnaise
    frites
    au four
Petits pois au beurre
    à la française
Épinards en branches
Tomates grillées
Champignons grillés
Choufleur mornay
    polonaise
Céleris braisés
Artichaut froid, sauce vinaigrette
    chaud, sauce hollandaise
Asperges en branche, sauce hollandaise
Haricot verts au beurre

Salades

Française
Verte

Buffet Froid

Poulet rôti
Caneton rôti
Côte de boeuf
Jambon
Galantine de volaille
Mayonnaise de homard

Entremets

Crêpes Suzette
Glaces: vanille, fraise, chocolat
Pêches ou ananas flambés au kirsch
Pêche Melba

Poire belle Hélène
Omelette à la confiture
    au rhum
Cold Trolley

Dessert

Corbeille des fruits

Savouries

Welsh Rarebit
Scotch woodcock
Canapé Diane
    Ivanhoe
Champignons sur croûte

Fromages

Cheddar
Red Cheshire
Edam
Brie
Caerphilly
Gorgonzola
Demi-Sel
Gruyère
Gouda

Café

Cona
Iced
Filtre
Irish

The French classical menu

In present times the full French classical menu is very rarely served except as a special dinner or banquet menu. The procedure is to have 4/5 courses for dinner and 5/6 courses for a banquet. There are thirteen courses altogether making up the French classical menu, each one following similar lines to the sections or courses of the à la carte menu. This form of menu shows the true art of menu compilation, where the balance must be perfect throughout the courses especially with regard to nutritional value, method of cooking, colour, garnishing, etc. Before attempting such a menu an establishment must ensure that the food preparation and service areas are adequately equipped.

63

1. **Hors d'oeuvre** are of a spicy nature in order to stimulate the appetite. The term Hors d'oeuvre is accepted as meaning a variety of pickled or well seasoned foodstuffs, from which the customer is able to make his or her choice. The hors d'oeuvres are either served from a rotating trolly or a tray, a small amount of each variety being placed on the plate to make up a portion. Examples of this form of Hors d'oeuvre are as follows:

Russian salad	Tomato salad
Potato salad	Beetroot
Anchovies	Fish mayonnaise
Choufleur à la grecque	Bismarck herring
Egg mayonnaise	Choux rouges

It must not be forgotten however that the term Hors d'oeuvre also covers any item to be served before the soup, such as melon, oysters, caviar, truite fumée, fruit and shellfish cocktails, etc. . . . usually known as **Hors d'oeuvre substitutes.**

2. **Soup (Potage)** may also act as an appetizer for the courses to come. Two soups are usually provided on the menu, one being a clear soup (consommé), and the other a thick soup; crème, velouté, purée. Special forms of soup may also be served: Bisque, Bortsch, Petite marmite, etc. Although there is a choice of a clear or thick soup for the menu, only one would be offered at each function. The clear soup (consommé) is always placed first on the menu.

3. **A Fish (Poisson)** course is always included in a dinner or banquet menu. The method of cooking and type of fish used may vary to some extent, but will normally be as follows—poached salmon, turbot, trout with its appropriate garnish, and accompaning sauce; hot shellfish—lobster, crayfish, Dublin Bay prawns; cooked meunière—sole, trout, salmon and the correct garnish; fried whitebait and sometimes fried sole.

Fish is a soft fibred and tender meat which is easily digested and helps to prepare the appetite for the heavier courses to come.

4. **Entrée** are generally small well garnished dishes which come from the kitchen ready for service. They are always accompanied by a very rich gravy or sauce. When a relevés follows the entrées then potatoes are not served with the latter, if however a relevés does not follow the entrées then potatoes and vegetables would be served with the entrée. Examples of this type of dish are as follows: tournedo, noisette, sweetbreads, garnished cutlets, vol-au-vent de volaille, etc. An entrée is the first meat course on the French classical menu.

5. **Relevé** are normally larger than entrées and take the form of butchers' joints which have to be carved. These joints are either poeled or roasted. A sauce or roast gravy and potatoes and green vegetables are always served with this course. This main dish may consist of any of the following items: Saddle of mutton, Baron of beef, Boned sirloin, Braised ham, etc.

6. **The Sorbet.** Because of the length of the French classical menu, this course is considered to be the 'rest' between courses, where the diners may obtain their 'second wind'. The Sorbet, therefore, must be able to counteract the richness of dishes already served and stimulate the appetite for those to come.

The Sorbet is a water ice plus Italian meringue, flavoured with champagne or a liqueur. The sorbet would be piped into a champagne glass and then this glass is served on an underplate with a teaspoon.

(At this stage of the meal cigarettes are passed, traditionally these are Russian cigarettes, and sometimes the first speech is given).

7. **Roast (Rôti)** always consists of roast game or poultry: chicken, turkey, duck, pheasant, quail, etc.—Each dish is accompanied by its own particular sauce and gravy, with a green salad served separately on a crescent shaped dish. The latter is placed on the top left hand corner of the cover.

8. **Vegetable (Légume).** At this stage of the meal the balance of the courses is gradually returning from heavy to light. We now have a vegetable dish served with only its accompanying sauce. Such vegetables are asparagus, artichokes and corn-on-the-cob, with hollandaise sauce or beurre fondue offered separately.

9. The **Sweet (Entremet)** may be hot or cold. Examples of such dishes are: soufflés, crêpes, coupes, poire belle Hélène, pêche Melba.

10. **Savouries (Savoureux)** may take the form of savoury items served hot on toast or as a savoury soufflé.

11. All types of **cheese** may be offered together with the appropriate accompaniments.

12. **Dessert.** All forms of fresh fruit and nuts may be served accompanied by castor sugar and salt.

13. **Café.** When coffee is served, petit fours will be placed on the table and liqueurs offered.

12 menu knowledge

This Chapter is a glossary of terms connected with the menu and its meaning and application. It is knowledge which the experienced waiter must have in order to carry out any service efficiently. At the same time he must be able to advise the guest on the translation of menu terms; the reasons why certain seasonal dishes may not be obtainable; how dishes are cooked and what are their accompaniments. The professional food and beverage service operator will always have this knowledge at his fingertips.

	Name	*Season*	*Menu terminology*
Fish (Poisson)	Barbel	June—March	Barbeau
	Bream (Sea)	July—End of December	Brème
	Brill	August—March	Barbue
	Cod	May—February best	Cabillaud
	Dab	July—December	Limande
	Eel	All the year (poor quality summer)	Anguille
	Flounder	January—May	Flet
	Haddock	All the year	Aiglefin
	Hake	September to February	Merluche
	Halibut	All the year	Flétan
	Herring	Best September—April	Hareng
	Lemon Sole	October—March	Limande
	Mackerel (Red)	December—May	Rouget
	Plaice	Best May—January	Plie/Carrelet
	Salmon	February—September	Saumon
	Salmon Trout	March—September	Truite saumonée
	Smelt	October—May	Éperlan
	Skate	October—May	Raie
	Sole	All the year (poor quality spring)	Sole
	Sturgeon	December—April	Esturgeon
	Trout (River)	March—October	Truite de rivière
	Turbot	February—September	Turbot
	Whitebait	February—September	Blanchaille
	Whiting	August—February best	Merlan

	Name	Season	Menu terminology
Shellfish **(Crustaces et Mollusques)**	Crab	Preferably Summer	Crabe
	Crayfish	October—March	Écrevisse
	Crawfish	January—July	Langouste
	Lobster	Preferably Summer	Homard
	Mussel	September—May	Moule
	Oyster	1st September— 30th April	Huître
	Prawn	September—May	Crevette rose
	Shrimp	All the year	Crevette grise
	Scallop	September—April	Coquille St. Jacques

MEATS

	Name	Season	Menu terminology
Butchers Meat (Viande)	Beef	All the year	Boeuf
	Lamb	Best Spring and Summer	Agneau
	Mutton	All the year	Mouton
	Pork	September—end of April	Porc
	Veal	All the year	Veau
Game (Feathered) (Gibier)	Wood Grouse	12th August— 12th December	Coq de bruyère
	Partridge	1st September— 1st February	Perdreau
	Pheasant	1st October— 1st February	Faisan
	Ptarmigan	August—December	Ptarmigan
	Quail	All the year	Caille
	Snipe	August—March 1st.	Bécassine
	Woodcock	August—March 1st.	Bécasse
	Teal	Winter—Spring	Sarcelle
	Wild Duck	September—March	Canard sauvage
	Wood Pigeon	1st. August—March 15th	Pigeon des bois
Poultry (Volaille)	Chicken	All the year	Poulet
	Duck	All the year	Canard
	Duckling	April—May—June	Caneton
	Goose	Autumn—Winter	Oie
	Gosling	September	Oison
	Guinea Fowl	All the year	Pintade
	Spring Chicken	Spring (cheapest)	Poussin
	Turkey	All the year	Dinde
Game (Furred)	Hare	1st. August—End of February	Lièvre
	Rabbit	Preferably Autumn— Spring	Lapin
	Venison	Male best May to September	Venaison
		Female best September to January	

	Name	Season	Menu terminology
Vegetables (Legumes)			
	Artichoke Globe	Summer—Autumn best	Artichaut
	Artichoke Jerusalem	October—March	Topinambour
	Asparagus	May—July	Asperge
	Beetroot	All the year	Betterave
	Broad Bean	July—August	Fève
	Broccoli	October—April	Brocolis
	Brussels Sprout	October—March	Chou de Bruxelles
	Cabbage	All the year	Chou
	Cauliflower	All the year	Chou-fleur
	Carrot	All the year	Carotte
	Celery	August—March	Céleri
	Celeriac	November—February	Céleri-rave
	Cucumber	best Summer	Concombre
	Chicory (Belgian)	best winter	Endive Belge
	Egg Plant	Summer Autumn best	Aubergine
	French Bean	July—September	Haricot vert
	Leek	October—March	Poireau
	Lettuce	best summer	Laitue
	Mushroom	All the year	Champignon
	Onion	All the year	Oignon
	Pea	June—September	Petit pois
	Parsnip	October—March	Panais
	Radish	Best summer	Radis
	Runner Bean	July—October	Haricot d'Espagne
	Salsify	October—February	Salsifis
	Sea Kale	January—March	Chou de mer
	Shallot	September—February	Échalotte
	Spinach	All the year	Épinards
	Swede	December—March	Rutabaga
	Sweetcorn	Autumn	Maïs
	Tomato	All the year (best summer)	Tomate
	Turnip	October—March	Navet
	Vegetable Marrow	July—October	Courgette
Fresh herbs (Fines herbes)			
	Bay-Leaf	September	Laurier
	Borage	March	Bourrache
	Chervil	Spring—Summer	Cerfeuille
	Fennel	March	Fenouil
	Garlic	All the year	L'Ail
	Garlic (Clove)	All the year	Une Gousse d'Ail
	Marjoram	March	Marjolaine
	Mint	Spring—Summer	Menthe
	Parsley	All the year	Persil
	Rosemary	August	Romarin
	Sage	April—May	Sauge
	Thyme	September—November	Thym
	Tarragon	January—February	Estragon

	Name	Season	Menu terminology
Fruit (Fruits)			
	Apple	All the year	Pomme
	Apricot	May—September	Abricot
	Blackberry	Autumn	Mûre
	Cherry	May—July	Cerise
	Cranberry	November—January	Airelle rouge
	Currant (Black & Red)	Summer	Groseille
	Damson	September—October	Prune de damas
	Gooseberry	Summer	Groseille à maquereau
	Greengage	August—September	Reine-Claude
	Grapes	All the year	Raisin
	Melon (Cantaloup)	May—October	Melon
	Nectarine	June—September	Brugnon
	Peach	All the year (best June—September)	Pêche
	Pear	All the year (best Autumn—Winter)	Poire
	Plum	July—October	Prune
	Pineapple	All the year	Ananas
	Raspberry	Summer	Framboise
	Rhubarb	January—July	Rhubarbe
	Strawberry	June—September	Fraise

Dessert Apples (English)

Beauty of Bath
Worcester Pearmain
Blenheim Orange
Cox's Orange Pippin
Charles Ross

Cooking Apples (English)

Bramley Seedling
Newton Wonder
Lanes Prince Albert
Arthur Turner

Dessert Pears (English)

Doyenne Du Comice
Conference
Louise Bonne of Jersey
William's Bon Chrétien
Beurre Hardy
Beurre Superfin

LESS COMMON VEGETABLES

Aubergine October—March

Commonly known as egg plant and is similar in shape to a young marrow. It has a glossy deep purple skin. The pulp is soft with a rich flavour and has seeds in the centre. It is a native of India. It may be used as a garnish for certain dishes and also for the preparation of a Greek national dish Moussaka. Member of the squash family—pumpkin.

Asparagus May—July

This is stick-like in shape 15-22 cm (6-9 ins) long tapers to a point, which is the choicest part. The point is of a deep purple, shading from green to white down the stalk. The plant is of the lily family. Asparagus is mainly produced in France, Belgium, Holland and Italy. Also English asparagus from Worcestershire. The most famous varieties from France (Lauris). Asparagus is a great delicacy and due to its careful growth and short season it is expensive.

Artichoke (Globe) May—September

Globe-like in shape, hence the name, it grows on a stalk $1\frac{1}{4}$ metres (4 ft) high. It is pale green in colour and is composed of tightly packed overlapping pointed leaves. If the leaves were removed the bottom and choicest part would be disclosed which is firm and white in colour. This is termed the *Fond*. The *fond* may be prepared and used separately for garnishes.

Artichoke (Jerusalem) November—March

This is a tuberous root similar to a small irregular potato. It has a brown skin and white flesh and has a sweet nutty flavour. It may be used as a vegetable, or in a soup, namely Crème Palestine. It is grown in England.

Broccoli October—April

This belongs to the cauliflower family but is smaller and more delicate. The flowers are purple on a dark green stalk. It would be served with melted butter or hollandaise sauce.

Cardons November—March

This is of the thistle family and grows similarly to celery. It is mainly cultivated for its roots and stalk, and is white in colour.

Celeriac September—February

Resembles a turnip in flesh but the skin is darker. It has a hard white flesh with celery flavour. It is usually eaten raw, and served as Hors d'oeuvre, or as a vegetable.

Pimento and chillies (of Capsicum family)

Pimentos are the large peppers, and chillies the smaller sized peppers. They are green and red in colour. They produce after processing various condiments, red pepper, (paprika,) and cayenne pepper. They are mainly obtained from the seeds which are very pungent. It may be used raw, cut in julienne as a salad base, but it is usually braised and stuffed with rice.

Cèpes

This is a fungus that belongs to the mushroom family. It is small, button shaped and the flesh is yellow in appearance and very firm. Used mainly as a garnish.

Endive (Belgium) March—June

Chicory. 12.5 cm (5 ins) long approximately consisting of tightly packed thin white leaves, the leaves have yellow tips. Similar to celery in growth. They may be eaten raw as a salad item. They may also be braised whole. Chicory, a member of the same family is used to blend with certain coffee brands.

Endive (frizzled) November—March

This is like a cabbage lettuce in shape with greener leaves and it has a yellow heart. It is sometimes called a chicory lettuce. It has a bitter flavour and the edges of the leaves are serrated.

Flageolets

These are a type of young fresh haricot beans mainly used for either garnishing or as a purée type soup.

Pumpkin

This belongs to the squash family and is like a very large round melon. It can be used in soups and pies.

Salsify (Salsifis)

This is similar in shape to a parsnip but longer and slimmer. Two varieties, one with a black skin, the other with a brown skin. The flesh is white. Served with melted butter. Sometimes called oyster plant.

Sea kale (Chou de Mer)

This has a white appearance and grows in a cluster with 2-3 stalks to a root. The stalks are tipped with a little purple fringe. Served usually à la crème or with melted butter.

Term	Definition
Ail	Garlic
À la broche	Cooked on a spit
À l'Anglaise	English style
Aspic	Savoury jelly
Assiette de	Plate of
Au bleu	Method of cooking trout
Au four	Baked in the oven
Au naturel	Uncooked
Aiguillettes	Long, thin, vertically cut strips of meat from the breast of ducks and other poultry.
Baba	Yeast sponge or bun
Bain marie	Hot water bath or well
Bard—barder	To cover or wrap poultry, game or meat with a thin slice of fat bacon so that it does not dry out during roasting.
Baron de boeuf	Double sirloin
Barquette	A boat-shaped tartlet case, filled in a variety of ways.
Beard—ébarber	To remove the beard from oysters, mussels, etc.
Béchamel	Basic white sauce
Beurre noisette	Golden brown butter
Bleu	Steak very underdone
Bombe	Iced sweet
Bordelaise	Rich brown sauce flavoured with red wine
Bouillon—court	Liquor for cooking fish.
Bind—lier	To thicken soups or sauces with eggs, cream, etc., to mix chopped meat, vegetables, etc., with sauce.
Bisque	A fish soup, made with shellfish.
Blanc	Water to which flour has been added, used to keep vegetables white, e.g. celery.
Blanch—blanchir	To part cook a food without colouring, e.g. Pomme frite.
Blanquette	A white stew
Bouchée	Small puff paste patty; tiny savoury or hors d'oeuvre tit-bit. Bouchées may be filled in a variety of ways. Bouchées à la reine.
Braisé	Braised
Braiser	To brown meat, game and poultry thoroughly and then finish cooking in a covered vessel with a little liquid or sauce. Vegetables are usually braised without browning in broth containing very little fat.
Braising pan—braisière	A covered dish
Breadcrumb—paner	To cover a piece of meat, fish, poultry, etc. with breadcrumbs after first dipping it in beaten egg or liquid butter. See breadcrumbs.
Breadcrumbs	Remove the crusts from stale white bread and rub through a coarse wire sieve. Used for breadcrumbing for deep and shallow frying, etc
Brioche	Type of yeast roll
Brochette	On a skewer
Brunoise	A name used to describe vegetables, ham, or chicken cut in tiny dice. It is also a garnish for clear soup.

71

Term	Definition
Butter—beurrer	To coat or brush the inside of a mould or dish with butter.
Carré	Best end
Caviare	Roe of female sturgeon
Célestine	Strips of savoury pancake
Champignons	Mushrooms
Châteaubriand	Double fillet steak
Chaudfroid	Sauce for cold buffet work
Cocotte	Small earthenware container
Concassé	Rough chopped (tomato)
Confiture	Jam
Citron	Lemon
Canapés	Small pieces of bread, plain, grilled, or fried, garnished and served mainly as hors d'oeuvres.
Caramel	Burnt sugar, commonly known as 'Black Jack'.
Caramelise—caraméliser	To line a mould thinly with caramel sugar; to coat fruit with, or dip it in, crack sugar.
Casserole	A fire-proof earthenware saucepan, casserole.
Chiffonnade	Leaf salads or vegetables cut in fine shreds and simmered in butter.
Choucroûte	See Sauerkraut—pickled cabbage.
Clarify—clarifier	To clear aspic or bouillon by mixing it with egg white beaten with a little water or mixed with chopped meat, bringing it to the boil and letting it simmer; broth is clarified by simmering gently and skimming off the impurities as they rise to the top.
Coat—napper	To cover a dish or a sweet entirely with a sauce a jelly or a cream. To mask, to dip.
Cocotte	Small round fire-proof dishes for cooking an egg, a ragoût, etc., also used to describe a larger oval casserole for cooking chicken, etc.
Court bouillon	Fish stock with white wine or vinegar and mirepoix
Croquettes	Minced fowl, game, meat or fish, bound with sauce and shapped like a cork. They are usually egg and breadcrumbed and fried crisp.
Croustades	Deep, scalloped tartlet cases which may be served with a variety of fillings.
Croûtons	Fried bread, used as garnish. For soups they are cut in small cubes, for other dishes in a variety of fancy shapes.
Courgettes	Baby marrows.
Darne	Thick slice of a round fish, including the central bone.
Du jour	of the day
Dariole	A small beaker-shaped mould
Daube	A method of cooking food very slowly in a hermetically sealed dish in order to preserve its full flavour.
Decant—décanter	To let liquid stand and then pour it gently into another container, leaving the sediment behind
Demi-glace	A basic sauce of fairly thin consistency, frequently used to improve other sauces, soups and stews
Devilled—à la diable	Generally applied to fried or grilled fish or meat prepared with the addition of very hot condiments and sometimes a highly seasoned spiced sauce
Dorer	To egg wash pastry with yolk or egg mixed with water. Some baked goods are brushed with milk

Term	Definition
Duxelles	A mixture of chopped onions, mushrooms and other ingredients, used for stuffing vegetables and in making sauces
Escalopes	Thin slices of flattened veal or beef
Entrée	A meat dish served with a sauce. Formerly regarded as intermediate dish, it is nowadays frequently served as the main course
Entremets	Sweet, dessert.
Étuver	A method of simmering food very slowly in butter or very little liquid in a closed casserole.
Farce	Stuffing
Filet mignon	Filet from the saddle of lamb
Fines herbes	Mixed herbs
Frappé	Chilled
Flambé	Flamed with spirit or liquer
Foie de veau	Calves liver
Foie gras	Liver of a fattened goose
Fromage	Cheese
Flame—flamber	To pour brandy or liquers over a dish and set them alight
Fleurons	Crescents and other fancy shapes of baked puff pastry. Used to garnish a variety of dishes.
Fricassée	A white stew in which the poultry or meat is cooked in the sauce.
Fumet	Essence of fish or herbs game or poultry.
Gâteau	Sponge cake
Glace	Ice-cream
Galantine	A fine cold dish of poultry or meat, boned, stuffed, braised in concentrated stock and coated and garnished with aspic.
Garnish	An ingredient which decorates, accompanies or completes a dish. Many dishes are identified by the name of their garnish.
Glaze—glacer	To dust a cake or sweet with icing sugar and brown under a grill; to simmer vegetables cut in fancy shapes in butter until they have a shining coating; to give meat a shiny appearance by frequent basting; to give cold dishes, cakes and sweets a shiny appearance by coating with aspic or jelly that is on the point of setting.
Gnocchi	Classified as a farinaceous type dish, made from semolina or other flour bases.
Gratin (au)	A dish is described as 'au gratin' when the top has been sprinkled with grated cheese, possibly mixed with breadcrumbs, and a little butter and is then browned on top under a grill or in a hot oven.
Hachis	Minced meat
Haché	Minced
Hang	To keep freshly killed meat or game in a cool place for a time so that it becomes more tender.
Hors d'oeuvre	Preliminary dishes intended to act as appetizers. Hors d'oeuvre may be hot or cold and are served before the soup.
Embrocher	To place on a spit for spit roasting or on skewers for grilling or frying.
Jardinière	Match stick shape cut of spring vegetables
Jus lié	Thickened gravy

73

Term	Definition
Julienne	Term used to describe vegetables cut in very fine strips. Used as a garnish in soups.
Knead—fraiser	To work dough on a pastryboard or marble slab with the ball of the hand.
Beurre manié	Butter and flour kneaded together and used to thicken soups and sauces.
Lard—larder, piquer	To draw strips of larding bacon through the middle of a piece of meat by means of a larding tube (larder); to lard the surface by means of a larding needle (piquer).
Lardons	Strips of fat bacon used for larding meat or fish.
Macédoine	Mixture of diced vegetables
Mise-en-place	Preparation beforehand
Macerate	To pickle briefly, to steep, to macerate or to souse. Generally applied to fruit, usually diced, sprinkled with caster sugar and liquers in order to improve flavour.
Maître d'hôtel butter	Herb butter. Served with grilled meat. Contains parsley and lemon.
Marinade	To soak meat, game etc., for a short while to improve flavour and make more tender.
Marmite	An earthenware pot in which soups and stews are cooked and served at table. The name is also given to some dishes cooked in such a pot.
Meat glaze—glace de viande	Boiled down bone broth of marrow bones, etc., reduced to the thickness of jelly, used for glazing cooked meats, and improving their appearance.
Medallion—médaillon	A round slice of meat, lobster, etc.
Mirepoix	A garnish of diced, browned onions, bacon and carrots with various herbs used to flavour soups, sauces, stews etc.
Mousse	A light and fluffy mixture, which may be sweet or savoury, hot or cold.
Mousseline	Purée strained extra fine and mixed with cream
Morilles	An edible fungus with a delicate flavour.
Nature	Plain boiled.
Poulet	Chicken
Poussin	Spring chicken
Purée	Passing food through a sieve. Term applied to soup and vegetables.
Panada	A dough used to bind forcemeat. Made from flour milk or water, eggs and butter.
Pasta	Pastes made from wheaten semolina in a variety of shapes and dried. Among the best-known are macaroni, spaghetti, vermicelli, noodles, ravioli
Paupiettes	Slices of meat rolled up with forcemeat
Paysanne	Vegetables cut in very thin slices. Size of a sixpence.
Pilaff	Rice cooked with meat, poultry or fish, etc.
Pipe	To force a soft mixture or dough through a forcing bag with a nozzle, plain or fancy, in order to arrange it in a desired pattern or shape.
Piquer	See Lard
Poach—pocher	To simmer dishes in a mould in a bain marie until done. To cook food in water that is kept just on boiling point without actually letting it boil.

Term	Definition
Poêlé	To casserole in butter in a covered dish with no liquid added. The lid is removed shortly before the end to allow the contents to brown. Used only for the better cuts of meat and poultry.
Profiteroles	Small balls of choux paste. Garnish for soup. Sweet of same name.
Quenelles	A kind of dumpling, made from various kinds of forcemeat and poached, made in different shapes, balls, ovals. etc.
Rôtir	To roast
Ris de veau	Calves sweetbreads
Ragoût—Ragoût	A rich, seasoned brown meat stew.
To reduce	To add wine or other liquid to a roux or to pan residue; to boil down to a desired consistency.
Roux	Flour stirred into melted butter, used for thickening soups and sauces. It may be white, blonde or brown.
Royale (à la)	A garnish
Salmis	Game birds and ducks, boned after roasting, placed in a rich sauce and served as a game stew.
Salpicon	Consists of one or more kinds of food, diced small and bound with sauce.
Sauerkraut—choucroute	Pickled, finely shredded white cabbage, preserved in brine and fermented with salt caraway seeds and juniper berries. A national dish of Germany and Alsace, served hot with bacon and sausages.
Sauteuse	A shallow pan with sloping sides and a lid in which food may first be fried and then braised.
Sauter	A quick cooking process. To brown quickly in a sauté or frying pan or toss in fat anything that requires quick cooking at considerable heat.
Shred—émincer	To cut meat or vegetables into thin slices or strips.
Skim dépouiller	To remove impurities and fat from the top of soups and broths being cooked for a long time by means of a skimming ladle.
Soubise	A smooth onion pulp served with various meat entrees.
Spaetzele—Spaetzeli	A Swiss and Austrian paste speciality made by pressing an egg noodle dough through a colander and boiling it in salt water.
Suprêmes	The best parts, e.g. suprêmes de volaille—chicken breasts and wings.
Tartare	Cold sauce, base of mayonnaise.
Tronçon	Portion of fish cut across the body (turbot)
Timbale	A half-conical tin mould; a dish cooked in such a tin.
Tabasco	A pungent Indian pepper sauce, also used extensively in countries with a hot climate.
Tournedos	Filled steak cut in round, neatly trimmed slices. Usually fried or grilled.
Truss	To bind or truss poultry or game birds for cooking to give them a better shape, using a special needle.
Velouté	Velvety, smooth. A rich white sauce made from chicken stock, cream, etc. Also a name given to certain cream soups.
Vol-au-vent	A round or oval case made of puff pastry.

13 accompaniments, cover and service for special dishes

Accompaniments are highly flavoured seasonings of various kinds offered with certain dishes. The object of offering accompaniments with certain dishes is to improve the flavour of the food or to counteract the richness in food, e.g. Apple sauce offered with roast pork. There are standard accompaniments for some dishes and the waiter must have knowlegde of all these so that when he serves a particular dish he will offer the correct accompaniments automatically. This is all part of the service a waiter should provide and shows that a waiter is thoughtful and efficient in anticipating and providing for all the guests' needs.

The following table shows a list of dishes with their standard accompaniments and the cover required for the correct service of each

DISH	COVER	ACCOMPANIMENTS	REMARKS
Hors d'oeuvre and hors d'oeuvre substitutes			
Hors d'oeuvre	Cold fish plate/fish knife and fork.	Oil and vinegar.	May be served from a tray with compartments or from a rotating trolly. When serving from the trolly, the trolly must be placed between the table and the waiter and rotated away from the guest. In this way the guest may see everything on the trolly in order to make his choice, and anything spilt will not fall on the guest. Each ravier should have its own service spoon and fork. When serving from a tray, it should be rotated on the waiters hand so that the item being served is in the ravier closest to the fish plate.

DISH	COVER	ACCOMPANIMENTS	REMARKS
Grapefruit cocktail (Cocktail de pamplemousse)	Coupe/doily on side-plate/grapefruit spoon or teaspoon	Castor sugar	Other fruit cocktails served as a Grapefruit cocktail, e.g. Florida cocktail.
Tomato Juice (Jus de tomate)	5 oz. goblet/small tumbler or club shaped glass. Placed on doily on a sideplate with a tea-spoon.	Worcester sauce.	Worcester sauce: bottle shaken; lid removed. Placed on doyley on a sideplate at the head of the cover. Serve tomato juice chilled and decorate edge of glass with a twist of lemon.
Fruit Juices (Pineapple, Orange, Grapefuit)	Glass as for tomato juice. Placed on a doily on a sideplate.	None.	Castor sugar is occasionally asked for as an accompaniment. If offered a teaspoon is also laid as part of the cover.
Oysters (les hûitres)	A soup plate or welled silver dish filled with crushed ice and placed on an underplate. Oyster fork, finger bowl filled with lukewarm water and slice of lemon and placed on a doily on a sideplate at the top left hand corner of the cover. Spare serviette.	Cayenne pepper Peppermill Chilli vinegar } Oyster Cruet Tabasco sauce Half a lemon. Brown bread and butter.	Oysters are normally offered 6 per portion. If another 6 are required then a fresh service would be laid. Oysters are served in the deep half of the shell set on the crushed ice surrounding the half a lemon.
Snails (les éscargots)	Snail tongs: left of cover. Snail fork: right of cover. Snail dish: which is round and has 6-12 indentations in it to hold the snail shells. Set on a doily on an underplate.	Brown bread and butter.	Snails shells are placed in the snail dish with their openings uppermost to stop garlic butter running out.
Potted Shrimps	Fish knife and fork/cold fish plate.	Cayenne pepper. Peppermill. Segments of lemon. Hot breakfast toast.	Normally 'plate served' from the larder or buffet. Shrimps removed from carton and placed on a bed of lettuce leaves on the cold fish plate.

DISH	COVER	ACCOMPANIMENTS	REMARKS
Plovers Eggs (Oeuf de Pluvier)	Small knife and fork/cold fish plate/finger bowl on a doily on a side-plate and containing lukewarm water and a slice of lemon. Spare sideplate for the shell. Spare serviette.	Brown bread and butter. Oriental salt.	Oriental salt—a mixture of cayenne pepper and salt of ratio 1:4. Plovers eggs are served cold and hard boiled. Approx. 3 per portion Placed in a special fold-'rose', of serviette on a doily on the cold fish plate.
Fresh Prawns (Les crevettes roses.)	Wine goblet/on doily on an underplate. Fish knife and fork. Cold fish plate. Finger bowl as for Plovers eggs. Spare serviette.	Brown bread and butter. Sauce mayonnaise.	The portion of prawns are placed over the rim of the wine goblet which would be filled with crushed ice. For special presentations of this dish silver dishes of diminishing sizes are placed one in another to form a cascade. This is called: Les crevettes roses en cascade.
Asparagus (Asperges au beurre fondue)	Asparagus rack: grid-serviette. Asparagus tongs—right of cover. Hot/cold joint plate. Joint fork. Finger bowl as for Plovers eggs and a spare serviette.	If served hot: hollandaise sauce or beurre fondue. If served cold: sauce vinaigrette.	The joint fork is placed upside down on the cover so that the joint plate when placed on the fork is tilted from right to left. The asparagus when being served should have the tips on the left hand side of the plate, the lower part, so that when the accompanying sauce is served it settles over the tips of asparagus. Asparagus may be served either as an hors d'oeuvre substitute or as a separate vegetable course.
Corn on the Cob (Mais naturel)	Hot fish plate. Corn on the cob holders.	Beurre fondue.	The corn on the cob holders may be placed on a sideplate at the head of the cover or inserted into the corn-on-the-cob by the waiter at his sideboard. corn-on-the-cob may be served as either

DISH	COVER	ACCOMPANIMENTS	REMARKS
			an hors d'oeuvre substitute or as a separate vegetable course.
Soups			
Petit Marmite	Special earthenware dish called a 'petit marmite'. Dessert spoon. Doily on an underplate.	Grated parmesan cheese. Grilled flutes. Poached bone marrow.	Beef and chicken flavoured. Garnished with turned root vegetables and dice of beef and chicken. The soup is eaten by the guest from the 'petite marmite' and not poured into a soup plate or consommé cup.
Croûte au Pot	As for petit marmite.	Grilled flutes. Grated parmesan cheese.	
Minestroni	Soup spoon. Soup plate. Underplate.	Grated parmesan cheese. Grilled flutes.	Clear soup heavily garnished with assorted vegetables and spaghetti.
Soup à l'Oignon	Soup spoon. Soup plate. Underplate.	Grated parmesan cheese. Grilled flutes.	French onion soup.
Potage St. Germain	Soup spoon. Soup plate. Underplate.	Croûtons	Green pea flavour.
Potage Germiny	Soup spoon. Soup plate. Underplate.	Cheese Straws	Is a consommé thickened immediately before serving with egg yolks and cream.
Crème de Tomate	Soup spoon. Soup plate. Underplate.	Croûtons.	The only 'cream' soup with which croutons are offered as an accompaniment.
Consommé	Dessert spoon. Consommé cup and saucer. Fish plate.	Depending on garnish.	
Consommé en tasse	As for Consommé.		Jellied clear soup.
Bouillabaisse	Soup plate. Underplate. Fish knife/fork. Dessert spoon.	Thin slices of french bread dipped in oil and grilled.	'Bouillabaisse', a Mediterranean fish, stew.

79

DISH	COVER	ACCOMPANIMENTS	REMARKS
Bortsch	Soup plate. Underplate. Dessert spoon.	1. Sour cream 2. Beetroot juice 3. Bouchées filled with a duck paste. Served in the order listed.	Bortsch is a duck flavoured consommé. Garnish with duck, diced beef and turned vegetables. Although a consommé type soup, a soup plate is used as part of the cover because of the large amount of garnish and accompaniments offered.
Turtle Soup (Tortue vraie) aux Xerès	Consommé cup. Consommé saucer. Fish plate. Dessert spoon.	Brown bread and butter. Segments of lemon. Cheese straws. Measure of sherry.	The segment of lemon may be offered in a lemon press. The sherry would either be added in the kitchen immediately before serving or from the gueridon at the table by heating the sherry in a ladle over a lamp.

Note All soups are normally silver served. If just one portion it would be taken to the table in the individual soup tureen on an underplate. Service would be from the left. Assuming the correct cover had been laid and accompaniments placed on the table the portion of soup would be poured from the tureen into the soup plate, the waiter ensuring he pours away from the guest. The underplate acts as a drip plate to prevent any spillage going on the tablecloth.

If a number of portions have to be served at one table then the soup is normally received in one large tureen from the kitchen. It would then be ladled into the individual plates at the sideboard or from the gueridon at the table. Before serving always ensure the edge of the soup plate is clean.

The silver service of a single portion of soup. Note the position of the hands when carrying both the soup plate on an underplate and the silver soup tureen on an underflat.

DISH	COVER	ACCOMPANIMENTS	REMARKS
Egg dishes			
Oeuf sur le plat	Oeuf sur le plat dish. Doily on underplate. Dessert spoon and fork (Side knife depending on garnish).		The egg is cooked in the oven in the oeuf sur le plat dish. Served to the guest in the dish in which it is cooked and received from the kitchen. A 'sur le plat' dish is round, white and has two ears.
Oeufs en cocotte	Cocotte. Doily on underplates Teaspoon.		The egg is cooked in the cocotte dish and again served to the guest in the dish in which it is received from the kitchen. A 'cocotte' is a round earthenware dish with two small ears.
Omelettes	Joint fork. Hot fish plate.		The joint fork is placed on the right hand side of the cover. On being served the ends of the omelette should be trimmed. It is usually easier to serve an omelette using two large forks rather than the recognised service spoon and fork.
Farinaceous dishes			

Note This includes all the Italian pastes such as spaghetti, macaroni, nouilles, ravioli, etc. Also the Gnocchi-Piedmontaise (Potato) Parisienne (Choux paste) and Romaine (Semolina).
    The Cover for all these with the exception of spaghetti, is the same.

DISH	COVER	ACCOMPANIMENTS	REMARKS
Spaghetti	Joint fork. Dessert spoon. Hot soup plate, on an underplate.	Grated parmesan cheese.	The joint fork is placed on the right hand side of the cover and the dessert spoon on the left.
Others	Dessert spoon and fork. Hot fish plate.	Grated parmesan cheese.	The dessert spoon is placed on the right of the cover and the dessert fork on the left.

DISH	COVER	ACCOMPANIMENTS	REMARKS

Fish dishes

DISH	COVER	ACCOMPANIMENTS	REMARKS
Grilled Herring (Hareng grillé)	Fish knife and fork. Hot fish plate.	Mustard sauce.	
Whitebait (Blanchailles)	As above.	Cayenne pepper. Peppermill. Segment of lemon. Brown bread and butter.	
Fried Scampi (Scampi frit)	As above.	Sauce tartare. Brown bread and butter. Segments of lemon.	
Poached Salmon (*Served hot*) (Saumon Poché)	As above.	Sauce hollandaise/ mousseline. — *hollandaise + cocam*	
(Served cold)	As above.	Sauce mayonnaise.	
Mussels (Moules marinière)	Soup plate. Underplate. Fish knife and fork. Dessert spoon.	Brown bread and butter. Cayenne pepper.	
Cold Lobster (Homard)	Fish knife and fork and lobster pick. Spare plate for the shell. Finger bowl containing luke warm water and a slice of lemon. Spare serviette.	Sauce mayonnaise.	The lobster pick would be used to help extract the flesh from the claw of the lobster.
Crawfish (L'angouste)	As for lobster with no lobster pick.	Sauce mayonnaise.	
Fried in batter (à l'orly)	Fish knife and fork. Hot fish plate.	Tomato sauce.	
Fish (fried)	Fish knife and fork. Hot fish plate.	Segments of lemon or slices of lemon with skin removed. Sauces Tartare. Remoulade. Gribiche.	The three sauces mentioned are all cold sauces with a mayonnaise base.
Fish (grilled)	As above.	Lemon as above. Cold sauces as above or hot sauces: Bearnaise. Tyrolienne.	

83

DISH	COVER	ACCOMPANIMENTS	REMARKS
Fish (poached)	As above.	Lemon as above. Hollandaise sauce Mousseline sauce Beurre fondue: (melted butter.)	

Meat

DISH	COVER	ACCOMPANIMENTS	REMARKS
Curry (Kari)	Joint knife and fork. Dessert spoon. Hot soup plate or joint plate.	Popadums: crisp, highly seasoned pancake. Bombay duck: dried fillet of fish from Indian Ocean. Mango Chutney: placed on a doily on an underplate. A joint fork would be on the inverted lid of the Mango Chutney jar to keep the underplate clean. Curry Tray: items which are generally hot or sweet in flavour. Such as chopped apple, sultanas, sliced bananas, desiccated coconut etc.	When curry is served on its own then the soup plate would be used as part of the cover. However, if the curry is to be accompanied by potato and vegetables then the joint plate replaces the soup plate. The rice and curry are always brought from the kitchen in separate containers. The rice should always be served first, making a bay in the middle in which the curry will be placed. Separate service spoons and forks should be used for both the rice and the curry. The poppadums and bombay duck are placed on doilies on sideplates at the head of the cover for the guest to help himself.
Roast Beef (Boeuf rôti)	Joint knife and fork. Hot joint plate.	French and English mustard. Horseradish sauce. Yorkshire pudding and roast gravy.	
Roast Lamb (Agneau rôti)	As above.	Mint sauce.	
Roast Mutton (Mouton Rôti) Saddle or Leg. Shoulder.	As above.	Red Currant Jelly. Onion Sauce.	
Roast Pork (Porc rôti)	As above.	Sage and onion stuffing Apple sauce and roast gravy.	

DISH	COVER	ACCOMPANIMENTS	REMARKS
Boiled Mutton (Mouton bouilli)	As above.	Caper sauce.	
Salt Beef (Silverside)	As above.	Turned root vegetables Dumplings and natural cooking liquor.	
Boiled Fresh Beef (Boeuf bouilli)	As above.	Turned root vegetables Natural cooking liquor Rock salt. Gherkins.	
Calves Head (Tête de veau)	As above.	Boiled bacon and parsley sauce, brain sauce or sauce vinaigrette.	
Mixed Grill and Grilled Steaks	Steak knife and fork. Hot joint plate.	French and English mustard. Beurre maître d'hôtel. Pomme paille, (straw potatoes). Watercress.	
Irish Stew	Soup plate on an underplate. Joint knife and fork. Dessert spoon.	Worcestershire sauce. Pickled red cabbage.	
Poultry			
Chicken (Poulet rôti)	Joint knife and fork. Hot joint plate.	Bread sauce. Roast gravy. Stuffing. Bacon rolls. Game chips. Watercress.	
Duck (Caneton rôti)	As above.	Sage and onion stuffing. Apple sauce. Roast gravy. Watercress.	
Wild Duck (Canard Sausage)	As above.	Orange salad. Acidulated cream dressing.	
Goose (Oie rôti)	As above.	Sage and onion stuffing. Apple sauce. Roast gravy.	
Turkey (Dindonneau)	As above.	Cranberry sauce. Bread sauce. Chestnut stuffing. Chipolatas. Gravy. Game chips. Watercress.	

DISH	COVER	ACCOMPANIMENTS	REMARKS
Game *(Furred)*			
Hare (Lièvre)	As above.	Heart shaped croûtes. Force meat balls. Red currant jelly.	
Venison	As above.	Cumberland sauce or Red currant jelly.	
(Feathered) All game such as Partridge, Grouse, Pheasant, etc.	As above.	Fried breadcrumbs. Hot liver paste spread on a croûte. Bread sauce. Gravy. Game chips. Watercress.	
Savoury			
All forms of Savoury	Side knife and a dessert fork. Hot fish plate.	Salt and pepper. Cayenne pepper. Peppermill. Worcestershire sauce.	It is generally accepted that where the savoury to be served is not a meat savoury—i.e. Scotch Woodcock or mushrooms on toast, then Worcestershire sauce would be omitted from the accompaniments to be offered to the guest.
Légumes			
Baked jacket potato (Pomme-au-four)	Hot side plate. Dessert fork.	Cayenne pepper. Peppermill. Butter.	May be served as a separate vegetable course or to accompany a main course. The waiter makes a cross-wise incision in the baked potato at the sideboard. A knob of butter is placed in the incision and it is seasoned. The baked potato is then placed on a hot side plate with the dessert fork and placed at top lefthand corner of the cover.

The following dishes will be covered in the chapter on Gueridon Service.

Hors d'oeuvre or **Substitutes**	1.	Smoked eel	Anguille fumée
	2.	Smoked trout	Truite fumée
	3.	Smoked salmon	Saumon fumé
	4.	Caviare	Caviare
	5.	Whole melon	Melon frappé
	6.	Globe artichoke	Artichaut
	7.	Pâté de foie gras	Pâté de foie gras
	8.	Shellfish cocktail	Cocktail de crevettes
Potage	9.	Turtle soup	Tortue vraie aux xerès
Fish	10.	Sole meunière	
		Sole grillé	
		Sole poché	
		Sole frite	
	11.	Saumon poché	
		grillé	
	12.	Blue trout	Truite au bleu
Steaks	13.	Double entrecôte steak	entrecôte double
	14.	Double fillet steak	châteaubriand
	15.	'T' bone steak	Porterhouse steak
	16.	Steak tartare	Steak tartare
	17.	Steak diane	Steak diane
Salad	18.	Green salad	Salade verte
	19.	Salad Dressings	Sauce vinaigrette
			Roquefort dressing
			Acidulated cream dressing
Poultry	20.	Chicken	Poulet rôti
	21.	Young chicken	Poussin
	22.	Duck	Canard rôti
Meat	23.	Boned sirloin of beef	Contrefilet de boeuf
	24.	Sirloin of beef	Aloyau de boeuf
	25.	Best end of lamb	Carré d'agneau
	26.	Saddle of lamb	Selle d'agneau
	27.	Leg of lamb	Gigot d'agneau
	28.	Leg of pork	Cuissot de porc
Entremets	29.	Fresh fruit	Dessert

14   accompaniments, cover and service for cheese, dessert and savouries

CHEESE

Introduction

Cheese is made from milk and is the natural way of preserving the nutrients in milk. It is made from pure, fresh milk, cream, or milk and cream mixed together. Many continental varieties are made from ass's, ewe's or goat's milk. The process of manufacture is carried out firstly by checking the milk for quality, then pasteurizing and following this it is ripened and curdled by the addition of a 'starter' (bacteria) and rennet. It is at this stage that the solids (curd) readily separate from the watery part (whey). The curds are packed into moulds to mature and become cheese. The degree of pressure determines the type of cheese. Cream cheeses are subject only to a light pressure whilst hard cheeses are subject to a heavier pressure.

The cheeses commonly used in cookery are Cheddar and Lancashire (English), Gruyère and Parmesan (European). The cheeses, normally served in the restaurant from the cheese board or trolley, may be a variety of any of the known cheeses which must be ripe and in good condition.

The character, texture and flavour in the cheeses varies according to the district in which it is made. There are two main reasons for this:
a) The type and quality of milk used which depends on the type of land where the cattle graze.
b) Difference in the method of manufacture.

All cheese made from full cream milk is graded. The time at which grading is done depends on the type of cheese. In the case of Cheddar the cheese must be at least four weeks old.

Cheese should be stored in a cool dark place with a good air conditioning. If not covered in its original wrapping it must be wrapped in greaseproof paper. It must be stored away from foods which absorb flavour. The various types of cheeses may be sub-divided as follows:
a) Hard
b) Semi-hard
c) Soft or Cream
d) Blue

Dependant on use, cheeses may be purchased either whole or pre-portioned. In present day establishments the latter is more often the case as there is less wastage and no loss in quality, flavour and aroma.

English cheeses

Cheddar

A hard cheese, creamy in colour. It has a unique 'nutty' flavour. It will adhere to the knife when cut. The approximate weight of a whole cheese is 40 kg (80 lb)

Cheshire

A mellow open-textured cheese. There is Cheshire red and Cheshire white, both with the same flavour, and both rather crumbly. There is also the famous blue, which is richer and more rare. Cheshire is known as a hard cheese.

Lancashire

A hard cheese which possesses a mild flavour when young and develops a full and rather pungent flavour as it matures. Its loose texture makes it one of the ideal cheeses for use in the kitchen. It is creamy white in colour.

Caerphilly

A semi-hard cheese made from skimmed full cream milk. Has a creamy white colour with a mild delicate flavour and smooth texture. This cheese matures quickly and is ready to eat in three to four weeks. Has a very thin rind. Country of origin: Wales.

Derby

A hard cheese which is close textured and a pale honey colour. It is similar to the Lancashire cheese in that it is mild when young but develops a fuller flavour as it matures. A sage-flavoured Derby cheese is also available all the year round but is traditionally a Christmas cheese.

Dorset Blue

A strong, hard pressed cheese, being close textured and made from skimmed milk. It is straw coloured with deep blue veins, is rather crumbly and has a rough rind.

Double Gloucester

A hard, straw coloured cheese. It is close textured and has a 'nutty' flavour similar to Cheddar. It is a slow ripening cheese.

Leicester

A hard mild flavoured cheese, with a rich russet colour and has a crumbly texture. Takes up to nine months to mature.

Wensleydale

There is a white, hard, and a blue viened Wensleydale cheese. The white Wensleydale has a soft flaky texture with a honeyed after taste, and is pale parchment in colour. The white matures quickly, the blue vein, slowly.

Stilton

A blue veined cheese which has a close texture and is intermingled with blue veins which give it its special flavour. The coat should be wrinkled and brownish grey in colour. Should be served by cutting it in a wedge from across the top.

European cheeses

Danish Blue

Is a blue veined cheese coming from Denmark. Made from cow's milk the whole cheese is two to three kilos (4-5 lb) in weight. May be purchased whole or in portioned segments and in each case they are wrapped in foil.

Brie

Is a soft or cream cheese the country of origin being France. Is made from cows milk, and the whole cheese averages 2-3 kilos (4-5 lb) in weight. For convenience however, it is cut into smaller wedge shaped portions of $\frac{1}{4}$ and $\frac{1}{8}$ kilo ($\frac{1}{2}$ and $\frac{1}{4}$ lb) and boxed. There are two sizes namely Petit Brie and Grand Brie.

Camembert

A soft or cream cheese coming from France. It closely resembles Brie. It is made in the Normandy district of France from cows milk and softens on ripening. It is a small flat round cheese yellow in colour with a very thin rind. It is packed in light wooden circular boxes and weighs about $\frac{3}{4}$ kilo ($7\frac{1}{2}$ oz). Should be served ripe.

Carre de l'Est

A soft or cream cheese produced in France. It is made from pasteurised cows milk, and packed in square boxes. Like Camembert it softens on ripening and is darker in colour than Brie. When ripe it has a mild flavour.

Edam

A hard cheese coming from Holland. Is globe shaped having a yellow or red rind. It is sold in grades of 40%, 30% and 20% fat. It is pale yellow in colour and has a waxy texture.

Gouda

A hard cheese produced in Holland. Is yellow in colour but paler than the Edam. Rind is yellow or red. Is a flat cheese with rounded edges and has a soft texture.

Demi-Sel

A soft or cream cheese from France. Is a sour milk cheese. Is flat and square in shape and comes wrapped in foil. Normally pre-portioned.

Gorgonzola

A blue cheese produced in Italy. The whole cheese weighs from 8-10 kg (16-20 lb). This cheese takes about eighteen weeks to ripen. It should have a white curd intersected by blue veins and have a softish semi-solid texture. Inclined to be slightly crumbly.

Emmentaler

A hard cheese from Switzerland. The whole cheese weighs over 50 kilos (1 cwt). It has a pale yellow in colour. It has cavities which should be holes or cavities that appear all over the cheese. The cavities are smaller than those in Gruyère but gives it a similar appearance.

Gruyère

A hard cheese produced in Switzerland and one of the most common ones to be used in the kitchen. This cheese is firm and dry and pale yellow in colour. It has cavities which should be shiny but not contain moisture.

Parmesan

A hard cheese from Italy. A dry cheese having an appearance of pinpricks all over it. Exclusively used for cooking purposes.

Pont l'Éveque

A semi-hard cheese made in France. Has a somewhat close curd with a thin rind. Obtains its full flavour on ripening. A square cheese sold in a wood chip box. Should yield to touch when ripe.

Port Salut

A semi-hard cheese made in France. The whole cheese is 1-2 kg (3-4 lb) in weight and has a hard rind.

Roquefort

Is a blue veined cheese made entirely from ewes milk. Country of origin is France. It is matured in the caves of Roquefort, and there obtains its unique characteristics. The whole cheese weighs about 2 kg (four pounds) and is foil wrapped. It is creamy but crumbly in texture.

These cheeses are the more popular ones that may be found on the cheese board or trolly in a catering establishment. The number and variety of cheeses displayed depends on the nature of the establishment and the area in which it is situated. It must be remembered that there are a large number of English and European cheeses which are made and eaten locally, and therefore never appear for sale in the shops or on the cheese board.

Cover, service and accompaniments

The cheese course is normally offered towards the end of a meal as an alternative to the sweet course. The cover to be laid is as follows:
Side plate
Side knife

Sometimes a small fork

In the service of this course the cover should be laid first and then the accompaniments set on the table as follows:
Cruet (salt, pepper, and mustard).
Butter in a butter dish on a doily on an underplate with a butter knife.
Celery served in a celery glass part filled with crushed ice, on an underplate.
Radishes, when in season, placed in a glass bowl on an underplate with a teaspoon.
Castor sugar for cream cheeses.
Assorted cheese biscuits (cream crackers, Ryvita, sweet digestive, water biscuits, etc.)

The cheese board or trolly will be presented to the customer, containing a varied selection of cheeses in ripe condition together with sufficient cheese knives for cutting and portioning the different cheeses. If cheese is wrapped in foil this must be removed by the waiter before serving. If the cheese rind is not palatable it is also removed by the waiter. This is not necessary in the case of Camembert and Brie as the rind of these two French cream cheeses is palatable. A Stilton should no longer be served in the traditional manner of scooping out and thereby wasting a large amount, but by cutting out thin wedges across the surface of the cheese. Recognition by the waiter of all cheeses on the cheese board or trolly is of utmost importance.

DESSERT (FRESH FRUIT AND NUTS)

Dessert is served on the lunch and dinner menu as an alternative to an entremet (sweet), whereas on a banquet menu it may be a course on its own being served between the savoury (savoureux) and cheese and biscuits (fromages assortis). On an à la carte menu, dessert is a section on its own.

Dessert may include all types of fresh fruits and nuts according to season, although the majority of the more popular items are available all the year round due to the up to date means of transport between various parts of the globe. Some of the more popular items are as follows—dessert apples, pears, bananas, oranges, mandarine, tangerine, black and white grapes, pineapple, and assorted nuts such as brazils, etc. Sometimes a box of dates may appear on the fruit basket.

The dessert is usually dressed up in a fruit basket by the larder section and may be used as a central piece on a cold buffet until required.

Cover for dessert

Fruit plate.
Fruit knife and fork: interlocked on the fruit plate.
Spare serviette.
One finger bowl: on a doily on a sideplate and containing luke warm water and a slice of lemon. It will be placed at the top right hand corner of the cover and may be used by the customer for rinsing his fingers.
One finger bowl: on a doily on a sideplate and containing cold water for rinsing the grapes. It will be placed on the top left hand corner of the cover.
Nut crackers and grape scissors; to be placed on the fruit basket.
Spare sideplate for shells and peel.

Accompaniments for dessert

Castor sugar holder on a sideplate.
Salt for nuts.

Service of dessert

If dessert is to be served as an alternative to a sweet one must ensure that crumbing down has been carried out. Before offering the fruit basket to the guest the waiter should make certain that the correct cover and accompaniments have been laid. The fruit basket is then presented to the guest who makes his or her choice of a portion of fresh fruit or nuts.

If it is silver service the guest chooses nuts as part of his portion then the nut-crackers would be removed from the fruit basket, placed on a sideplate and left on the table at the head of the cover.

If grapes are chosen then the waiter rests the fruit basket on the table supporting it with one hand and cuts off the selected portion of grapes with the aid of the grape scissors. These are so made that they will grip the stem once the portion has been cut and removed from the main bunch, and thus by holding the portion with the grape scissors they may be rinsed in the finger bowl at the top left hand corner of the cover, and then placed on the fruit plate. If gueridon service is being used the procedure will be the same but take place from the gueridon or trolly.

In gueridon service the Station head waiter completes the service of fruit by removing the peel and/or core from such fruits as apples, pears, oranges, pineapples etc. This procedure is carried out on the gueridon next to the guests table.

Service of pineapple

If one is commencing with a whole pineapple first remove the upper stalk and then cut 1-2 slices per portion approximately 6 mm ($\frac{1}{4}$ in) thick. Trim round the edges of each pineapple slice and then remove the core. Cut into four equal pieces and arrange neatly on the fruit plate. At this stage, if required, kirsch may be poured over the prepared pineapple and it is then ready to serve. Replace the upper stalk onto the top of the pineapple in the fruit basket as this helps to retain the juices and moisture of the pineapple.

Service of apples and pears

Take the selected fruit and insert the prongs of a fruit fork into the core of the apple or pear, from the base. Holding the fruit fork in the left hand and using a fruit knife peel the apple in a circular fashion, and the pear lengthways from top to bottom. When all the peel is removed cut the apple and pear in quarters with the aid of the fruit knife and fork and remove the core taking care all the time not to damage or bruise the fruit. Cut into slices and arrange neatly on the fruit plate and serve. Preparation may be taken a stage further by heating the prepared fruit in a pan containing sugar syrup and then flambé with kirsch. This would only be done if gueridon service was being carried out.

Service of oranges

Cut a thin slice from the top and bottom of the orange. This ensures that it will stand firmly on the board for peeling which will be carried out according to the thickness of the peel. With the aid of a fruit knife and fork remove lengths of the orange peel by cutting from top to bottom. One must ensure that the pith is removed at the same time as the peel. Then using the fruit knife and fork remove all segments of the orange fruit leaving only the pith that holds the segments. Arrange the segments neatly on a fruit plate and serve.

Fresh cream may be served with all types of fruit but is normally charged extra. The fresh cream may be served in a cream jug which is placed on the table, or from a sauce boat and offered to the guest by the waiter with the aid of a sauce ladle or dessert spoon.

SAVOURIES (SAVOUREUX)

A savoury as the term indicates is a savoury item served on varying shapes of toast; in tartlettes (round) and barquettes (oval); in bouchées; flan rings or as an omelette or soufflé.

On the lunch and dinner menu the savoury is generally served as an alternative to a sweet, whilst in a banquet it may be a course on its own, coming between the entremet (sweet) and dessert (fresh fruit and nuts). In a full à la carte menu the savouries are listed in a section of their own.

Cover for savouries

Hot fish plate.
Side knife.
Dessert fork.

Accompaniments for savouries

Cruet: to be replaced if previously removed when clearing the main course.
Cayenne pepper ⎫ each item placed on a sideplate
Peppermill   ⎬ on the table.
Worcestershire sauce: Shake bottle and remove lid, stand on sideplate on table. Only to be offered if a meat savoury.

Service of savouries

If a variety of hot and cold sweets are being ordered by a party of people then the cold items must be served first followed by the hot items. One must ensure the fish plate is hot for the savoury; the correct cutlery is laid before serving; the necessary accompaniments are all on the table before service commences. The savouries will be pre-portioned by the kitchen. If the savoury is being eaten as an alternative to a sweet off the lunch or dinner menu, then before the cover or accompaniments are laid crumbing down should take place.

Savouries on toast

Anchovies on Toast:
Toast the bread and lay the anchovy fillets side by side. Trim the toast. Finish with the heated oil from the anchovies. Decorate with seived hard boiled yolk of egg and chopped parsley.

Sardines on Toast:
Split sardines in half and remove backbone. Lay head to tail on toast. Finish with the oil from the sardines.

Roes on Toast:
Shallow fry the roes and dress on toast. Sprinkle with lemon juice, coat with beurre noisette and serve.

Haddock on Toast:
Poach haddock and flake. Mix with a cream sauce. Spread on toast, decorate and serve.

Mushrooms on Toast:
Peel, wash and slice mushrooms. Shallow fry and dress on toast. Sprinkle with chopped parsley and serve.

Moelle sur Toast:
Slice the chilled marrow 6 mm ($\frac{1}{4}$ in) thick. Poach gently in a little white stock. Drain well and dress on hot buttered toast. Season and coat with beurre noisette, sprinkle with chopped parsley and serve.

Welsh Rarebit:
$\frac{1}{8}$ litre ($\frac{1}{4}$ pt) bechamel (thin). Reduce $\frac{1}{4}$ litre ($\frac{1}{2}$ pt) beer to an $\frac{1}{8}$ litre ($\frac{1}{4}$ pt) and add to bechamel. Stir in 113 grammes (4 oz) grated cheddar. Season with salt, cayenne pepper and Worcestershire sauce. Bind with a liaison of one yolk. Pour on to fingers of toast and glaze.

Buck Rarebit:
A Welsh rarebit garnished with a poached egg.

Canapés

Are shaped pieces of bread approximately 6 mm ($\frac{1}{4}$ in) thick, brushed over with melted butter and placed under a salamander and coloured on both sides. Could be shallow fried.

Canapé Baron:
Garnish with slices of fried mushrooms, grilled bacon and poached bone marrow.

Canapé Ritchie:
Creamed haddock, garnished with slices of hard boiled egg.

Canapé Quo Vadis:
Grilled roes garnished with small mushroom heads.

Canapé Nina:
Half small grilled tomato, garnished with mushroom head and a pickled walnut.

Canapé Charlemagne:
Garnish with shrimps bound with a curry sauce.

Angels on Horseback:
Poached oysters, wrapped in streaky bacon and grilled on skewers.

Devils on Horseback:
Stoned cooked prune, the inside stuffed with chutney and sprinkled with cayenne. Wrap in streaky bacon and grill on a skewer.

Croûtes

Are shaped pieces of bread approximately 6 mm ($\frac{1}{4}$ in) thick. Shallow fry.

Croûte Derby:
Spread with ham pruée and garnish with a pickled walnut.

Croûte Windsor:
Spread with ham purée and garnish with small grilled mushrooms.

Croûte Diane:
Partly cooked chicken livers (fried) wrapped in streaky bacon and grilled on a skewer.

Scotch Woodcock:
Scrambled egg garnished with a trellis of anchovy and studded with capers.

Note Most of the above can be named either Canapés or Croûtes.

Tartlettes (round) or Barquettes (oval)

These are normally made from unsweetened short crust pastry.

Charles V:
Soft roes mixed with butter and covered with a cheese souffle mixture. Bake in the oven.

Favorite:
Fill with cheese souffle mixture and slices of truffle, Garnish with slices of cray-fish tails or prawns.

Haddock: Fill with diced haddock bound with a curry sauce. Sprinkle with breadcrumbs and gratinate.

Bouchées

Have various fillings such as shrimp, lobster, prawn and haddock.

Indienne:
Filled with curried shrimps and chutney.

Omelettes:
Two/three egg omelettes. Have various flavours such as parsley, anchovy, cheese, fines herbes (mixed herbs) etc.

Soufflés

Made in soufflé dishes. Various flavours such as mushrooms, spinach, sardine, anchovy, haddock, cheese etc.

Flan

Made from unsweetened short crust pastry.

Quiche Lorraine:
Flan made from unsweetened short crust pastry and filled with rashers of streaky bacon and slices of cheese. Covered with a savoury egg custard mixture and baked in the oven. Serve hot.

15   control systems

A control system covering the sale of all food and drink in a catering establishment is essential to achieve maximum returns. The type of control system used varies from one establishment to another. A catering establishment offers to the guest various services from different departments; the kitchen, dining room, dispense bar, cocktail bar, lounge and floor service. So that the control may be efficient, the system will vary in each department according to its needs. All food and beverage service staff should be made aware of the importance of control and the great loss that may occur in materials and money if the system is not properly operated. How this is carried out depends on management and the degree of training and instruction that is given to staff on the job. In a large establishment a control and accounts department would be in overall charge of the efficient running and working of the control systems used. In a smaller establishment this would be taken over by the assistant manager or even the manager himself who would carry out the daily and weekly checks that were necessary. All control systems should be as simple as possible, making it easier for the food and beverage service staff to operate and for the control and accounts department staff to check for any errors and omissions and to have them immediately rectified.

The function of a Control System

A control system should work on the following basis:

1. There must be efficient control on all items issued from the various departments.
2. The system should reduce to the minimum any pilfering and wastage.

3. Management should be provided with any information they require for costing purposes, so that they may estimate accurately for the coming financial period.
4. The cashier should be able to make out the guests' bill correctly so that he is neither overcharged nor undercharged.
5. The system should show a breakdown of sales and income received in order that adjustments and improvements may be made.

The main control systems in use in catering establishments are:

a) Triplicate checking system.
b) Duplicate checking system.
c) Waiter billing machine.

So that the control may be efficient, the system will vary in each department according to its needs.

There are many variations on these according to the requirements of a particular establishment.

a) *Triplicate Checking System*

This is a control system used in the majority of medium and large first class establishments. As the name implies the food check consists of three copies.

To ensure efficient control the waiter or waitress must fill in the information required in the four corners of the check: This is

1. Table number
2. Number of covers
3. Date
4. Signature of waiter/ress taking order.

On taking the order it is written from top to bottom of the food check. Where only a table d'hôte menu is in operation the guest would

FOOD CHECK (Before and after order is taken)

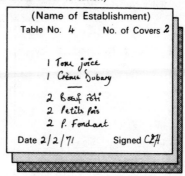

initially only order their first and main course. A second new food check is written out for the sweet course, this being taken after the main course is finished. A third new check will be completed if any beverage such as coffee is required. The operation for an à la carte menu is similar, though the guests may order course by course according to their requirements. It must always be remembered that all checks should be legible and that where an à la carte menu is in operation the prices of the dishes must be put on the check. Abbreviations may be used when taking the order as long as they are understood by everyone and not misinterpreted by the kitchen causing the wrong order to be put up, and therefore a delay in the services to the guest.

The Food Check
1. The top copy of the food order goes to the kitchen and is handed to the Aboyeur at the hotplate.
2. The duplicate goes to the cashier who makes out the guests bill.
3. The flimsy, or third copy, is retained by the waiter at his sideboard as a means of reference.

Any checks or bills which have to be cancelled should have the headwaiter's or supervisor's signature on them; so also should checks and bills which have alterations made to them. In certain instances it is necessary to write out special checks. These would be as follows:

1. Where it is necessary to write out more than one food check for a meal, e.g. where a sweet check is written out after the first and main course has been served.

At the head of this check would be written the word *Suivant* which means the 'following' check, and showing that one check has already been written out for that particular table.

2. When an extra portion of food is required because sufficient has not been sent from the kitchen, a special check must be written out headed *Supplement*. This means to supplement what has already been previously sent. It should be signed by the head waiter or supervisor and normally there is no charge (n/c), but this depends on the policy of the establishment concerned.

3. Where a wrong dish has been ordered and has to be sent back to the kitchen and replaced a special check must again be made out. If the service being carried out is from an à la carte menu then the prices of the two dishes concerned must be shown. Two main headings are used on this special check, *Retour*, or 'return' and the name of the dish going back to the kitchen, and *En place* or 'in its place', and the name of the new dish to be served.

4. It occasionally happens that the waiter or waitress may have an accident in the room and perhaps some vegetables are dropped. These must be replaced without any extra charge to the guest. Here a check must be completed headed *Accident*. It will show the number of portions of vegetables required and should be signed by the head waiter or supervisor in charge. No charge (n/c) is made.

The Cashier
On receiving the duplicate copy of the food check from the waiter the cashier opens a bill in duplicate according to the table number on

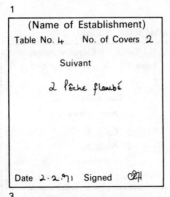

1

(Name of Establishment)

Table No. 4   No. of Covers 2

Suivant

2 Pêche flambé

Date 2·2·71   Signed CPH

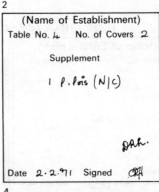

2

(Name of Establishment)

Table No. 4   No. of Covers 2

Supplement

1 P. Pois (N/C)

DRh.

Date 2·2·71   Signed CPH

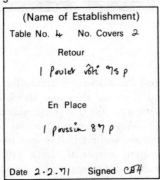

3

(Name of Establishment)

Table No. 4   No. Covers 2

Retour

1 Poulet rôti 95 p

En Place

1 poussin 87 p

Date 2·2·71   Signed CPH

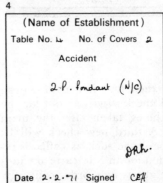

4

(Name of Establishment)

Table No. 4   No. of Covers 2

Accident

2·P. fondant (N/C)

DRh.

Date 2·2·71   Signed CPH

the food check. All the sets of bills are serial numbered for control purposes. As checks are received by the cashier from the food or wine waiter she enters the items ordered onto the bill together with the correct prices. When this is done the bill and duplicate checks are pinned together and may be placed into a special book or file which has its pages numbered according to the number of tables in the room. The bill and duplicate checks are placed in the page corresponding to the table number. As further checks are received the items are entered onto the bill and the checks then pinned with the others to the bill.

When the guest requests his bill the waiter must collect it from the cashier who must first check that all items are entered and priced correctly and then total it up. It is advisable for the waiter to double check the addition. The top copy of the bill is presented to the guest on a sideplate and folded in half with one corner turned up. On receiving the necessary payment from the guest the waiter returns the bill and cash to the cashier who will receipt both copies of the bill and return the receipted top copy plus any change to the waiter. The waiter then returns this to the guest. The receipted duplicate copy with the duplicate checks pinned to it is then removed from the special book or file and

put on one side until service is completed.

At the conclusion of service all the items from all the bills are entered onto a cashiers summary sheet. This shows an analysis of all cash taken and must be balanced by the cashier before going off duty. Once it is balanced it would be handed to the control and accounts department together with all the duplicate bills and their checks, and the cash received through the service plus the float. A receipt must be obtained for the cash handed in.

It is worth noting at this stage where services are provided to residents in the lounges and on the floors, cash does not always change hands for the service rendered and therefore all checks written out must be signed by the resident concerned to show he has received a particular service. These checks would then be immediately passed on to the control and accounts department. It is their job to co-ordinate and marry up all checks, bills and money coming in via the various service departments. In this way all residents bills are up to date and all services provided are charged for. When a resident signs a check for a service rendered the waiter must ensure the correct room number is placed on the check so that the charge can be made on the right bill.

TRIPLICATE CHECKING SYSTEM

Food checks normally white in colour
Wine checks normally pink in colour

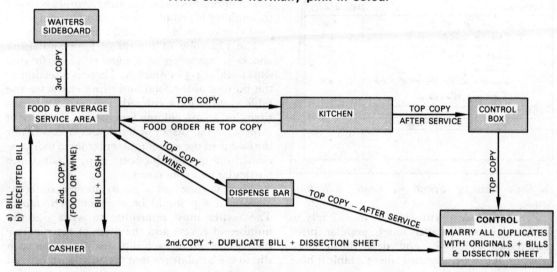

CASHIERS SUMMARY SHEET

BILL No.	TABLE No.	No. OF COVERS	ROOM No.	AMOUNT PAID	CREDIT	KITCHEN	BEVERAGE (COFFEE)	WINES	LIQUEURS	BEERS AND MINERALS	CIGARS AND CIGARETTES	FLOWERS	EXTRAS	SUNDRIES	TOTAL
0631	6	3	64		2.05	1.00	10p	53p	17p		25p				2.05
0632	10	2		2.52		1.20	15p	47p	53p		17p				2.52
						2.20	25p	1.00	70p		42p				4.57

£4.57

All bills to be entered in numerical order according to the serial numbers

The Bill

(Name of Establishment)		
Serial No. 057531		
Table No. 4		Date 2/2/71
2 Couvert @ 87p		1·74
2 Café @ 10p		0·20
Wines — 1×1b @ 70p		0·70
Spirits —		
Liqueurs — 2 Tia Marias @ 23p		0·46
Beers and Minerals —		
057531		£3·10
Service Charge 10%		0·31
	Total	£ 3·41

Duplicate Checking System or *Check Bill Book System*

This is a control system which is more likely to be found in the smaller hotel, popular price restaurants and café, and department store catering. It is generally used where a table d'hôte menu is in operation and sometimes a very limited à la carte menu. As the name implies there are two copies of each of these food checks, each set being serial numbered. A check pad, or bill pad, as it is sometimes termed, usually contains a set of 50 or 100 food checks. The top copy of the food check is usually carbon backed, but if not then a sheet of carbon must be placed between the top and duplicate copy everytime a fresh order is taken.

For control purposes the top copy may have printed on it a waiters number or letter. This would be the number or letter given to a waiter on joining the staff. The control and accounts department would be informed of the person to whom the number applied, and he would retain it throughout his employment. Also on each set of food checks would be printed a serial number.

The top copy of the set of food and drink checks is made up of a number of perforated slips usually 4-5 in number. There is a section at the bottom of the food and drink check for the table number to be entered. The top copy sometimes has a cash column for entering the price of a meal or the dishes ordered, but if this is not the case then the waiter must enter them independently on to the duplicate copy against the particular dish concerned.

When writing out a guests order a different perforated slip would be used for each course. The waiter must remember to write out the number of covers and the price of the meal or dish concerned on each slip. Before sending each slip to the hotplate see that the details are entered correctly on the duplicate copy together with the price. Since the duplicate copy acts as the guests bill the waiter has to ensure that everything served is charged and paid for.

As the service of a meal commences the waiter/ress tears off from the top copy of the food and drink check the perforated slip showing the first course ordered. This is taken to the hotplate and the required dish is put up. As soon as this happens the aboyeur will tear off the waiters number (21) on the end of the slip and place it with the dish concerned. This then shows which

Serial No.	Waiters No.	
0693	21	
0693	21	
0693	21	
0693	21	
0693	21	
0693	21	
Table No. ____ Date ____ Total	£	

TOP COPY

Serial No.	Waiters No.	
0692	21	21
0692	21	21
0692	21	21
0692	21	21
0692	21	21

ALTERNATIVE TOP COPY

0692	2 Covers @ 62½p	21	
	2 Tomato Soup		21
0692	2 Covers @ 62½p	21	
	2 Sole frit		21
0692	2 Covers @ 62½p	21	
	2 R. Lamb		21
	2 R. Pots		
	2 Beans		
0692	2 Covers @ 62½p	21	
	2 Vanilla Ices		21
0692	2 Covers @ 62½p	21	
	2 Coffees		21
0692	2 Covers @ 62½p	21	
	½ × 16		21

waiter it is for. If there is no waiters number at the end of the perforated slip then the perforated slip itself is left with the order until collected by the waiter. The Aboyeur will then retain the slip showing the course just served. As soon as the first course is served and allowing time for this course to be consumed the second perforated slip is taken to the hotplate by the waiter. This dish will then be collected as required. This same procedure is carried on throughout the meal.

It may happen that there are insufficient perforated slips on the top copy of the food and drink check for a particular guests requirements. Very often the waiter does his own wine waiting and thus he takes the wine order and enters it on a separate perforated slip. When there are not sufficient perforated slips a supplementary check pad is brought into use. This pad is made up of single slips on which the waiter writes his order and his number and then collects the items concerned from a particular service point. He must ensure that the charge for such items is entered on the guests bill—the duplicate copy of the food and drink check.

When a guest requires his bill the waiter checks everything, is entered on the duplicate copy of the food and drink check and then totals the bill. It is presented to the guest as previously mentioned. One of two methods of payment may now occur. The guest may pay at the cash desk on the way out or he may pay the cash direct to the waiter who will give any change that is necessary. The cashier usually keeps the bills on payment but if a guest wishes to have a receipt then a special bill is written out and receipted for him.

Depending on the system used a waiter may enter the details of his bills from the stubs on his check pads into an account slip. This account slip plus the stubs and cash received are then passed on to the control and accounts department who marry them all up.

2/2/71	No. 21
D.R. Smith	
0692	2·50
0693	0·77
0694	1·53
0695	1·20
	£6·00

WAITER'S ACCOUNT SLIP

If the waiter makes out and presents the bill to the guest and it is then paid by the guest to the cashier on leaving the establishment, then the cashier will draw up a daily summary sheet or analysis sheet to show the daily takings and also a waiter's analysis sheet showing each individual waiter's takings.

Control is effected by the control and accounts department marrying up the checks used to order food and drink from the bars, stillroom and kitchen against the bills issued by each waiter.

It will be useful at this stage to point out the basic differences between the triplicate and duplicate control systems. These are as follows:

	Triplicate	*Duplicate*
1. Type of establishment	First class establishments usually operating an extensive à la carte menu.	Popular price restaurants, café and department stores when a table d'hôte menu is in operation with possibly a limited à la carte.
2. No. of copies of food check	Three	Two
3. The Bill	Cashier makes out the bill, which is in duplicate.	The bill is the duplicate copy of the food and drink check and is made out by the waiter.
4. Payment of the bill	The guest pays the cashier via the waiter who returns the receipted bill and any change to the guest.	The guest may pay the cashier direct or pay the waiter according to the policy of the establishment.
5. At the end of service the cashier	Completes her summary sheet and hands it in with any cash and the duplicate bills and checks to the control and accounts department.	In addition to this the waiters account slip and the stubs from his check pad must be handed in, by the waiter, together with the cash received by him.

Waiter Billing Machine

This is a fairly new innovation on the catering scene. Although the machine itself is expensive to install, it has the advantage of allowing the waiters to take their own cash, and thus doing away with a cashier. From this point of view a cashier's wages are being saved and thus the machine may pay for itself within a year. Basically its operation is very simple. The machine will give an analysis of sales according to the needs of the establishment concerned. This is done by simply pushing a particular button depending whether the sale is food, drink, beverage, cigars, cigarettes or sweets.

On commencing a 'service' the waiter should have for control purposes:

1. Key: with his waiter letter upon it.
2. Folder: to hold the required stationery.
3. Sets of food order pads plus bills: serial numbered in consecutive order.
4. Waiter paying - in slip.
5. Float.

Each waiter on commencing his employment will be given a 'letter' which he will carry with him throughout his employment. This type of control system may be said to be a form of duplicate checking as only two copies are used. The top copy has the food order written on it and this sheet is again divided into a number of perforated slips, usually 5 in number. When the order is taken each course is written on one of the perforated slips. Before this slip is taken to the hotplate for the dish concerned to be put up the whole bill must be placed in the billing machine and the appropriate keys pushed so that the correct price is printed on the order opposite the appropriate dish. The top copy is treated with a special chemical and the order and price will come through on the duplicate copy which acts as the bill. Every time a waiter has to use the billing machine he must firstly insert his own billing machine key into the appropriate locking position and finally press the button with his own letter on. When a check is carried out, this enables the control and accounts department to know who has used the machine on each occasion should they wish to analyse sales. To use the machine the following simple procedure must be carried out:

1. Insert key into the correct locking position.
2. Place whole order and bill in machine.
3. Press keys to denote price of the dishes concerned.
4. Press the button concerned according to whether the order is food/beverage/drink etc. to show what the cash received was for.
5. Press waiter's 'letter'.

This is done so that when the Aboyeur receives a perforated slip the price is printed against the appropriate dish. If this is not the case then the aboyeur will refuse the perforated slip. It is a means of control showing that the cash for a dish has been rung up and therefore it must be paid in by the waiter before service is finished. The procedure for service of a meal when this system is in use is as for duplicate checking. On requesting his bill the duplicate copy or bill is totalled up and the total entered in the appropriate box. The bill is then presented to the guest in the usual manner, and payment is made direct to the waiter concerned. The waiter retains all the cash received until the service is completed. The slip at the foot of the top copy also has the total amount entered in it, and is handed to the guest as a receipt for cash paid. The waiter retains the bills until after service and they are then all totalled together showing the grand total of cash taken by a particular waiter. This information is then entered on the 'Waiter's paying-in slip'. This would then be double checked against the reading on the billing machine, and the two totals should agree. Any discrepancies must be accounted for. The perforated slips from the hotplate may also be checked against the reading on the billing machine.

As has already been mentioned there are many variations to the basic duplicate checking control system. These are too numerous to mention individually but two are described below very simply in order to give one some idea of the possible variations *available*.

ORDER (Top Copy)

Order written this side   Price of dish typed this side

TABLE No.	COVERS
1.	
B	
2.	
B	
3.	
B	
4.	
B	
5.	
B	

The Cathedral Restaurant
No. 00404

£
Please pay waiter/ress

ORDER (Duplicate Copy)

TABLE No.	COVERS
1.	
B	
2.	
B	
3.	
B	
4.	
B	
5.	
B	

The Cathedral Restaurant
No. 00404

£
Please pay waiter/ress

PAY IN SLIP		
WAITRESS G		DATE 7/2/71
Machine Total £		
Signed Bills		
Bill No.	£ · p	
012	1·77	
013	2·17	
014	1·53	
015	2·23	
TOTAL SIGNED BILLS		£ 7·70
CASH	£ · p	
£5 Notes	10·0	
£1 Notes	3·0	
50 pence	1·0	
Silver	0·73	
Copper	0·12	
Cheques	2·17	
TOTAL CASH		£ 17·2
TOTAL CASH PAID IN		£ 17·2
Bills Used From 010 To 026		

The first alternative shows the menu order and customers bill combined on one sheet. Each party of guests would be allocated what we may term a 'menu and customer bill'. When the order is taken the guests requirements would be written down in the column next to the price column. Thus if a party of two guests requested two cream soup, one mushroom omelette and chips and one fried cod and chips it would be noted down as follows by the waiter.

'Quick service' menu and customer bill

Soup		
Cream soup	6p	2
Hot Dishes		
Omelette served with chips or Bowl of salad Plain		
Cheese		
Ham		
Mushroom		1
Tomato	17p	
Fried Cod and Chips	18p	1

The guest may order just a hot snack and beverage; a complete three-course meal with all the ancillary items such as rolls and butter or he may like to order only his first and main course and leave his sweet and beverage order until his main course in finished. This depends entirely on the individual and the time he has available. Once the order has been taken the 'menu and customer bill' is retained by the guest and the waiter orders verbally over the hotplate. All cold drinks and food stuffs are immediately to hand for the food and beverage service staff thus reducing any delay in the service to the minimum. Once the meal is finished the guest takes his 'menu and customer bill' and hands it to the cashier. The cashier then rings up the cost of the dishes consumed according to the 'menu and customer bill' and totals the sum outstanding. This is then paid by the guest. The cashier keeps each menu customer bill for checking purposes after service. Thus in the example given above the amount rung up on the cash register would be as follows:

	p
2 Cream Soup at 6 p	12
1 Mushroom Omelette at 17 p	17
1 Fried Cod an Chips at 18 p	18

Amount owing	47 p

Each 'menu and customer bill' has a waiters letter or number printed on it denoting who carried out the service of a particular meal, and is also serial numbered. This in itself is an added form of control which may be checked by the cashier or accounts department after every service is completed.

The advantages of this form of service and control are that the menu is limited to items which can be provided quickly and are still well presented and palatable. Administration as far as the waiter is concerned is reduced to the minimum and the control system may be learnt very quickly by a new member of staff because it is so simple. No waiter handles any cash whatso ever, this all being done by one person, the cashier. The turnover of custom where this form of service is in operation is usually very high.

A further simple form of checking is shown by the diagram below, which may be used in cafés and quick turnover restaurants and department stores. The menu is very limited with little or no choice. The waiter takes the order and marks down the guest's requirements; calls for the order verbally over the hotplate and when the guest

'QUICK SERVICE' MENU AND CUSTOMER BILL

SOUP: Cream soup	6p		SALAD BOWL: Lettuce, egg, tomato, cucumber, potato	10p	
HOT DISHES:			SWEETS: Milk pudding,	6p	
Omelettes served with chips or bowl of salad plain	15p		Fruit tart, custard	9p	
cheese mushroom	17p		ICES: Vanilla, chocolate, coffee	4p	
			SUNDAES: Peach melba	15p	
			Knickebocker glory	19p	
Fried cod and chips	16p		SUNDRIES: Roll	2p	
Pork sausage and chips	17p		Ryvita	2p	
Buck rarebit	11p		Butter	1p	
VEGETABLES: Peas, beans	5p		BEVERAGES: Tea, per cup	2p	
POTATO: Creamed, roast	5p		Coffee, per cup	4p	
SALADS: Egg Mayonnaise	15p		Minerals	4p	
Cold Ham	23p		Squashes	4p	
Grated Cheese	19p		Milk	3p	

PLEASE PAY CASHIER

WAITRESS No. _____

Number of Persons _____

B.00491

---

requests his bill, prices the order sheet and hands it to the guest. The guest then hands it in to the cashier on leaving and pays the required amount. There is only one copy of this order and bill combined and it is retained by the cashier, for control purposes, once the guest has made the necessary payment. The stub at the top of the check may be retained by the waiter in the bill pad and will only have entered on it the total amount owing for each party served. This is an added measure of control and the stubs may be handed in after service and be married up with the bill paid.

In conclusion it must be remembered that control in one form or another is all important, the final method of control being used depending upon the policy of the establishment concerned. No system is fool-proof but if sufficient care and caution is observed then any loss will be cut to a bare minimum.

			12
		Tea, coffee etc. Bread and butter Cakes and pastries Soups Fish Meat Vegetables Sweet dishes and ices Sundries	
		Total	12

16   breakfast service

Breakfast is traditionally an English rather than a Continental meal, originating from the days of the private house and family service when it was a very substantial meal consisting of some six or seven courses, including such items as chops, liver, game and even steak as the main part of the meal. For the European a Continental breakfast is of a much lighter nature and takes the form of a light snack, as their midday meal is generally taken earlier and is much more substantial than in England.

In London the current trend is for hotels to serve a 'Continental breakfast' inclusive in the room rate, and to serve the 'full English breakfast' at an à la carte charge. In provincial hotels a three-course 'full English breakfast' is still served and may or may not be included within the room-rate.

Breakfast may be served in the hotel restaurant or dining room, in a breakfast room aside for this one meal, or in the guest's bedroom or suite. The Floor waiter (Chef d'étage) will serve breakfasts in the bedrooms or suites and a *Breakfast brigade* will serve in the other rooms. The staff for this may be drawn from the normal restaurant brigade on a weekly or daily rota, or there may be a special breakfast brigade working daily from 7.00 am. until 11.00 am. In a provincial hotel serving 80 full English breakfasts the brigade may consist of one Head waiter and four waiters or waitresses, depending on the type of establishment.

Checking system

The double checking system is normally used for breakfasts, both on the floors and in the restaurant. It is the Head waiters or Floor waiter responsibility to see that signed bills, booked to a room number, are sent to the Bill office as often as possible during the service of breakfasts and are not kept until the end of service. This will ensure that any guests who are leaving immediately after breakfast will have been charged the correct amount on their hotel bill, or it may happen that they will settle their account and leave the hotel by the time the breakfast bills arrive at the Bill office.

Café complet

This term is widely used on the continent and means in effect a Continental Breakfast with coffee as the beverage. *Thé Complet* is also used, in this sense, with tea as the beverage.

Café simple ou Thé simple

On the other hand the guest may order a Café simple or Thé simple in which case he requires the beverage (coffee or tea) with nothing to eat.

The breakfast menu

A full English breakfast menu may consist of from two to eight courses, and the order of courses will follow that laid down in the classical French menu. The specimen breakfast menu shown may be found in a first class hotel, but the extent and variety of any menu will obviously depend on the type of establishment in which it is being served.

CATHEDRAL HOTEL

BREAKFAST
Chilled Fruit Juices
Orange, pineapple, grapefruit, tomato

Stewed Fruits
Prunes, pears, apples, figs
Cereals
Porridge and all proprietary brands of
breakfast cereals
Fish
Finnan haddock, grilled herring, bloaters,
Fried or grilled kippers, fried smelt,
Fried or grilled plaice or sole,
Kedgeree
Eggs
Fried, poached, scrambled, boiled,
Omelettes—plain or savoury
Meat
Fried or grilled bacon, pork sausages,
Kidneys, tomatoes, sauté potatoes
Cold Buffet
York ham, calves tongue, breakfast sausage
Breads
Toast, rolls, croissants, brioches, ryvita,
Hovis and procea
Preserves
Marmalade, honey, plum, cherry
Beverages
Tea, coffee, chocolate

Date

Cover

The term 'Breakfast cover' may therefore be
divided into two types when discussing the
service of the breakfast meal, these being:
a) A Continental breakfast cover.
b) A full English breakfast cover.

Cover for a Continental breakfast

This meal will consist of hot croissant/brioches
or hot toast, butter, preserves, and coffee or tea.
With this in mind the cover would be as follows:
1. Side plate.
2. Side knife.
3. Serviette. Normally placed on the side plate
   and under the side knife.
4. Bread boat containing the croissant or
   brioche in a serviette to keep them hot, or a
   toast rack on an underplate.
5. Butter dish on a doily on a sideplate with a
   butter knife.
6. Preserve dish on a doily on a sideplate with a
   preserve spoon.
7. Breakfast cup and saucer and a teaspoon.
8. Stands or underplates for coffee/tea pot and
   hot milk/hot water jug.

A breakfast tray laid for a continental breakfast.

9. Ashtray.
10. Table number.
11. Sugar basin and tongs.
    If tea is to be the beverage then the following additional items would be needed:
12. Slop basin.
13. Tea strainer.
14. Jug of cold milk.

Cover for a full English breakfast

This meal will consist of a number of courses, usually three or four, with a choice of dishes from within each course, as shown on the specimen breakfast menu. The cover will therefore be a modified Table d'hôte cover as follows:

1. Joint knife and fork.
2. Fish knife and fork.
3. Dessert spoon and fork.
4. Sideknife.
5. Sideplate.
6. Breakfast cup, saucer and teaspoon.
7. Slop basin.
8. Tea strainer.
9. Jug of cold milk.
10. Sugar basin and tongs.
11. Stands or underplates for tea pot/coffee pot and hot water jug/hot milk jug.

12. Butter dish on a doily on an underplate with a butter knife.
13. Preserve dish on a doily on an underplate with a preserve spoon.
14. Cruet: salt, pepper, mustard and mustard spoon.
15. Sugar castor.
16. Ashtray.
17. Serviette: either laid flat between the joint knife and fork or placed on the sideplate under the side knife.
18. Toast rack on an underplate.
19. Table number.
20. Bread boat containing the croissant or brioche in a serviette to keep them warm.

The majority of the items listed for the two types of breakfast would be placed on the table as part of the mise-en-place, before the guest is seated. A number of items however, are not placed on the table until the guest is seated, and these include:

a) Butter dish and butter.
b) Preserve dish with preserve.
c) Jug of cold milk.
d) Toast rack with toast and/or bread basket with hot rolls.

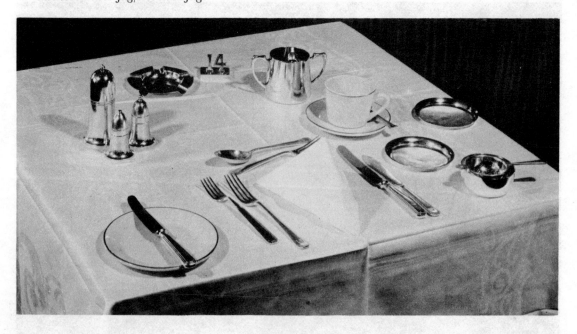

Full English breakfast cover as laid during the pre-service preparation period. Note: the cover laid is a Table d'hote cover without the soup spoon, the positioning of the items, to the right of the cover for the convenience of the guest.

Breakfast served in the restaurant

The basic mise-en-place for the service of breakfast is normally carried out the evening before, after the service of dinners has finished. To ensure protection against dust until the breakfast brigade come on duty the corners of the cloths may be lifted up and over the basic mise-en-place. It will be completed the following morning before the actual service of breakfast commences.

It is advisable to be on duty in plenty of time in order to check your station and to complete the necessary mise-en-place. This will include the turning up of the breakfast cups the right way, and the laying up of the breakfast buffet with items usually served for the first course such as chilled fruit juices, cereals, and compote of fruit together with all the necessary glasses, plates and cutlery required for the correct service. Also found on the breakfast buffet would be preserves and butter if they were not to be obtained from the stillroom. Jugs of iced water and glasses should be ready on the buffet throughout the meal especially if the establishment is catering for American visitors. Cereals would be dispensed at the buffet direct from the packet and on no account should they be served at the table. The exception to this is when individual packets of cereal are in use and these may then be placed on the table as required. For economy reasons, preserves may be served in either individual pots or in there original jars placed in a suitable container. Finally check that the table is correctly laid, that fresh mustard has been made and placed in its appropriate container on the table, that all other mise-en-place is complete and everything is ready for service.

The guest will be escorted to a particular table by the Head waiter, the chairs pulled out and the guest seated. The breakfast menu will be presented and, giving a few minutes for the guest to make his choice, the waiter takes the order.

The food order is written on one check and is sent to the kitchen, the beverage on another check which is sent to the stillroom. While the orders are being attended to in the various departments, the waiter must remember first of all to remove any unwanted cutlery from the cover and where appropriate lay fresh cutlery and any accompaniments that may be required, e.g. Worcestershire sauce if the first course is to be tomato juice. The first course will then be laid on the table.

When the first course has been consumed and the cutlery, plate or glasses cleared, the beverage will be served. The teapot and hot water jug or the coffee pot and hot milk jug will be placed on the stands or underplates to the right hand side of the lady in the party, or in case of an all male party, by the senior gentleman present. The handles of the pots should be placed in the most convienient position for pouring. Hot fresh toast and/or hot rolls will then be placed on the table before serving the main course.

The main course at breakfast is usually plated and all necessary accompaniments should be on the table before it is served. On clearing the main course the waiter should move the side-plate and knife in front of the guest and then enquire if more toast, butter, preserve or beverage is required.

Breakfast served in apartments

The guest may place his order for breakfast in his room with either the Floor waiter (Chef d'étage) or the night porter, the night before. If with the latter, the floor waiter must collect these orders as soon as he comes on duty. Alternatively the guest may order his breakfast on the morning concerned by telephoning to or ringing for the Floor waiter, whichever system is used in the hotel.

To lay up a breakfast tray is the same procedure, with a few exceptions, as for laying up a table for a full English or Continental breakfast in the restaurant, although as most orders for the service of breakfasts in the apartments are known in advance the tray may be laid according to the order.

The main difference between laying a tray and a table for the service of breakfast are as follows:
a) A tray cloth replaces the tablecloth.
b) Underplates are usually left out because of lack of space. This need not necessarily be so if a Continental breakfast is being served in apartments. Where adequate space is available underplates should be used.
c) There will be no ashtray or table number on the tray.

For standing orders for breakfast in the apartments, the trays should be laid up the night before, placed in the pantry and covered with a clean cloth. The floor waiter must make sure that the kitchen has the order, signed by him, stating the time, number of covers, and room number.

The beverage, toast and first course will normally be prepared by the floor waiter in his service or floor pantry together with the preserves and other accompaniments that may be required according to the order given. The main course is sent up already plated from the kitchen, by the service lift. Before taking the tray to the apartment check to see that nothing is missing and that the hot food is hot. The beverage and toast should be the last items on the tray for this reason. The positioning of the items on the tray is all important. The items should be placed so that when being carried by the floor waiter in the traditional manner the tray may be evenly balanced on the hand. Also, the position of the items should be such that everything may be easily reached and to hand for the guest i.e. beverage and breakfast cup, saucer and teaspoon to the top, centre right of the tray. This helps the balance of the tray and is in the correct position for pouring. Any bottled proprietary sauce required on the tray should be laid flat to avoid accidents when carrying the tray. On arriving at the apartment door, knock loudly, wait for a reply, enter and place the tray on the bedside table. If there are two or more people partaking of breakfast in the apartment then it may be necessary to lay up a table, or trolly, and to serve the breakfast in the same way as in the restaurant.

After approximately 45 minutes the floor waiter must return to the room, knock and wait for a reply, enter and ask if it is convenient to clear the breakfast tray away.

It is important to note that all trays and trollies should be cleared from the rooms and corridors as soon as possible, otherwise they may impede the chambermaids in their work, and may also inconvenience the guests.

When breakfast service is finished all equipment must be washed up in the floor pantry and foodstuffs such as milk, cream, butter rolls and preserves should be returned to the stillroom or placed in the refrigerator or store cupboard in the pantry for re-use. The pantry is then cleaned and the mise-en-place carried out for the day.

Other special points to note when serving breakfasts

a) Hot or cold milk, or cream should be offered when serving porridge.

b) Cream is not normally served with stewed fruit unless asked for.

17 the service of afternoon teas

The old English tradition of taking afternoon tea at 4.0 o'clock is slowly dying out and in its place the trend is towards 'tea and pastries' only, the venue changing from the hotel lounge to the coffee bars and tea gardens. This trend is due to two main factors, the first being the problem of the staffing of the afternoon period between lunch and dinner, and the second being a simple case of economics in that in order to make the **service of afternoon tea** pay the hotelier would have to charge a price unacceptable to the public.

However afternoon tea is still served in many establishments and in a variety of forms which may be classified into three main types:

a) Full afternoon tea as served in a first class hotel.

b) High tea as served in a popular price restaurant or café.

c) The reception or buffet tea.

Full afternoon tea

This is usually served in the hotel lounge by the Lounge waiters or by a small **brigade** drawn from the restaurant on a rota basis. The lounge tables will be used, and are covered with an afternoon tea cloth which may be white or coloured. A buffet table may be set up in one corner of the lounge, preferably with immediate access to the **stillroom** and **service area.** It would be set up as a sideboard with all the necessary equipment for serving and relaying the afternoon teas.

The menu will usually consist of some or all of the following items which are served in the order in which they are listed.

Menu
1. Hot buttered toast or toasted tea cake or crumpets
2. Assorted afternoon tea sandwiches— Smoked salmon, cucumber, tomato, Sardine, egg, Gentleman's relish
3. Buttered scones, brown and white bread and butter, fruit bread and butter, raspberry or strawberry jams
4. Gâteaux and pastries

With reference to the menu above:
1. Toast, tea cakes and crumpets are obtained from the **stillroom** as ordered and are served in a soup plate or welled dish with a silver cover on an underplate. An alternative to this would be the use of a muffin dish which is a covered silver dish with an inner lining and with hot water in the lower part of the container. It is essential that all these items are served hot. When serving hot buttered toast for afternoon tea, the crusts from three sides only are removed, and the toast is then cut into 'fingers' with part of the crust remaining attached to each 'finger'.
2. The sandwiches are sent from the **larder** already dressed on silver flats, and these are set out on the buffet prior to service.
3. The scones and assorted buttered breads are obtained from the **stillroom,** and are dressed on doilies on silver flats and are also set out on the buffet. Preserves are also obtained from the **stillroom,** either in individual pots or in preserve dishes, both of which are served on a doily on an underplate and with a preserve spoon.
4. Gâteaux and pastries are collected from the Chef Patissier already dressed up on doilies on silver flats or salvers. An alternative to this would be the use of a pastry trolly.

Cover for afternoon tea

1. Side plate.
2. Paper serviette.
3. Side or tea knife.
4. Pastry fork.
5. Tea cup and saucer and a teaspoon.
6. Slop basin and tea strainer.
7. Sugar basin and tongs.
8. Tea pot and hot water jug stands or under-plates.
9. Jug of cold milk.
10. Preserve on a doily on an underplate with a preserve spoon.
11. Ashtray

Items 9) and 10) may be brought to the table only when the guests are seated and are not part of the basic mise-en-place.

Service of afternoon tea

As soon as the order has been taken, the top copy of the check is sent to the stillroom for the beverage and any toasted items that may be required. Whilst these are being prepared, items (9) and (10), of the cover listed above are set on the table.

The beverage will be served first making sure that the teapot, hot water jug and milk jug are placed to the right of the hostess of the party and with the handles correctly positioned for easy pouring. The toasted items are served next and are followed in turn by the other savoury items and then the assorted buttered breads with the appropriate preserve.

The sideplate will then be changed before serving the pastries. There are three alternative methods for the actual service of the food, this depending on the type of establishment and style of service employed, and also the number of staff available. These are as follows:

a) Silver service direct from the various silver flats.
b) As for a) but with all the flats on a trolly which is wheeled from table to table.
c) The waiter plates up the food at the buffet with the appropriate portions and the plates are all set on the table. This method has obvious disadvantages in that it is time wasting and uneconomical.

Checking system

Double checking is normally used for the service of afternoon tea, the top copy of the check going to the stillroom and the bottom copy being the bill, against which the waiter will collect payment, in the case of chance customers. In the case of hotel guests, it will be signed by them, and then have the appropriate room number entered on it and will be sent to the bill office at the end of service. Afternoon tea may be either table d'hôte or à la carte.

Service of high tea

In department stores and popular price restaurants a high tea may be available in addition to the full afternoon tea. It is usually in a modified à la carte form and the menu will offer, in addition to the normal full afternoon tea menu, such items as grills, toasted snacks, fish and meat dishes, salads, cold sweets and ices. The meat dishes normally consist in the main of pies and pasties, whereas the fish dishes are usually fried or grilled.

Cover for high tea

1. Serviette.
2. Joint knife and fork.
3. Sideplate.

4. Sideknife.
5. Cruet: salt, pepper, mustard, and mustard spoon.
6. Tea cup, saucer and teaspoon.
7. Sugar basin and tongs.
8. Slop basin and tea strainer.
9. Tea pot and hot water jug stands or underplates.
10. Jug of cold milk.
11. Preserve on a doiley on an underplate and with a preserve spoon.
12. Ashtray.

As for the afternoon tea cover the jug of cold milk and the preserve on a doily on an underplate will only be brought to the table when the guests are seated and are not part of the mise-en-place. Any other items of cutlery that may be required are brought to the table as for à la carte service.

In the case of a high tea, bread and butter is a normal accompaniment. Because of the hot snacks offered on a high tea menu there should be available on the waiters sideboard a good variety of proprietary sauces such as, Tomato Ketchup, H.P. sauce, Worcestershire sauce and A.1. sauce. In the case of both afternoon tea service and high tea there will normally be a

choice of Indian, Ceylon, China, Russian or iced tea available. For methods of infusion and service reference must be made to the section on beverage (page 49).

Checking system

Double checking is again the system of control used for the service of high teas. Sections of the top copy going to the stillroom for the beverage, and to the kitchen for the hot snack ordered. The bottom copy is the bill against which the waitress will collect payment. An alternative method of payment is for the bill to be presented to the guest, who in turn pays the cashier on his way out of the restaurant, the cashier having receipted the bill and returned any change necessary. The charge for high tea is generally à la carte.

Service

For the service of a high tea the beverage would again be served first, followed by the hot snack ordered with its accompaniment of bread und butter. When this has been consumed and cleared the service then follows that of a full afternoon tea.

Reception or buffet tea

These are offered at special functions and private parties only, and as the name implies the food and beverage are served from a buffet table and not at individual tables. The buffet should be set up in a prominent position in the room making sure that there is ample space on the buffet for display and presentation and for the guests to make their choice. As well as being in a prominent position the buffet should be within easy access of the stillroom and wash-up so that replenishment of the buffet and the clearing of dirties may be carried out without disturbing the guests. Another important factor when setting up the buffet is to ensure there is ample space for customer circulation and that a number of occasional tables and chairs should be placed round the room. These occasional tables should be covered with clean, well starched linen cloths and have a small vase of flowers and an ashtray on them.

Setting up the buffet

The buffet will be covered with suitable cloths making sure that the 'drop' of the cloth is to within 1.25 cm ($\frac{1}{2}$ inch) of the ground all the way round the buffet. If more than one cloth is used the creases should also be lined up and where the cloths overlap one another the overlap should be facing away from the entrance to the room. The ends of the buffet will be 'box' pleated with the aid of drawing pins which must be used under the folds of the cloth so that they do not show thereby giving a better overall presentation of the buffet.

The normal afternoon tea cutlery, china and serviettes are then laid along the front of the buffet in groups with the tea cups, saucers and teaspoons concentrated in one or more tea service points as required. Sugar basins and tongs may be placed on the buffet or on the occasional tables that are spread round the room. The tea would be served at the separate tea service points along the buffet from silver urns which would be kept hot with methylated spirit burners. Milk would be served separately from silver milk jugs.

A raised floral centrepiece should be the focal point around which the dishes of food would be placed. Cake stands may also be used for presentation and display purposes.

Service

During the reception some of the staff will be positioned behind the buffet for service and replenishment of the dishes of food and the beverage. Others will circulate round the room with the food and also clear away the dirties as they accumulate. As the dishes on the buffet become depleted they should be quickly replenished or cleared away so that the buffet looks neat and tidy at all times.

Cost

At this type of function no checking system will be needed, but a bill will be made out afterwards and sent to the host, the price having being quoted beforehand when the function was booked.

18 the dispense bar

The term 'Dispense Bar' is recognised to mean any bar situated within a food and beverage service area which only dispenses wine or other alcoholic drinks to be served to a guest consuming a meal. However, it should be noted that in many establishments, because of the planning and layout, wine and other alcoholic drinks for consumption with a meal are sometimes dispensed from bars situated outside the food and beverage service area itself. In other words from one of the public bars. All drink dispensed must be checked for and controlled in some way and this will be dealt with in the section on cellar control. All alcoholic drinks are served by that member of the restaurant team known as the *Sommelier* or the wine butler, unless it is the custom for the food service waiter to serve his own guests with the drink they require.

Equipment

In order to carry out efficiently the service of all forms of drink requested the bar should have available all the necessary equipment for making cocktails, decanting wine, serving wine correctly, making fruit cups and so on. The equipment should include:

1. Assorted Glasses.
2. Measures—4/5/6 out.
3. Ice buckets and stands.
4. Cocktail shakers.
5. Boston shaker.
6. Hawthorn strainer.
7. Bar mixing spoon.
8. Small ice buckets and tongs.
9. Wine baskets.
10. Soda syphons.
11. Water jugs.
12. Coloured sugars.
13. Assorted bitters: peach, orange, augoustura.
14. Cutting board and knife.
15. Optics.
16. Assorted fruit: mint, cocktail cherries, olives.
17. Bottle opener.
18. Cork extractor.
19. Ice crushing machine.
20. Ice pick.
21. Bar glass.
22. Ice making machine.
23. Lemon squeezing machine.
24. Drinking straws.
25. Swizzle sticks.
26. Cocktail sticks.
27. Strainer and funnel.
28. Carafes.
29. Coasters.
30. Cooling trays.
31. Refrigerator.
32. Small sink unit, or bar glass washing machine.
33. Service salvers.
34. Wine and cocktail lists.
35. Wine knife and cigar cutter.
36. A plentiful supply of glass cloths, serviettes and service cloths.

The bar

There are certain essentials necessary in the planning of every bar, and it is as well to bear these in mind now. They are factors which should be given prime consideration when one has to plan a bar or set up a bar for a particular function. They are as follows:

1. *Area*: The barman must be given sufficient area or space in which to work and move about. There should be a minimum of 1 metre (3 ft) from the back of the bar counter to the

storage shelfs and display cabinets at the rear of the bar.

2. *Layout:* Very careful consideration must be given, in the initial planning, to the layout. Everything should be easily to hand so that the barman does not have to move about more than necessary to give a quick and efficient service.

3. *Plumbing and power:* It is essential to have hot and cold running water for glass washing. Power is necessary to provide the effective working of cooling trays, refrigerators and ice making machines.

4. *Storage:* Adequate storage must be provided in the form of shelves, cupboards and racks, for all the stock required and equipment listed.

5. *Safety and Hygiene:* Great care must be observed in that the materials used in the make-up of the bar are hygienic and safe. Flooring must be non-slip. The bar top would be of a material suited to the general decor, hard wearing, easily wiped down, with no sharp edges. The bar top should be of average working height—approximately one metre (3 ft) and a width of 0.6 metres (20 ins).

6. *Site of the bar:* A major factor is the siting of the bar. The position should be chosen so that the bar has the greatest possible number of sales.

Apéritifs

This term covers a wide range of drinks which may be served before a meal. A large number of aperitifs must be stocked within the dispense bar in order to cater for the majority of tastes. The wine butler of sommelier would present the wine list to the host for an apéritif order immediately before the butter is placed on the table, and the rolls and melba toast are offered to all the guests. This then gives the wine butler time to serve the apéritif order, and the guests time to consume them, before the first course is served. Some of the more popular apéritifs are as follows:

Sherry Dry (e.g. Tio Pepe) Medium (amontillado) Sweet (e.g. Double Century) Cream (e.g. honey cream and Bristol cream)	The normal measure for a glass of sherry is a '3 out' measure, and served in an Elgin shaped glass. The colour of sherry varies from very pale for a dry sherry to a rich dark golden brown colour for a sweet or cream sherry.
Martini Dry (pale in colour) Sweet (dark in colour)	Has a base of a blend of light white wine. Has a base of a blend of full-bodied red wines, or white wine with colouring added. Dry Martini is served on ice using one '3 out' measure and garnished with a twist of lemon peel, or an olive. Sweet Martini is served on ice using one '3 out' measure and garnished with a cocktail cherry on a stick. Glass: either a cocktail glass, a 14.20 centilitre (5 oz) goblet or a 'club' shaped glass.
Gin and Italian	As a guide it would be made up of one '6 out' measure of gin and one '6 out' measure of Italian or sweet martini. The exact proportions are according to taste. Garnished with a cocktail cherry on a stick, and served on ice in a 18.93 centilitre (6⅔ oz) Paris goblet or a highball glass.
Gin and French	As above, but using French or dry martini instead of sweet martini. Garnished with a twist of lemon peel or an olive.
Dubonnet Red (rouge) White (blond)	Serve one '3 out' measure on ice and garnish with a slice of lemon, in a 18.93 centilitre (6⅔ oz) Paris goblet or a highball glass. Dubonnet is of French origin and made from a base of either sweet red wine flavoured with quinine, or white wine.
Campari	Serve in a 18.93 centilitre (6⅔ oz) Paris goblet or a highball glass. Use one '6 out' measure on ice and garnish with a slice

of lemon. Top up according to the guests requirements with soda or water (iced). Campari is a pink bitter sweet Italian aperitif, having a slight flavour of orange peel and quinine.

Pernod

Is of French origin, being a clear liquid obtained by means of distillation of oils. Use one '6 out' measure and add iced water poured over a sugar lump held in a tea-strainer. The reaction of the ice cold water hitting the distilled liquid (Pernod), affects the oils in the Pernod, and turns the once clear liquid milky in appearance. The proportion of Pernod to iced water should be approximately 1 : 5. Serve in a 18.93 centilitre (6⅔ oz) Paris goblet or a highball glass.

Gin and Bitter Lemon

Use one '6 out' measure of gin plus a bottle of bitter lemon which would be added at the table according the the guests requirements. Serve well iced in a 18.93 centilitre (6⅔ oz) Paris goblet or a highball glass.
The service would be similar for such drinks as gin and tonic, whisky and ginger ale, etc.

Pink Gin

Two drops of Angoustura bitters swilled around in the glass and then tipped out. Place in ice and pour over one '6 out' measure of gin. Serve with iced water according to taste.

Wines

Immediately the food order has been taken the wine list should again be presented to the host so that he may order wine for his party, to go with the meal they have ordered. The Sommelier or Wine butler should be able to advise and suggest wines from the wine list to the host if the occasion arises. This means then that the wine butler must have a good knowledge of the wines contained within the wine list in order that he may 'sell' them on behalf of the management. When he writes out the order it must be clear and legible. The top copy goes to the bar and the duplicate to the cashier. It should be remembered that all red wines are served at room temperature, white and rosé wines chilled and sparkling wines well chilled. The following basic procedure takes place when a bottle of wine has to be served.

White Wine
1. Obtain the wine from the dispense bar.
2. Take to the table in an ice-bucket.
3. Present the bottle to the host showing the label.
4. Ensure the correct glasses are placed on the table for the wine to be served.
5. See that a clean serviette is tied to the handle of the ice-bucket.
6. Cut the foil, remove and wipe the top of the cork with the serviette.

7. Remove the cork in the accepted fashion. Smell the cork in case the wine is 'corked'. This happens when the wine has been affected thorough a faulty cork and it cannot be served. Place the cork in the ice-bucket.
8. If the wine concerned is a Château bottled wine then the cork would generally be placed on a sideplate at the head of the hosts cover. This cork would have the name of the Château concerned and the year of the wine printed on it.
9. Wipe the inside of the neck of the bottle with the serviette.
10. Wipe the bottle dry.
11. Hold the bottle for pouring in such a fashion that the label may be seen. Use your waiters' cloth, folded, to catch any drips.
12. Give a taste to the host pouring from the right. The host should acknowledge that the wine is suitable. Correct taste bouquet and temperature.
13. Serve ladies first, then gentlemen and the host last, always commencing from the hosts right.
14. Fill each glass two/thirds full. This leaves room for an appreciation of the bouquet.
15. Replace the remaining wine in the wine-bucket and refill the glasses when necessary.
16. If a fresh bottle is required then fresh glasses should be placed upon the table.
17. As one finishes pouring a glass of wine, by twisting the neck of the bottle and raising it

at the same time one prevents any drips from falling on the tablecloth.

Red Wine

If the red wine to be served is young—up to 7 years old—it need not be served from a wine basket as there will be little or no sediment. If over 7 years old then more care must be taken, and a wine basket used to prevent disturbing, as far as possible, any of the sediment. It is at the discretion of the Dispense barman and the Wine butler whether a wine basket is necessary or not. The cork should be removed from the bottle of red wine as early as possible so that the wine may attain room temperature naturally. Under no circumstances should the wine be placed on the hotplate or in the bain-marie to get it to the required temperature quickly. If the red wine to be opened is young the bottle may stand on an underplate on the table and be opened from this position, the basic procedure being similar to opening a bottle of white wine. If an older bottle of red wine is being opened from a basket then the wine waiter must place a sideplate, inverted, underneath the neck-end of the wine basket. This tilts the bottle slightly and keeps the neck-end of the wine bottle raised. The reasons for this are twofold. Firstly the sediment is kept in the base of the bottle, and secondly when the cork is removed it prevents any wine from spilling onto the tablecloth. Apart from the points mentioned the basic procedure for opening the wine bottle is as listed above.

Sparkling Wine

When we think of sparkling wines our thoughts immediately turn to Champagne. The same method is used for opening all sparkling wines. The wine should be served well chilled in order to obtain the full effect of the secondary fermentation in the bottle, namely, effervesence and bouquet. The pressure in a Champagne bottle due to its maturing and secondary fermentation will be (about 70 lbs per sq inch). Therefore, great care must be taken not to shake the bottle otherwise the pressure builds up, and as soon as the 'wire cage' is removed the pressure shoots the cork out. This has been the cause of many accidents in the past and great care is demanded here. After presenting the bottle to the host it will be replaced in the wine cooler. The neck of the bottle should be kept pointed to the ceiling during the

opening process to avoid any accidents to guests should the cork be suddenly released. It is advisable to hold a serviette over the cork with ones hand over the serviette when commencing to open the bottle. Unwind the wire cage and remove carefully. Holding the cork in the serviette twist the bottle slowly to release the cork. Serve into tulip shaped glasses, from the right hand side of each guest.

Glasses

As a guide to everyday service it should be noted that the following wines are served in the following types of glasses.
Bordeaux, Burgundy, Loire and most other wine area's 18.93 centilitre (6⅔ oz) Paris goblet.
Hock (brown bottle): long brown stemmed Hock glass.
Moselle (green bottle): long green stemmed Moselle glass.
Note Many establishments now use a long clear stemmed glass for both wines.
Champagne: tulip shaped glass.

Measures

Since the 1st. August 1966 it has been law that a bar must have on show a notice stating the size of measure or optic used and these must be Custom and Excise stamped or sealed. These measures or optics may be what are termed:

'4 Out' measure or optic⎫ or in a multiple of any one quantity, such as a 'double' or 'treble'. This law relates to the sale of gin, rum, whisky and vodka only.
'5 Out' measure or optic
'6 Out' measure or optic⎭

The above law is one of the requirements of the Weights and Measure Act, 1963. The terms mean:
'3 Out' of one gill or quarter of a pint (14.20 cl).
'6 Out' of one gill or quarter of a pint (14.20 cl).

One obtains approximately 6 glasses of wine from one bottle of wine and 3 glasses of wine from one half bottle. A bottle of wine itself holds 26⅔ fl. ozs. (75 centilitres), and there are 6 bottles to 1 gallon (4.546 litres) of wine.
'3 Out': 1⅔ fluid oz or 4.735 cl: 16 to a bottle.
'4 Out': 1¼ fluid oz or 3.551 cl: 21 to a bottle.
'5 Out': 1 fluid oz or 2.841 cl: 26 to a bottle.
'6 Out': 5/6 fluid oz or 2.367 cl: 32 to a bottle.

New laws will have to be introduced to revise the 1/6th of a gill measure now in use. The possible replacement may be the 2.5 centilitre measure which would give 30 measures from the (75 centilitre) $26\frac{2}{3}$ fluid oz. spirit bottle. This measure is therefore only slightly larger than the existing one. Home manufactured spirits are already bottled in 75 centilitres and this bottle size is therefore likely to remain. The wine bottle content will possibly also remain as it is at present as it now comes in 70-75 centilitre bottles. Packaging may differ being reduced from cases of 1 dozen to cases of 10 for all wines and spirits. For beer the 25 centilitre and 50 centilitre measures would possibly replace the $\frac{1}{2}$ and 1 pint measures

Measures per bottle:
The following is a guide as to how many measures, for control purposes, one obtains from the following bottles of:

1. Spirits   32
2. Brandy   26/30
3. Martini   16
4. Liqueurs   26 (or varies according to bot. size)
5. Sherry   16
6. Dubonnet   16
7. Pimms   14
8. Campari   20

The Wine List

The function of the wine list is similar to that of the menu and should be regarded by both management and the food service operator as a *selling aid*. Therefore careful thought must be given to its planning, design, layout, colour and overall appearance for presentation purposes. Something which catches the eye will cause the individual to look at it further, whereas if the wine list is drab it will possibly cause the loss of many sales. Simply speaking the contents are listed in the order in which they may be consumed, namely:

1. Cocktails.
2. Apéritifs.
3. Cups.
4. Wines.
5. Liqueurs.
6. Beers, minerals and squashes.
7 Cigars.

The wines are listed area by area, with the white wines of one area first and followed by the red wines of that area In all wine lists sparkling wines, and therefore the Champagnes, are listed first of all the wines available. It is most important that in all wine lists the prices are clearly shown. The Sommelier should have a good knowledge of all the wines available and their main characteristics. He should also have an extensive knowledge of which wines are most suitable to offer with certain foods.

Liqueur trolly

Liqueurs are generally offered from a liqueur trolly at the table. The wine butler should present the trolly immediately the sweet course is finished to ensure that any liqueurs required will be on the table by the time coffee is served. Again the wine butler must have a good knowledge of liqueurs, their bases and flavours, and their correct mode of service. Normally all liqueurs are served in an elgin shaped liqueur glass which holds one '6 out' measure.

If a person asks for a liqueur to be served 'frappé' then it is served on crushed ice. A larger glass will then have to be used. Two/thirds fill it with the crushed ice and pour over the '6 out' measure of liqueur. Place in two short drinking straws and serve, e.g. Creme de Menthe frappé. If a liqueur is requested with cream, then the cream is slowly poured over the back of a teaspoon to settle on the top of the selected liqueur, without mixing with it. Under no circumstances should the liqueur or cream be mixed together, e.g. Tia Maria with cream.

The basic equipment required on the liqueur trolly is as follows:

1. Assorted liqueurs.
2. Assorted glasses: liqueur/brandy.
3. Draining stand: measures '6 out' and '3 out'.
4. Service salver.
5. Jug of double cream.
6. Teaspoon.
7. Drinking straws.
8. Cigars.
9. Cigar cutter.
10. Matches.
11. Wine list and check pad.

Customs and Excise Badge

In certain instances one finds 25 centilitre (half-pint) and 50 centilitre (pint) beer mugs and glasses have stamped on the side of them a Customs and Excise badge which states exactly how much that mug or glass should hold.

When one asks for a half-pint or pint of beer it must be served in a Customs and Excise stamped glass, as you have stated the exact amount that you require.

If however you only asked for a 'glass of beer' it need not be put up in a Customs and Excise stamped glass, and even though you are paying for a pint of beer the actual liquid content may be slightly less as you have not stated the exact amount you require. A weights and measure inspector can enter licensed premises at anytime if it is believed that alcoholic liquor is being incorrectly served.

19 dispense bar beverages — non-alcoholic

These beverages may be classified into 5 main groups.

1. Aerated Waters.
2. Natural Spring Waters or Mineral Waters.
3. Squashes.
4. Juices.
5. Syrups.

1. *Aerated Waters*

These beverages are charged or aerated with carbonic gas. Artificial aerated waters are by far the most common. The charging with carbonic gas imparts the pleasant effervescent characteristic of all these beverages. The flavourings found in different aerated waters are imparted with various essences. Some examples of these aerated waters are as follows:

Soda water	which is colourless and tasteless.
Tonic Water	colourless and quinine flavoured.
Dry Ginger	golden straw colour with a ginger flavour.
Bitter Lemon	pale cloudy colour with a sharp lemon flavour.
'Fizzy' lemonades Orange Ginger Beer Coca-Cola etc.	Are other flavoured waters which come under this heading.

All these aerated waters may be served on their own, chilled, and in either tumblers, Paris goblets, highball glass or a 34.08 centi-litre (12 oz) short stemmed beer glass depending upon the requirements of the guest and the policy of the establishment. They may also accompany other drinks,

e.g. Whisky and dry ginger
    Gin and tonic
    Vodka and bitter lemon
    Rum and coca-cola

2. *Natural Spring Waters*

These waters are obtained from natural springs in the ground, the waters themselves being impregnated with the natural minerals found in the soil and sometimes naturally charged with an aerating gas. The value of these mineral waters, as they are sometimes termed, has long been recognised by the medical profession. It should be noted at this stage that one may often find a bottle of Malvern water on the bar top as well as the soda syphon. The guest may then help himself to whatever he wishes. Where natural spring waters are found there is usually what is termed a Spa, where the waters may be drunk or bathed in according to the cures they are supposed to effect. Many of the best known mineral waters are bottled at the springs. The mineral waters are usually classified according to their chemical properties. These are as follows:

Alkaline Waters. These are the most numerous of all the mineral waters. It is said they help the treatment of gout and rheumatismn.
e.g. Perrier
    Malvern
    Vichy
    Evian
    Saint-Galmier
    Aix-les-bains
    Aix-la-chapelle
    Selters

Aperient Waters. So named because of their saline constituents, these being in the main

sulphate of magnesia or sulphate of soda.
e.g. Cheltenham
  Montmirail
  Leamington Spa
  Seidlitz

Chalybeate Waters. These mineral waters are of two kinds, being either carbonated or sulphated. It is recognized that they act as a stimulant and a tonic.
e.g. Forges
  Passy
  Saint Nectaire
  Vittel

Lithiated Waters. These are rich in Lithia salts.
e.g. Baden-Baden
  Carlsbad
  Saint Marco
  Salvator

Sulphurous Waters. These waters are impregnated with hydrogen.
e.g. St. Boes
  Harrogate
  Challes

Service of Mineral Waters
These are normally drunk on their own for medicinal purposes. However as has been previously mentioned some mineral waters may be mixed with other alcoholic beverages to form an appetising drink.

Table waters

These waters are recognised to be much less highly mineralised than other natural spring waters, and are mainly alkaline. They are still used on the continent far more than in this country, although here their popularity is growing slowly. They may be taken between meals or at meal time, either alone or mixed with light wines or spirits. When taken regularly these table waters stimulate and act as a tonic, *e.g.* Apollinaris, Buxton, Malvern, Perrier, Saint Galmier, Aix-la-chapelle.

Service: They should be drunk well chilled, to approximately 7-10 °C (45-48 °F). If drunk on their own serve in a 18.93 centilitre (6⅔ fluid oz) Paris goblet.

Continental and English mineral waters

Perrier	Malvern
Vichy	Cheltenham
Evian	Leamington Spa
Saint Galmier	Bath
Aix-la-chapelle	Harrogate
Aix-les-bains	Buxton
Saint Nectaire	
Vittel	
Baden-Baden	
St. Boes	

Squashes

Squashes may be served on their own, mixed with spirits or cocktails, or used as the base for such drinks as fruit cups. They are indispensable in the bar and an adequate stock should always be held.
e.g. Orange   Squash
  Lemon
  Grapefruit }
  Lime   } Juice.

Service: From the Bar:
A measure of squash poured into a tumbler or 34.08 centilitre (12 oz) short stemmed beer glass containing ice. Top up with iced water or the soda syphon. Decorate the edge of the glass with a slice of fruit where applicable. Place in the drinking straws

From the Lounge:
All the items required to give efficient service must be taken by the wine butler or lounge waiter on a service salver. These would include:
1. Tumbler or 34.08 centilitre (12 oz) short stemmed beer glass containing a measure of squash.
2. Straws.
3. Jug of iced water   } on an underplate
                          } because of the
4. Small ice-bucket and tongs } condensation.
5. Soda syphon.
6. Coaster: to place the glass on in the lounge.
  At the side table in the lounge the coaster would be placed down and the glass containing the squash placed on the coaster. The waiter would then add ice and enquire whether the guest wishes iced water or soda to be added. The drinking straws would be placed in the glass at the last moment if required. It may be necessary to leave the iced water and ice bucket

on the side table for the guest. If this is the case they will be left on underplates.

Juices

The main types of juices held in stock in the dispense bar are as follows:

Bottled or *Canned*

1. Orange juice:
2. Pineapple juice:
3. Grapefruit juice:
4. Tomato juice:

These are normally purchased in small bottles termed 'babies' which contain 11.36 centilitres (4 fluid ozs). They may also be obtained canned.

Fresh

A. Orange juice:
B. Grapefruit juice:
C. Lemon juice:

It is very often necessary that a small stock of these, made from fresh fruits, be kept. They would be used for cocktails and for mixing with spirits.

Service: All juices should be served chilled in a 14.20 centilitres (5 fluid oz) goblet.

Tomato juice

Should be served chilled in a 14.20 centilitre (5 fluid oz) goblet on a doily on an underplate with a teaspoon. The Worcestershire sauce would be shaken, the top removed, placed on an underplate and offered as an accompaniment. The goblet may have a slice of lemon placed over the edge of the glass as additional presentation.

Fresh fruit juice

If fresh fruit juice is to be served in the lounge then the service would be similar to the service of squash in the lounge with one exception. In addition to the items mentioned previously a small bowl of castor sugar on an underplate with a teaspoon will have to be taken to the table.

Syrups

The main use of these concentrated sweet fruit flavourings is as a base for cocktails, fruit cups or mixed with sodawater as a long drink. The main ones used are:

1. Grenadine: Pomegranate flavour
2. Cassis: blackcurrant
3. Citronelle: lemon
4. Gomme: white sugar syrup
5. Framboise: raspberry
6. Cerise: cherry

20   beer

Beer may be said to compare with tea in that it has been called our national 'alcoholic' beverage, whereas tea is looked upon as our national 'non-alcoholic' beverage. Beer has been a major part of our alcoholic diet for thousands of years, and is even more so today. In Britain today there are in the region of 140,000 licensed establishments able to sell drink. The total figure is made up approximately as follows:

1.   75 000 public houses and hotels.
2.   27 000 licensed or registered clubs.
3.   30 000 off-licences.
4.   5 000 restaurants.
5.   3 000 combined restaurants and residential premises.
6. 140,000 licensed establishments in Britain.

Of this approximate total, brewery companies own 48 percent or just under half. Of the 75,000 public houses and hotels, the brewery companies own 78 percent or 58,000. The public house is the brewers' front window or shop.

Beer consumption grows every year. The world beer consumption in 1968 was 11,790 million gallons, a rise of 3 percent. Of this total the British beer drinkers share was 1,132 million gallons. We in this country are one of the worlds leading draught beer drinkers together with New Zealand and Australia. The average yearly consumption of everyone in this country last year was 40 pints of draught bitter and 50 pints of draught mild. A further fact brought out from this is that the British beer drinker contributes to the national exchequer £400 million per year in the form of duty.

The public house itself depends largely on the personality of the landlord and his wife as to whether it will sell at full capacity or not. The husband and wife team play a large part, together with adequate organising and administrative control and good staff relations. There are three main classifications of public house landlord, namely: managers, tenants, and those who own or lease free houses.

Managers
The manager works as an employee of the brewery or other company owning the public house. He is paid a salary and all profits go to the owners of the public house. It is normal for the manager to receive commission on any increase in sales, and this acts as an incentive.

Tenants
Tenants will pay rent to a brewery and are generally expected to purchase all their beer, wines and spirits from that brewery. This rule is not kept to as rigidly as in the past which allow the tenant a little more variation in his selling power, enabling him to attract a wider sector of the public. The tenant has an incentive to increase sales as he receives all profits made. It is as well to note here that some breweries have agreements to stock each others products thus increasing the variety available.

A tenant requires a certain amount of capital or 'ingoing' as it is termed before he may take over a public house. This capital is usually a sum between £1,500 and £5,000. However depending on the public house itself, the site, area and future potential the 'ingoing' could range from a few hundred pounds up to £10,000. This sum covers purchasing from the previous tenant all fixtures, fittings, furnishings in the public part of the premises, and all the remaining stock. Also included in this sum is a security deposit required by the brewery.

Owner or *Lease Holder*

Here the owner can purchase his drink where he wishes and sell as wide a range as he thinks necessary according to his situation. The 'free house' as it was known in the past are gradually reducing in number mainly due to the large amount of capital outlay that is initially involved. This can range anywhere from £25,000 to £35,000.

In order to improve the overall efficiency of all licensees the National Trade Development Association, (N.T.D.A.), has opened, as recently as 1966, a residential training centre at Buxton in Derbyshire. This is jointly financed by the Brewers Society and the Hotel and Catering Industry Training Board. It has been so successful that a second centre has only recently been opened at Shaftesbury on the Wiltshire-Dorset borders. The success of these new ventures is shown by the number of applicants which far exceeds the present number of places available. Three main types of course are at present being run:

1. A two week course for newcomers to the trade.
2. A one week refresher course to bring already experienced managers and tenants up to date in new techniques and future trends, and also to recap on past knowledge and how to put it to use more efficiently.
3. A one week condensed catering course on such things as bar snacks hot and cold, bar buffet work and the dishes available, and bar equipment.

Although the basic traditional methods are still used in the brewing of beer, there are being introduced many new techniques and equipment which will speed up the brewing process and do away with many of the old time-wasting jobs. Perhaps the best example of modern methods of production are to be found in the new brewery at Luton where stainless steel has been used throughout to facilitate the highest possible standards of hygiene, and where the cleaning of the fermenting vessels is carried out automatically. The brewery water—**liquor** —as it is technically called, is pumped up from a specially constructed well.

The whole production process is controlled by programmed equipment so that each phase is carried out at the exact time required and can be corrected if necessary. By this centralised control consistency of brew from batch to batch is far greater. There are eight main phases of production which are programmed:

1. Malt intake.
2. Malt blending and milling.
3. Wort production and the addition of hops.
4. Fermentation and yeast control.
5. Maturation.
6. Blending.
7. Beer dispatch.
8. Vessel cleaning.

Centralised programmed control and modern construction materials for the necessary equipment has allowed the go-ahead brewery to achieve constant quality and consistency and at the same time to make economies in its production.

One of the main changes has been in the storage of draught beer. Tank beer, with fixed tanks in the cellars of a public house, is in certain instances replacing the traditional barrel or cask of beer. The tanks come in two sizes:

1. Five barrel: 409 litres (720 pints).
2. Two and a half barrel: 205 litres (360 pints).

It will cost approximately £500 to install such a tank in a public house cellar, and is only feasible where the volume of sales are sufficiently high.

Wooden barrels and casks have now largely given way to stainless steel casks, but even so a cask usually has to be racked for a day or two before its contents have settled sufficiently to allow the beer to be at its best condition for serving. Tank beer or bulk storage beer is chilled and filtered at the brewery as is keg beer. One of the problems of tank beer is the cleaning of the tank itself before each delivery. This problem is partially overcome by the use of disposable plastic bags to line the tanks. The cost of such a bag is 50p each approximately, but this cost is regained in the cleaning time saved. What are the advantages of bulk or tank beer?

1. The landlord is saved the job of moving barrels about, and also the job of cleaning his bulk tank.
2. There is no need for a cellarman as the beer does not have to be racked. The beer itself may be served immediately after delivery as long as his cellar is maintained at the correct temperature.
3. Beer transported, stored and then sold in this manner has consistency, the only problem to the brewer being that the more he chills and filters beer before sending it to the public house, the more flavour is lost.

It would only be fair to say that since its introduction 4/5 years ago the popularity of tank beer has receeded slightly. One of the main reasons being that it is not economical to the smaller public house and very largely depends on the site and area of each house and the amount of trade involved. Popularity has gone from the tank to the keg, which has the great advantage of being able to site it in almost any corner. The handling of the keg is easier because it is made of aluminium rather than stainless steel and is therefore lighter. The beer is forced from the keg under pressure received from a gas cylinder. Where kegs are used in very busy houses they may be linked up to give a chain effect to ensure that the beer will not run out every 15/20 minutes. The present trend for the future seems to be indicated by the wider use of kegs, and where volume justifies it, the use of bulk or tank beer.

Brewing

The basic materials used in the brewing process are as follows:

1. *Malt*
   The best cereal for use in the production of beer is barley. This cereal goes through a process which converts it to what is termed Malt.

2. *Hops*
   These are specially grown for brewing and the best are produced in Kent, Sussex and Worcestershire. The part of the hop which is used is the flower. The flower contains an oil which gives beer its flavour.

3. *Sugar*
   Specially graded and refined sugars are used which aid the fermentation and the production of alcohol and also add sweetness.

4. *Yeast*
   Yeast is a living thing and is added to the beer at a set time to cause fermentation. Yeast × Sugar produces alcohol and gives off a gas CO_2. During fermentation the yeast multiplies and this new yeast is collected and used for future brews.

5. *Finings*
   This is a substance obtained from the sturgeon which is commonly called isinglass,

and used for attracting the sediment to the bottom of a cask. In other words it is used to clear and brighten a fermented beer.

6. *Primings*
   This is a solution of sugar and hops added to some beers at racking. The function of this solution is to develop the condition of the beer by the remaining yeast reacting with the sugar to give off CO_2 in the cask.

7. *Water (Liquor)*
   Usually drawn from a special well and may have certain minerals in its make-up which helps a beer develop its own special characteristics.

Draught Beers

These are usually racked into casks which have been sterilised. The casks of beer are then allowed to mature in the cellars before distribution to the trade. Light beers need not be stored as long as the stronger beers. Sometimes the beers are rolled in the cellars to encourage the working of a slight secondary fermentation. As soon as this occurs a porus peg is inserted to ease the pressure of the gas given off. This peg will later be replaced by a hard peg as soon as this slight secondary fermentation has eased and the beer is in condition.

Bottling

The object of bottling is to supply a beer which is consistent in flavour and character and will remain in good condition for a reasonable length of time. Bottled beer may be classified basically into two groups. Firstly those beers that have matured before being bottled and secondly those beers that finish maturing in the bottle. Immediately before and after bottling the beer is stored at a constant temperature of 13-15° C (55-58° F). During this maturing period very often a slight deposit may form and therefore it is most important for the landlord to ensure that all his beer is stored at a constant temperature, namely 13-15° C (55-58° F). If the temperature is any colder then a **'chill haze'** may appear. Some bottled beer is subjected to a slowly rising temperature up to 60° C (140° F), for 18 minutes, and then slowly cooled again. This surpresses all the organisms that may be present in the beer and allows the beer to remain in a sound condition over a longer period of time.

Brewing Process

1.		Barley	Barley
		↓	↓
2.		Ripened.	
		↓	
3.		Soaked.	
		↓	
4.		Spread on floors to germinate.	
		↓	
5.		Placed on malting floors, dried and toasted. Coloured from pale to very dark according to the brew.	
		↓	↓
6.	This process up to this stage changes the starch in the cereal to sugar. The barley is now termed MALT.		Malt
		↓	
7.		The malt is cleaned.	↓
		↓	
8.		Then crushed. Now called GRIST.	Grist
		↓	↓
9.		The grist is now mixed with hot water. (LIQUOR).	Liquor
		This mixture—grist + hot water—is termed MASH.	Mash
		↓	
10.		The mash is now allowed to infuse.	
		↓	↓
11.		The extract is drained off to a clean container called the Copper.	
		↓	
12.		HOPS and SUGAR are now added.	Hops & Sugar
		↓	
13.		This liquid is now boiled to concentrate it, and is now termed WORT.	Wort
		↓	
14.		The extract is strained off to remove the hops.	
		↓	
15.		Cooled to approximately 16°C (60°F)	↓
		↓	
16.		and run into a fermenting vessel (VAT).	Vat
		↓	↓
17.		Yeast is added and fermentation takes place. Fermentation = Yeast × Sugar produces alcohol and gives off CO_2.	Fermentation
		↓	
18.		Yeast reproduces itself and is collected for re-use.	
		↓	
19.		The gas CO_2 given off is collected and used in bottled beer.	
		↓	
20.	After 36 hours in the fermenting vessel the wort is run off into fermenting squares.		
		↓	
21.		Surplus yeast is skimmed off. Some is left on as a dust cover.	
		↓	
22.	On completion of the fermentation the yeast is cooled as the process of fermentation has heated the wort.		Cooling
		↓	↓
23.		It takes approximately 7 days from mashing to the wort becoming BEER.	Beer
		↓	↓
24.		The beer is now allowed to mature.	Mature
		↓	↓
25.		Racked into casks/keg/tank.	Cask/Keg/Tank
		↓	↓
26.		The FININGS are now added to brighten the beer.	Finings
		↓	
27.		The Beer is allowed to settle.	↓
		↓	
28.	Tasted for quality and consistency before being sent out to the trade for SALE.		Sale

The Bottling process

1. Bottles sterilised.
2. Beer filtered to ensure it is sterile and bright.
3. Bottles filled.
4. Crowning: each bottle is sealed with a crown cork.
5. Pasteurised.
6. Labelling.
7. Packing.
   Dispatch to the trade.

Service of beer

Beer should be served at a temperature of 13-15° C (55-58° F). The only beer served *chilled* is lager. It is often found in practice, however, that many different varieties of bottled beers are served chilled. Also draught beer on its route from the keg/cask to the pump, often passes through a chilling unit. Draught beers should have a small head on them, and the barman should ensure that he serves the correct quantity of beer with a small head, and not a large head to make up the quantity required. One may note the good condition of beer if the head or froth clings to the inside of the glass.

When pouring bottled beer it should be poured down the inside of the glass which is held at a slight angle. It should be poured slowly. This is especially important where a beer works a lot and may produce a large 'head' quickly if it is not poured slowly and carefully. Such beers are Guinness and stouts. All the glasses used should be spotlessly clean with no finger marks, grease or lipstick upon them. Pouring beer into a dirty glass will cause it to go flat very quickly. More care must be taken when pouring beer in hot weather as this causes the beer to work much more. The neck of the bottle should not be placed in the beer when pouring, especially where two bottles are being held and poured from the same hand. Where bottled beers have a sediment, when pouring, a little beer must be left in the base of the bottle holding the sediment back. There should always be adequate beer mats and coasters on the bar top and in the lounge on the occasional tables.

Types of beer

Draught	Bottled
Mild	Brown Ales
Bitter: Ordinary and Best	Pale Ales

Guinness	Guinness and Stouts
Bass	Bass
Worthington	Worthington
Lager	Lager
Keg	Strong Ales

Types of beer glasses

1. Half pint/pint tankards for draught beers.
2. Pint tumblers for draught beers.
3. Tumblers for any bottled beer.
4. 34.08 centilitre (12 oz) short stemmed beer glass for bass/worthington/guinness.
5. Lager glass for lager.
6. 22.72/28.40/34.08 centilitres (8/10/12 fluid oz) Paris goblets for brown/pale/strong ales.

It is worth noting here that draught beer is served by 25 centilitre (half pint) and 50 centilitre (pint) measures.
Bottled beer, however, is served in the following sizes:

nips	22.72 centilitres (7/8 fluid oz).
half-pint	28.40 centilitres or 0.284 litres (10 fluid oz).
pints	56.80 centilitres or 0.568 litres (20 fluid oz).
quarts	113.60 centilitres or 1.136 litres (40 fluid oz).

Canned beer, a fairly recent innovation in this country, is mainly found in half-pints, although it is possible to get larger sizes for special occasions such as parties, anniversaries etc. The sale of canned beer is mainly through the off-license trade and the grocery shop chain stores who have a large annual turnover of sales to the everyday shopper. The advantages of canned beer are:

1. Storage.
2. Disposable after use.
3. No breakages.
4. Long shelf life.
5. Minimum risk of deterioration.

Mixed Beer Drinks

1. Mild and bitter
2. Stout and mild
3. Brown and mild
4. Light and mild
5. Shandy: draught bitter and lemonade or ginger beer
6. Black velvet: Guinness and champagne
7. Black and tan: half stout and half bitter.

The Barman

The barman is the salesman and he can 'make or break' a selling situation. His uniform is generally a white coat, white shirt, black trousers and either a long black tie or bow tie. As with the food and beverage service operators his uniform must be spotless, and his appearance immaculate. His hands are on show all the time he is serving and therefore they must be clean with no nicotine stains and clean nails. He should never smoke or drink whilst on duty and must be constantly alert in order to anticipate his guests needs. He must handle all glasses correctly, goblets by the stem tumblers by the base and tankards by the handles. The bar top and any occasional tables should at all times be kept clean, wiped down and all the dirty glasses removed. The barman is also responsible for his display shelves and storage area. When restocking his shelves all old beers must be brought to the front and the new beer placed at the rear. His display area, if clean and well presented, may effect more sales and increase the turnover for the establishment.

Draught Beer Containers

1 pin	=	20.457 litres	(4½ gallons)
1 firkin	=	40.914 ,,	(9 gallons)
1 kilderkin	=	81.828 ,,	(18 gallons)
1 barrel	=	163.656 ,,	(36 gallons)
1 hogshead	=	245.484 ,,	(54 gallons)
1 keg	=	45.46 ,,	(10 gallons)

Cellar Management

The service of beer in good condition depends on a number of factors all of which are equally important if sales are to be maintained and possibly increased. These factors, determining good cellar management, are as follows.

1. Good ventilation.
2. Cleanliness.
3. Even temperature of 13-15°C (55-58°F).
4. Strong draughts and wide ranges of temperatures should be avoided.
5. On delivery all casks to be placed immediately upon the **stillions**.
6. Casks remaining on the floor should be **bung** uppermost to withstand the pressure better.
7. **Spiling** should take place to reduce any excess pressure in the cask.
8. Tapping should be carried out 24 hours before a cask is required.
9. Pipes and engines should be cleaned at regular intervals.
10. Beer left in pipes after closing time should be drawn off.
11. Returned beer should be filtered back into the cask from which it came.
12. Be careful not to overstock the cellar.
13. All spiles removed during the service should be replaced after closing time.
14. All cellar equipment should be kept scrupulously clean.
15. Any ullage should be returned to the brewery as soon as possible.

In conclusion it should be remembered that beer is a living thing; great care has to be taken, and is taken, in its production, packaging and distribution to the trade. From delivery it is up to every landlord to cherish his cellar and its contents to ensure that the beer is served in good condition.

21 bar and cellar control

Bar control

An efficient system of control must operate between the wine waiters and the dispense barman in order that the correct drinks are served at the right table; that they are charged on the right bill and that a record is kept of all drinks issued from the dispense bar. At the same time a system of control allows management to assess the sales of each bar over a financial period and see whether it is making a profit or loss.

The usual system of control is a duplicate check pad. The colour of the check pad may be pink or white but is generally pink. This acts as an aid to the cashier and the control and accounts department in differentiating quickly between food (white) and drink (pink) checks.

When the wine order is taken it is written in duplicate. The wine waiter must remember to fill in the four items of information required one in each corner of the check. These are as follows:
1. Table No. or Room No.
2. No. of Covers
3. Date
4. Signature

Abbreviations are allowed when writing the order as long as they are understood by the dispense barman and cashier. It should be remembered that when wines are being ordered only the bin number is written down together with the number of bottles required. The bin number is an aid to the dispense barman and cellarman in finding, without delay, the wine required by a guest. Each wine in the wine list will have a bin number printed against it. All drinks ordered should also have the price printed against them, and then at the base of the check the total amount of cash owing for the order given should be written and circled. This is an aid to the cashier who must check all prices before entering them on the bill.

On taking the order the wine waiter will hand the top copy to the dispense barman and the duplicate to the cashier. Alternatively the wine waiter may hand both copies to the dispense barman, who retains the top copy, puts up the order and leaves the duplicate copy with the order. This enables the wine waiter to see which is his order when he comes to collect his drinks, and after serving them he hands the duplicate copy of his order to the cashier.

WINE CHECK (Pink)

top copy to dispense barman

(Name of Establishment)

Table No. 10   Covers 3

2 Sweet sherries @ 17p   0.34

1 Pale ale @ 9p   0.09

½ ⨯ 16 @ 37p   0.37

1 ⨯ 40 @ 95p.   0.95

£ 1.75

Date 2/2/71   Signed CRA

duplicate copy to cashier

Goods ordered, received and issued from the cellar

When any alcoholic or non alcoholic drinks need to be purchased for an establishment, to keep up the level of stock, this will be done by the cellarman. The cellarmans order will be written in duplicate on an official order form. The top copy will be sent to the supplier and the

duplicate remains in the order book for control purposes when the goods are delivered In some instances there may be three copies of the order sheet If so they are distributed as follows:
1. Top copy: supplier
2. Duplicate copy: control and accounts dept.
3. Third copy: remains in the order book

When the goods are delivered to an establishment they will be accompanied by either a delivery note or an invoice. Whichever document it may be the information contained on them will be exactly the same, with one exception: Invoices show the price of all goods delivered whereas delivery notes do not. The goods delivered must first of all be counted and checked against the delivery note to ensure that all the goods listed have been delivered. An extra check may be carried out by the cellarman by checking the delivery note against the copy of the order remaining in the order book. This is to make sure that the items ordered have been sent and in the correct quantities and that extra items have not been sent which were not listed on the order sheet, thereby incurring extra cost without immediately realising it. At this stage all information concerning the goods delivered will be entered in the necessary books for control purposes.

No drinks will be issued by the cellarman unless he receives an official requisition form, correctly filled in, dated and signed by a responsible person from the department concerned. The cellarman should have a list of such signatures and will not issue anything unless the requisition sheet is signed by the appropriate person on his list. In order to aid the cellarman all requisitions should be handed into him at a set time each day, when all issues will be made. In certain instances however, depending on the organisation of an establishment, it may be necessary to issue twice per day, once before opening time in the morning and again before opening time in the evening. All requisition sheets are written in duplicate. The top copy going to the cellar for the items required to be issued, and the duplicate to remain in the requisition book for the barman to check his drink on receipt from the cellar.

Cellar control

In any catering establishment where a large percentage of the income received is through the sale of drink, a system of cellar control and costing must be put into operation. The system put into operation would depend entirely on the policy of each establishment. Some or all of the books listed below may be necessary depending upon the requirements of management:
1. Order book
2. Goods inward book
3. Cellar ledger
4. Bin cards
5. Goods returned book
6. Stock book
7. Departmental requisition book
8. Daily consumption sheets.

The cellar is the focal point for the storage of alcoholic and non-alcoholic liquor in an establishment. All the service points for such liquor, such as the lounge, lounge bar, cocktail bar, saloon bar, buttery, dispense bars and floor service would draw their stock on a daily or weekly basis from the cellar, this being determined largely by the amount of storage space available and the turnover of sales. All the bars within an establishment will hold a set stock of liquor which is sufficient for a period of one day or one week. At the end of this period of time they requisition for the amount of drink consumed in that one day or week, thus bringing their total stock up to the set stock required.

In the cellar where bin cards are used then every time a wine is received or issued it will be entered on the appropriate bincard and the remaining total balance shown. Thus the bin cards should show at any given time the total amount of each particular wine held in stock. They will also show where applicable a maximum and minimum stock this being a guide to the cellarman when ordering and dependant on the storage space available.

BIN CARD

Name of Wine		BIN No.	
Date	Received	Balance	Issued

In the dispense bar, as all drink is checked for before issue, a daily consumption sheet is completed each day after the service by copying down the sales shown on the top copy of the wine checks. The consumption sheet will list the complete stock held in the dispense bar.

Bin cards may also be completed for checking the wines. At the end of the week the consumption sheets may be totalled up, thereby showing the total sales for that period. These totals may then be transferred on to a bar stock book for costing purposes. Where drink consumed is not checked for in any way then either a daily or weekly stock is taken so that the amount to be requisitioned from the cellar may be noted. This then brings the bar stock back up to its required level.

DAILY CONSUMPTION SHEET

NAME OF DRINK	BIN No.	MON.	TUES.	WED.	THURS.	FRID.	SAT.	SUN.	TOTAL

STOCK BOOK

NAME OF DRINK	BIN No.	OPENING STOCK	RECEIVED	TOTAL	CLOSING STOCK	CONSUMPTION	PRICE PER UNIT	£	p.

The following diagram may help to show very simply the basic steps in bar and cellar control:

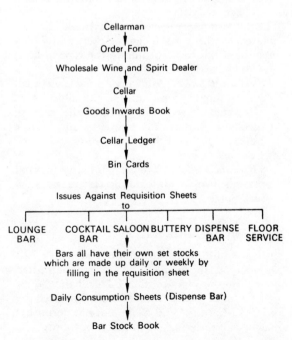

Cellarman

↓

Order Form

Wholesale Wine and Spirit Dealer

↓

Cellar

Goods Inwards Book

↓

Cellar Ledger

Bin Cards

↓

Issues Against Requisition Sheets
to

| LOUNGE BAR | COCKTAIL BAR | SALOON | BUTTERY | DISPENSE BAR | FLOOR SERVICE |

↓

Bars all have their own set stocks which are made up daily or weekly by filling in the requisition sheet

↓

Daily Consumption Sheets (Dispense Bar)

↓

Bar Stock Book

22   the licensing laws

The Licensing Act, 1964.

The Annual Licensing Meeting is always held in the first fortnight in February. In addition there must be held at least 4, but no more than 8, licensing sessions at regular intervals throughout the year.

Licensed premises must, in order to sell alcoholic liquor, obtain what is called a *Justices Licence* of the type required for the business carried on.

This may be:

1. *Full On License.* This allows the licensee to sell all types of alcoholic liquor for consumption on and off the premises. An 'On' licence may be limited by the licensing justices as to the type of alcohol that may be sold. *i.e.* Beer only.

The following are three new types of licence created by the 1961 Licensing Act, and which must be obtained according to the type of business to be carried out.

2. *Restaurant Licence* Allowing the sale of alcoholic liquor for consumption with table meals.
3. *Residential Licence* This allows the sale of alcoholic liquor to residents in Private hotels, Guest and Boarding houses.
4. *Combined Licence*
   (*Restaurant* and *Residential*) For a residential establishment with a public restaurant, such as a hotel.

Licensed Restaurants

Such establishments are allowed an extra half an hour, at the end of the normal permitted hours, for the consumption of alcoholic liquor with a meal. This liquor must however be ordered before the end of the normal permitted hours. No ordering of liquor, but only the consumption of liquor, may take place during the extra half an hour. *E.g.* if the end of the normal permitted hours is 3.0 p.m. then consumption may be until 3.30 p.m. At 3.30 p.m. it would be the wine waiters responsibility to ensure that all glasses and bottles are removed from the table.

The Resident

A resident in licensed premises is allowed to consume alcoholic liquor at any time, *i.e.* resident in an establishment holding either a residential or combined restaurant and' residential license. The residents guests may also consume drink outside of the normal permitted hours provided the resident orders and pays or signs the bill and the guest does not.

Permitted Hours

This is the time during which alcoholic liquor may be served and consumed on the premises. There are occasions in certain areas where the licensing justices may grant earlier opening hours or an extension of the normal permitted hours, *e.g.* Market day, New years eve, Air show etc. These provisions concerning permitted hours came into force on March 1st, 1962. The permitted hours are classified into two sections.
Weekdays:
London
11.0 a.m. to 3.0 p.m.   A total of 9½ hours.
5.30 p.m. to 11.0 p.m.
England & Wales
11.0 a.m. to 3.0 p.m.   A total of 9 hours.
5.30 p.m. to 10.30 p.m.

It should be noted here that there may be an earlier opening hour, not earlier than 10.0 a.m., in order to vary the position of the afternoon break. A period of '10 minutes' is allowed at the end of the morning and evening periods as drinking-up time.

Sundays

The Sunday opening hours are the same for both London, and England & Wales.

12.00 noon. to 2.0 p.m.   A total of 5½ hours.
7.0 p.m.   to 10.30 p.m.

There are a number of variations which may apply to the basic permitted hours shown above. This would depend whether your establishment had been granted one of the following types of licence/certificate, according to the type of business you may wish to carry on.

1. Special Order of Exemption

This is an extension of the normal permitted hours of on-licensed premises for any special occasion, *e.g.* Wedding, buffet dance, etc.

2. Occasional Licence

This allows a licensee already holding an 'on' licence to sell similar liquor at premises other than his own. This license would be granted for social functions held on unlicensed premises and allow the sale of alcoholic liquor in such premises *e.g.* Dances, engagement parties, 21st. birthday parties etc.

3. General Order of Exemption

This allows a licensee to be exempted from the normal permitted hours during a certain day, or for a certain time. Such a notice must be displayed outside the premises for all to see.

4. Supper Hour Certificate

This is a grant by the licensing justices, once they are satisfied that the premises are suitable, of an additional hour to the permitted hours in a licensed restaurant for the sale and consumption of alcoholic liquor with a meal. This certificate also allows any other bars and dispense bars to remain open for the additional hour after the end of the permitted hours. The half an hour drinking up time in the licensed restaurant would still be allowed after the additional hour.

5. Special Hours Certificate

Where this certificate is in force the permitted hours in such licensed premises will be extended until:

West End of London 3.0 a.m. with consumption
            until 3.30 a.m.
Elsewhere   2.0 a.m. with consumption
            until 2.30 a.m.

This certificate only applies to certain establishments who provide music and dancing with substantial refreshment (table meal). Such music and entertainment must be 'live'.

6. Extended Hours Certificate

This extension is for the benefit of premises which qualify for a Supper Hour Certificate and which also provide regular musical or other entertainment (live), together with the 'table meal'. Here the sale of liquor is ancillary to both the 'table meal' and the entertainment. The refreshment and entertainment must be provided in a part of the premises normally set aside for the purpose. This certificate extends the permitted hours up to 1.00 a.m. The service of drink must cease when either the entertainment or service of 'table meals' cease. The service of drink must in any case finish at 1.00 a.m. There is a 'drinking up' time of thirty minutes allowed after the service of drink has ceased. The Extended Hours Certificate expires on April 4 of each year and must be renewed at the February annual licensing session of that year.

Protection of Young Persons

1. For knowingly selling drink to 'under 18's', the penalty for a first offence is £ 25 and £ 50 for the second offence with the possible loss of the licence.
2. It is an offence for a young person, 'under 18', to consume alcoholic liquor on licensed premises.
3. The penalty for selling liquor without a licence is either £ 200 or 6 months.
4. It is also an offence for 'under 18's' to attempt to purchase alcoholic liquor on licensed premises.
5. A young person, 16 years of age and under 18 years of age, if consuming a substantial meal (knife and fork meal) in a licensed restaurant is allowed to purchase and consume with that meal beer, cider or perry.
6. A person of 18 years and over is allowed to work with and consume alcoholic liquor in licensed premises during the permitted hours.

Miscellaneous

1. A non-licensed restaurant must not sell or supply alcoholic liquor. The restaurant however may act as the agent for the guest, buying the alcoholic liquor required outside the restaurant and with the guests money.

The liquor must be paid for in advance, otherwise it is assumed that an illegal sale has taken place. The restaurant must not purchase the alcoholic liquor required at their own 'off' license as this would bring them an 'indirect' profit. The restaurant must make no profit out of such a transaction.

2. A club in which intoxicating liquor is supplied must apply to a magistrates court for a Certificate of registration, to be renewed annually.

3. The permitted hours for 'off-licensed premises' and 'off-sales departments' will commence at 8.30 a.m. and may continue until the end of the normal permitted hours for licensed premises pertaining in the area. It is not essential for 'off-sales' to remain open for all of this period.

23 speciality catering

We shall now look at some aspects of 'Speciality Catering'. The rate of progress at the present time in all aspects of the catering trade is such that there is always something new coming on to the market. It may be in the form of a complete speciality catering unit, or a single piece of equipment used within a food and beverage service operation to increase efficiency and production. All speciality catering units are aimed at one section of the population in order to give maximum efficiency at minimum cost. The following are some different forms of speciality catering.

HOSPITAL CATERING

Hospital catering comes within that section of the catering industry classified as Welfare catering. Hospital catering employs in the region of 36,700 people as against a total labour force in the hotel and restaurant industry of 625,000.

Apart from the School meals service, Hospital catering is one of the largest catering organisations within Welfare catering. Approximately 500,000 staff are employed in the hospital service and of these about 36,700 are full-time catering staff. This complement of catering staff produce and serve meals to about 400,000 patients involving in the region of 750,000 mid-day meals and the equivalent number of breakfasts, teas and evening meals.

The total number of full-time catering staff may be broken down as follows:

(*Approximately*) 910 Catering officers and assts.
115 Housekeeper caterers
260 Dietitians
430 Kitchen superintendants and assts.
2,220 Head cooks and assts.
9,590 Cooks of other grades
11,680 Other kitchen staff
720 Dining room supervisors
10,530 Other dining room staff
250 Clerical staff

It is suggested that the cost of catering staff is in the region of £30 million plus per annum. Added to the expenditure of £45 million plus on provisions, this total of £75 million represents approximately 10% of the cost of the hospital service.

The development of the hospital catering service goes back to the National Health Act of 1947. Before this time all hospitals were dependant on income from patients fees, private donations, proceeds from garden parties and so on. Due to this the service of food varied considerably from one hospital to another, and went generally from bad to worse. Very little consideration was being given to an attractively served meal; the correct nutritional value; a wide variety of food; or all food being served freshly cooked and piping hot.

The long term effect of the 1947 Act was that gradually considerable change took place. 'Regional' Boards were organised who were directly responsible to the Ministry of Health. The responsibility of the catering services were transferred from the matron to the hospital catering officer. A wage scale for hospital catering staff was introduced into the Whitley Council wages proposals for nursing and ancillary professions. Hospital catering staff generally work on a straight shift system and have to provide a 24 hour service. The training of hospital catering staff was carried out at the School of Hospital Catering at St. Pancras Hospital which was established in 1951. In 1965 the school moved to Bayswater and is now called the Staff College for Hospital Caterers. Because of initial bad planning before 1947 and the slow growth and development of the hospital catering service the major food service problems were for all meals to reach the patient quickly, to look attractive and to have the correct nutritional value. To this end the Ganymede system was introduced.

The Patient

When in hospital likes and dislikes become more important to the patient and this is an important factor that the catering officer must not overlook. Patients may be said to fall into six categories:

1. *Medical* who are usually in hospital for a long time. As recovery here may often be long and tedious, the patient is often inclined to lose his appetite and interest in food. Therefore he must be tempted to eat by serving nourishing and appetising food.
2. *Surgical.* Only stay in hospital for a short time and invariably they begin to improve 3 to 4 days after their operation. These patients need good nourishment with a high protein diet and this will involve the service of special diets.
3. *Geriatrics.* Many old people require hospital treatment and have special needs. Therefore generally speaking they should be provided with soft and easy to eat foods such as stews, roasts, minced meats, etc. They should receive plenty of protein and vitamin C, the latter normally in the form of stewed fruits. It is very necessary for these meals to be attractively served up.
4. *Orthopaedics.* These patients are not normally physically ill but may often be unable to move without help. These patients need a good varied diet with good helpings, attractively served.
5. *Maternity.* Patients need good nourishing food often to include extra milk, eggs, butter, fresh fruit and vegetables.
6. *Pediatrics.* Is the hospitalisation of children. As children nowadays commence to eat adult food earlier there is little problem in catering for children. The only slight difference being that an early supper or high tea of a rather light nature is often

served to children. A varied diet containing a good percentage of protein is essential.

The timing of patients mealtimes generally follows the same pattern.

Breakfast	7.30-8.00 a.m.
Dinner	12.00 noon
Tea	3.00-3.30 p.m.
Supper	6.00-6.30 p.m.
Later hot drink	Anytime between 8.00-10.00 p.m.

These times are normally followed as they will not coincide with nurses and doctors meal-times or visiting times. In some hospitals ward waitresses are being introduced in order that meals may be served at a more realistic time. An average of £1.75 per week per head is allowed for food costs in hospitals.

The Ganymede system

The Ganymede System is a method of food service used in hospital catering. It was originally American but the patent has now been bought by a British firm. This system is installed in a number of hospitals in this country and also in hospitals in various countries in Europe and as far away as South Africa. It was first introduced in this country into Bethnal Green hospital in 1964. The cost of installation including a wash-up area and various machines required within the system is approximately £25,000. This is one of the disadvantages—the high cost of conversion of existing premises. When all the dishes listed on the menu are prepared and cooked, the Ganymede Dri-Heat system takes over. Production is 8/10 meals set up per minute, and each meal may be different in its make up according to the patients choice. One initial problem caused by this system was staff, since a large number of staff is required around the conveyor belt for setting up the meals. This is generally overcome by using house-porters, and making use of a number of house-maids from various wards, for a period of 30 minutes over the luncheon and dinner service period.

The equipment required is all based around a conveyor belt and consists mainly of heated and cold plate dispensers; machine which holds the pellets; dispenser for the bases; electric portable bain-marie for holding various dishes of vegetables, etc.; tray dispenser; quick fry tops and hot-plates nearby for excess equipment in case it is required.

In the Ganymede system the service points consist of mobile, heated bains marie and cold stations. They are set at right angles to a conveyer belt so that the operator can see the tray card — which indicates the meal components — without turning her head. Pre-wrapped cutlery may be put on at the start or selected cutlery with a serviette may be added near the end of the belt. The tray is checked by a supervisor before dishes are lidded.

The advantages of this system are that the patient receives his meal presented appetizingly on the plate and piping hot. Labour and administration costs can be reduced to some extent. Time originally spent by the house-maids in the ward 'plating up' meals can now be put to better use by completing other duties. The patient is able to select the meal he requires from a given menu. It has been estimated that there is a saving of 4 hours per day in the wards because of the easier and speeded up means of service to the patient, and as little or no washing-up is done in each ward but in a central wash-up area.

The menu, with a choice, is given to each patient at 8.00 a.m., and he then marks off his requirements for lunch, dinner and breakfast the following day by putting 'X' in the appropriate box. These menus are then collected by the ward sister who sends them down to the catering manager. He, by means of an automatic machine, is informed of the number of portions of each dish required, and then this information is passed on to the kitchen by 9.00 a.m. At service time, depending on the type of dish, extra portions are available in case required. The patient may also mark on the card if he requires a large or small portion. By this system of dry heat service a meal will keep in perfect condition for up to 45 minutes. Therefore if for some reason a patient is not available when meals are brought to the ward, but comes in 30 minutes later, his meal is still satisfactory. The private patient's choice of menu is larger and more varied than the main wards, and here the menus are often printed in part French and part English. The evening meal for private patients is termed 'Dinner', but for other wards it is 'Supper'.

To commence the service of the meal a supervisor stands at the end of the conveyor belt and checks each meal before it is placed in an unheated trolly to go to the wards. The meal required, with the aid of a pellet (metal alloy disc), will remain at the correct temperature for approximately 45 minutes. The pellet, $\frac{1}{4}$ kg ($\frac{1}{2}$ lb) in weight, is placed in the base and the plate on top, allowing the air to circulate, which in turn circulates the heat from the pellet. Before use the bases are heated to 104° C (250° F.), the pellet to 152° C (400° F.), and the plate to 104° C (250° F.).

One member of staff stands at each of the service points along the conveyor belt and deals with a certain item of food as listed on the menu. As each tray progresses along the belt with the patients chosen menu upon it, the appropriate members of staff place the necessary portions of food on to the plate. A suggested order of items on the tray is—cutlery in a serviette and a menu; main dish; sauce; vegetables; potatoes; sweet; sauce and soup. Beverages are made and dispensed from the ward kitchens.

The china plates in use are specially made to absorb the required heat without cracking. Bowls used for soups and hot sweets are plastic and have a vacuum in the bottom which helps the soup or sweet to retain its heat for the required period of time. Care must be taken when using this equipment as the bowls, being specially made, cost in the region of £ 1 each. Bakelite trays are used as they are light and easily cleaned. All cutlery used is generally stainless steel.

For nutritional purposes as much food as possible is fresh. To some extent however this form of service lends itself to the use of pre-portioned wrapped foods e.g. for butters, preserves, sugars, marmalade, salt and peppers and creams. This again is more hygienic, cuts out wastage, and helps to reduce costs and storage problems to a minimum.

A system similar to the Ganymede System has been introduced in some hospitals.

The Helitherm tray service

This is a Swedish system working on similar principals to the Ganymede using a selective menu, tray service, and run on an assembly line. By this method the food is kept hot by specially insulated trays. This system is expensive to install and very often difficult in existing premises. One of the main advantages of the system is its flexibility, in that there are no heated pellets or special ovens required so that the trays may be used in smaller units. Perhaps the one disadvantage of the Helitherm tray service is that the menu does not travel directly towards the server as in the Ganymede system and therefore some difficulties may arise in the server reading the menu. Both systems will complete approximately 8-10 trays per minute.

The cold dishes will be served from one side and hot foods from the other side of the assembly line. The bain-maries are placed against the conveyor belt which means the operator fills the plate by means of a forward movement as against a sideway movement employed in the Ganymede system. This now means that if there is a shortage of staff in the Helitherm tray service system one server may possibly be able to serve from more than one section.

At the beginning of the belt one operator puts the menu in its holder and a hot plate on the tray. As the tray passes down the moving belt the servers place the required portions of food on to the plate. At the end of the belt the tray is checked and lids put in place. The trays are then put into trollies and sent to the various wards.

Hospitals have also experimented with Smethursts Ltd. 'Top Tray system' which was introduced to the catering industry in 1963/4. The 'Top Tray system' consists of complete deep-frozen meals prepared in central kitchens and re-heated in radiant heat ovens at the service points. The main disadvantages are the fairly high cost per meal and the fact that there are limits to the variety of food which may be prepared in this way. One main advantage is that the food may be prepared in 'off peak' hours and then brought into use as and when required. Labour costs can be reduced, and the labour force can be deployed to other necessary duties without the usual pressures of a 'service period'.

Micro-wave ovens are already making an appearance in hospitals to provide quick re-heating facilities for food at certain periods of the day and night, when if labour were employed, the wages bill would be sky-high. All forms of dishes required can be prepared the day before in 'off-peak' hours in a central kitchen and blast-frozen. When required the following day the dishes are ready for service only 1 minute after going into an oven at full heat. The skill and craftsmanship of the food preparation staff are still required in the preparation of each dish, which can be done and completed when not under pressure. The final reconstitution can be carried out by unskilled staff in a matter of seconds.

Automatic vending is another aspect of food and beverage service which is creeping into the hospital catering service. Because of the necessity of a 24 hour service in the hospital to patients, surgeons, doctors, and the nursing staff, the introduction of automatic vending machines for beverages, both hot and cold, and hot and cold snacks, cuts labour costs.and ensures a constant and reliable service. In this way staff are able to get a drink or snack as and when they wish. The vending machines must be replenished and cleaned daily and have regular maintenance. For maximum sales they must be sited correctly. Whether the time will come when complete meals will be dispensed from an automatic vending machine in a hospital remains to be seen.

It can be seen that the new systems are devised to boost the morale of the patient by continually presenting him with well cooked food, attractively plated-up and piping hot. At the same time over the period of a week or a fortnight the patient has a wide and varied selection of dishes from which to choose.

Hospital Staff Menu

Breakfast
Porridge or cereal
Grilled bacon
Apple fritters
Toast
Preserve
Beverage
or
Porridge or cereal
Welsh rarebit or
Boiled egg
Toast
Preserve
Beverage

Luncheon
Tomato juice
Roast lamb, mint sauce
Cauliflower, carrots,
Roast or creamed potatoes
or
Scotch egg,
Florida salad with crisps
Plum pie & custard, milk pudding
or
Ice cream
Beverage
or
Chicken soup
Fried fillet of haddock
Sauce tartare,
or
Beef hot-pot
Chipped or creamed potato
Peas and tomatoes
Cabinet pudding, jam sauce
Milk pudding
or
Ice cream
Beverage

Dinner
Vegetable consommé
Fish pie
or
Rissoles & bacon,
Chipped potato's
Peas.
Stewed plum and semolina
Beverage
Kidney soup
Fried sausage
or
Fried egg
Creamed potato
Baked beans
College pudding and Jam sauce
Beverage

A cover that might be found in a popular priced or speciality restaurant. The equipment required is: Place mat — Fish plate — Napkin — Joint knife — Joint fork — Wine glass.

Note:

No tablecloths are required. Here we find the wood grained formica topped table which allows for easy cleaning; paper napkins replace linen ones, and additional cutlery would be added to the guests cover as required, according to his order.

POPULAR CATERING

This is an aspect of catering difficult to define accurately and there are many variations within the scope of the term, although it may be said to denote the preparation and service of hot and cold snacks or meals, and beverages at popular prices, within the reach of the average persons pocket. The type of establishment where this form of catering is found may vary from a first class establishment, with one popular service area, to the medium class establishment, down to the department store, and speciality catering unit. In each case, however, the management are aiming at maximum turnover in a minimum period of time. In order to do this efficiently, as in all forms of food and beverage service, it is necessary for all staff to be made aware of the art of salesmanship and the social skills necessary in

order to be able to sell effectively. It is not possible to discuss here all the variations of popular catering. The popular catering set-up will give an insight into some of the main factors controlling the make-up and working of such a unit. It must firstly be remembered that these types of establishments may take the form of 'Steak Bars', 'Salad Bowls' or other forms of 'Speciality Units' and both the name of the establishment and the decor must be suitable to attract the desired customer. The name may very often take the form of a catch phrase which it is hoped will take the public imagination and therefore be remembered. Seating capacity in the restaurant may be approximately 100 covers. Furniture and furnishings should be of a high standard and have a main colour theme. Banquette seating provides for the maximum number in a limited area.

Staff over the service periods consists of perhaps 4 waiters each with a station of approximately 24 covers. There would be one Head waiter or Manageress who would be responsible for the overall administration and organization as well as taking bookings and greeting and seating guests. Each waiter would serve their own drink. This would be collected from a dispense bar which serves both the lounge area and the restaurant. Each waiter would keep his own tronc, thus they all work on an incentive basis, the higher the turnover of customers the more they receive in tips.

The menu would be a limited à la carte at reasonable prices. All the food is cooked from a call-order unit situated within the room, thus all is on show to the guest. The equipment used should facilitate a speedy turnover of meals, e.g. infra-red grills, micro-wave and convection ovens. All meat and fish is bought pre-portioned and at set weights, which is an aid to standardising costing. Great use would be made of convenience foods, all vegetables being frozen, and soups powdered and condensed. It is in this type of food service that an ever-increasing amount of ancillary items are being offered in a pre-portioned and wrapped form. This includes sugars, butters, cheese, biscuits and so on. By controlling the food as strictly as possible in the ways mentioned above, using pre-portioned foods and being careful in the type of dishes offered on the limited à la carte menu one does not need to employ the professional chef de cuisine to oversee and control the kitchen. This allows a saving of some £ 2,000 per annum, and the service does not suffer.

Small tables would be used to seat two guests, and these may be joined together to seat larger parties. The tables would be formica topped, which facilitates easy cleaning, and disposable place mats and paper serviettes are used thereby saving on linen costs. All cutlery used would be of stainless steel and the china heavy, but with a pleasant design.

The beverage served—coffee—would be collected from the stillroom area of the service counter and then kept hot on heaters on the sideboards. An alternative to this would be to have banks of coffee machines in the room with the coffee being made as required. This ensures a completely fresh cup of coffee being served at all times.

Checking and control may be by means of a National Cash Register where each waiter has a key letter. He presses this letter after he enters the price of the dishes ordered on the bill by means of the keys on the cash register. The waiter must total the bill and give the bottom of the bill to the customer as a receipt. The waiter receives all cash from the guests, and at the end of service this is paid in. The person who collects all the cash can check the National Cash Register by means of a special master key and see how much cash each waiter has taken. This would be checked against the cash amounts handed in. The cash register may also break down the total amount of cash taken into totals for food, alcohol, beverages, etc.

A limited wine list is offered, and also wine by the carafe and the glass. The type and variety of wine would depend on the clientele served. Another important aspect is the uniform of the food service staff. This should tone in with the décor and very often in this form of establishment a nylon overall for waitresses and nylon jacket for waiters toning in with the colour scheme is as pleasing to the eye as the traditional and formal waiting uniform.

In this type of service there is a saving on linen, silver service equipment, cutlery and labour costs, in comparison with the more formal forms of food and beverage service.

All forms of popular catering may not contain all the aspects mentioned above. The different aspects will vary according to the particular situation. The trend in food and beverage service is towards, giving a well cooked and presented meal in pleasant surroundings which is served efficiently and quickly with a maximum turnover in a limited period of time.

INDUSTRIAL CATERING

It is not many years ago that workers in industry had to be satisfied with literally a 'crust of bread and glass of water' to carry them through the long working day of perhaps 16-18 hours. Over the last half-century, however, many developments have taken place which now ensure that all staff receive during their meal-break an attractively presented meal, with good sized portions that are nutritionally well balanced.

Many of the large industrial firms now provide catering facilities for their staff equal to those found in any first class establishment.

The staff dining room in a Marks and Spencer store where a three-course lunch is available for the staff for as little as 5p (1971)

There are two methods by which an industrial firm can set up a catering operation for the benefit of its staff.

These are

1. By handing out the catering rights to contract caterers.
2. By setting up a catering department within the firm itself.

Where contract catering is in operation the firm concerned is expected to produce meals at a given rate per head, or they may have a set amount to budget upon annually over the period of the contract. The contracts may run in terms of a year, or 3 or 5 years as the case may be.

Both of these methods are used, and it depends on the size, situation, number of workers and the requirements of a firm as to which method they choose. The main meals to be provided are morning coffee, luncheon, and afternoon tea with biscuits. Very often in the larger industrial firm with its own catering department a number of evening functions are also carried out. These take the form of cocktail parties and dinners for visiting representatives from other firms or countries, and social evenings for the firm's staff association such as dinner dances or dances with a cold buffet. Where shift duties are involved catering to the needs of the worker may be over a 24 hour period. To this end automatic vending has taken over to some extent.

The number of staff employed in a catering set up would depend on the firm itself and its requirements. In a large catering concern there would be a need for catering management and supervisory staff, chefs, waiters or waitresses, barmen, storekeepers, linen-maids, besides all the maintenance and cleaning staff. It is appreciated therefore that it would be difficult to state exactly how many catering staff work in any particular aspect of industrial catering such as factories, office blocks and large commercial firms. As an approximate guide, however, we may suggest:

1. An establishment with 2500 staff: Total of 170 catering staff. This allows 1 member of catering staff to 15 members of staff.
2. An establishment with 500 staff: Total of 50 catering staff.

From these figures it should be noted that the larger the total number, the smaller number of catering staff required. The number of catering staff serving at the counter would depend on the size of the menu, and the style of service offered, whether plain or multipoint counter service. One of the most important factors to remember is that speed of service and turnover are essential to maintain a constant flow. Each member of the serving staff should know exactly what his or her job entails and that all food should be served piping hot. In this form of food service the time factor is very important as the staff to be fed usually only receive a lunch break of 30 minutes. Another delay in the service would be the use of a cashier. The handing over of money and giving of change all takes time, but to overcome this problem many firms use a ticket system for the meals service which does away with the cashier as the tickets are collected at the beginning of the queue. A number of the ancillary items to the meal are generally offered free of charge and with no restrictions on the amount taken. Such items would be rolls, butter, cheese and biscuits, sauces, and pickles.

Most menus offer a choice within each course. A higher class of menu would be offered in the Directors' dining room or Senior Staff dining room than the menu offered to the majority of staff in the cafeteria. As we have already said speed of service is essential for cafeteria service. Waitress service would be offered in the dining rooms for supervisory grades and senior staff which would be a little slower in operation. The directors' dining room could well compare with a private suite in a first class establishment and might be a full silver service. Here all forms of alcoholic drink would be available and served by an experienced barman from a static or portable bar.

In this form of catering, luncheon is the main meal served. The time allocated for the service of lunch is usually 12.00-2.30 p.m. Where very large numbers have to be catered for in a limited area, the service would be staggered over half-hour periods to avoid any hold-ups. Beverages would possibly not be served with the meal but in a separate staff lounge where a range of hot or cold beverages and snacks would be available. This is where automatic vending machines have taken over to some extent. If the machines are sited correctly and maintained regularly then they do away with a certain amount of labour and also help to reduce certain costs, namely wages, washing-up, pre-preparation and so on. Morning coffees and afternoon teas would be served in the staff lounge and also from various service points on the different floors. The service is more often than not carried out by a member of the catering staff from a trolly. The preparation of the beverages and washing-up of all cups, saucers, teaspoons and sideplates would be done either in the service points on the different floors or from a central distribution point and sent to the different floor service points by lift.

The service staff generally consist of waitresses for all the dining rooms. Those working in the Directors' dining room and Senior dining room are usually fully experienced in full silver service. The waitresses working in the Supervisors dining room would possibly carry out a form of plate-silver service, which has already been described. The covers laid are table d'hôte and any special equipment would be brought to the table as required. In the Directors dining room the ratio of waitress to staff is approximately 8 staff to 1 waitress, whereas in the Supervisors' dining room the ratio would increase to 15 staff to 1 waitress. In the cafeteria where counter service is functioning the service staff required in the actual room would be women with trollies to clean all the dirty equipment and wipe down the tables. This is an important function and the supervisor in charge must ensure that the dirty china and cutlery is speedily returned to the wash-up so that there is no hold-up due to shortage of equipment. These ladies must also ensure that the tables are adequately stocked with cruets, sauces, ashtrays, jugs of iced water and glasses. Depending on the situation these women very often only work part-time, over the luncheon period. A modern trend here is to have tables with inserts in them made to hold exactly the tray carried by the consumer with his meal. When the meal is finished the consumer deposits the tray and dirty cutlery onto a conveyor belt which passes the tray and its contents to the wash-up. This gives some saving in the table area required per head and saves on labour costs for clearing the tables. All washing-up will be done by machine.

Most industrial establishments provide uniforms for serving staff and dining room staff which will be laundered free of charge. Some firms go as far as providing shoes for all catering staff to wear, which would be comfortable to the feet and safe to wear in the kitchen, i.e., no high heels. The majority of catering staff work a 40 hour week from 8.30 a.m. to 4.00 p.m. with a half hour break for lunch. In some instances the food service staff do not report till 10.00 a.m. but may work later when there are evening functions. It is more usual however for staff to be employed on a casual basis for all forms of evening functions and they will then be paid so much for the evening or so much per hour. Every employee is allowed two weeks holiday per annum plus so many extra days according to the length of service with a particular firm.

Apart from the excellent catering facilities many firms provide for their staff; they also spare no expense where social amenities are concerned. Many firms have 'Sports Clubs': tennis, football, cricket, athletics, billiards, rowing, etc. together with other sections for dancing, opera and music and so on. Most of these clubs incorporate licensed bars on the premises open during normal licensing hours to staff and their friends and families. Always on call in case of emergency would be a qualified nursing staff in case of accidents at work or during any social activity. They would also carry out a searching medical examination on all new members of staff before they would be accepted for the job applied for.

The menus, as in all branches of the catering trade, must be varied to satisfy and attract most of the staff. The final decisions on the menu are taken by the chef in conjunction with the catering manager after considering any suggestion put by the staff committee. This committee meets at regular intervals to comment on the meals provided, and the service, and offer any suggestions for improvement. They speak and represent the staff as a whole in this connection.

Depending on the size of the firm a member of staff would be concerned with buying supplies on a day to day basis or in bulk from a wholesaler, if there is sufficient storage space. Many of the fresh foods with a limited storage life would be purchased day by day as required. A wide variety of convenience foods: frozen, powdered mixes, and pre-portioned foods, are being used. There are advantages in their storage, since there is no deterioration or shortage of certain commodities and they can be easily prepared without skilled staff.

Not only do good conditions and amenities make the staff happy and contented in their work, but another most important factor to be borne in mind is the cost of the meal supplied. Most firms subsidise the meals served to staff, some more than others. Some firms may charge $12\frac{1}{2}$ p-$17\frac{1}{2}$ p per head but offer a fairly wide range of choice which would be well served in pleasant surroundings. Other firms may charge less, perhaps 5 p-$7\frac{1}{2}$ p per head, but then the choice would be much more limited. In some instances the staff are not charged at all for their meal, the whole cost being borne by the firm.

Industrial catering menus

Cafeteria

Starters	Soups or juices
Fish	Grilled lemon sole
Salad	Corned beef
Toast Dish	Scotch woodcock
	or
	Savoury
Main Dish	Roast beef and yorkshire pudding
	or
	Lamb pot pie
Entrée	Egg florentine
Vegetables	Roast and mashed potato
	Runner beans and carrots
Sweets	Steamed jam roll
	Sago pudding
	Ice cream and gooseberries
	Fresh bananas
Beverage	Tea or coffee
Starters	Soups or juices
Fish	Turbot meunière
Salad	Tongue
Toast dish	Savoury rice
	or
	Mushrooms on toast

Main dish	Roast pork, stuffing and apple sauce
	or
	Tomato beef casserole
Entrée	Shepherds pie
Vegetables	Chipped and mashed potato
	Peas and tomato
Sweet	Treacle tart
	Steamed raisin sponge
	Macaroni pudding
	Ice cream and meringue
Beverage	Tea or coffee

The following items available daily at no extra charge.

a) Selection of rolls, bread, ryvita, with butter.
b) Individual salad in lieu of vegetable or potato.
c) Cheese, biscuits and butter.
d) Custard sauce wherever applicable.

What are the future trends in this sphere of the catering industry? As far as insight allows it seems that gradually we are going to turn over to a 'service' industry rather than 'preparation and service'. By that I mean we will be using all forms of convenience, preportioned and prepared foods which need only limited handling and by un-skilled staff. The problems of 'space available', 'labour' and 'costs' will be forever with us and to reduce this to the minimum we have to think in terms of large central distribution kitchens, blast-freezing meals, micro-wave cookery, top-tray, automatic vending and so on.

JEWISH CATERING

This is catering for a special section of the community where all procedures are laid down according to their dietary laws. It is known as 'Kosher' cooking. It is as well to have a brief insight and awareness of what is involved as a number of Jewish catering firms employ Gentiles, that is chefs and other staff from outside the faith. These people must abide by and have respect for the strict dietary laws and traditions laid down according to the Jewish religion. The dietary laws are derived from two of the five books which are the basis of their religion, Deuteronomy and Leviticus. It is from these that the standard rules are formulated. Very simply they are as follows:

1. The division is between those animals which may be eaten and those which may not.
Clean
a) Those animals which have cloven hooves and chew the cud.

e.g., the cow but only the forequarter
b) Any fish with fins and scales are permitted.
c) Hens eggs are allowed, but any blood specks showing must be removed.
Unclean
i) Animals with only one of these qualifications (a) above are unclean.
ii) Not the hindquarter as this holds the reproductive organs, and are unclean.
iii) Shellfish are not allowed as they creep and crawl along the ground. In other words it is regarded as a scavenger.
iv) Any birds or animals of prey are not allowed.
v) Eggs and milk of any unclean animals and birds.
vi) Gelatine made from the bones and hoofs of animals.
vii) Certain fats.

2 Another of the basic laws is that blood must not be eaten. The reason for this is that the blood represents the 'life' of an animal. In order that the 'clean' meats may be eaten the animals are slaughtered in a particular way so that the blood is drained out of the animal. This method of slaughter is called *Shechitah* and it would be carried out by the butcher or *Shochet* as he is called. *Shechitah* denotes the cutting of the jugular vein, causing all the blood to be immediately drained away and therefore rendering the meat acceptable. Very often the meat has all the fat and veins removed before being used.

To make the meat *Kosher* means to ensure that all the blood has been removed in the correct fashion and the meat prepared by soaking for a short period of time; washing it; sprinkling with salt and then allowing it to stand for one hour. Finally the meat is rinsed and ready for use. It will now be realised that the butcher or *Shochet* must be an expert at his profession ensuring that all meat is fit for consumption by someone of the Jewish faith.

All these procedures, from the slaughter until the meat is ready for use, are carried out under the supervision of the *Shomahs* or representatives of the Court of the Chief Rabbi. The *Shomahs* form two committees or groups known as the *Beth Din* and the *Kashrus*. Both these groups deal only with food their members or *Shomahs*, ensuring that all food procedures are correctly carried out according to the strict laws of the Jewish faith. All food which has been *Koshered* is marked by a small metal tab on a piece of wire. This acts as a seal.

3. A further dietary law forbids the use of milk and meat together. This law is carried out very strictly and the *Shomahs* watch stringently over all catering operations to ensure that the staff do not mix up meat and milk equipment. This therefore means that whenever catering for Jewish functions one virtually needs two pieces of every item of equipment. This is not only in the kitchen but also in the food service area. All this equipment must be marked and a colour is normally used to differentiate between meat from milk items, blue crockery for meat and red for milk. The only item of equipment which is neutral is glassware. Some examples of equipment which must be duplicated are spoons; ladles; whisks; knives; bowls; cloths; sinks, etc. During the service of a meal the *Shomahs* must ensure that all food served is Kosher. After a meat meal no milk foods are eaten for approximately 4 hours. After a milk meal, as it is easily digested, meat may follow fairly quickly.

No cooking may be carried out by anyone of the Jewish religion from sunset Friday to sunset Saturday, as Saturday is the Jewish Sabbath. Therefore all foods are cooked the day before, dished up, and then eaten cold on the saturday. All male Jews when eating in a house must have their heads covered by a small headpiece or skull-cap. At the beginning of every meal a prayer is said; followed by the procedure known as 'break-bread' and then the washing of hands. The loaf used in a special plaited loaf. No smoking is allowed in the house on the Sabbath. Any special functions such as weddings, engagements, anniversaries, birthdays, and *Barmitzuahs* are supervised rigidly by the *Beth Din* and *Kashrus* commitees. There are certain periods of the year when a Jew does not marry. The Barmitzuah is the coming of age of a son of a family and the function given to celebrate this occasion. The son comes of age at 13 years and this will be celebrated in both the synagogue and the home. The children normally celebrate on the saturday and the parents on the sunday. A menu to be offered on the occasion of a Barmitzuah for the Sunday might be as follows:

Menu
Fruit cocktail
Smoked salmon hors d'oeuvre
Egg mayonnaise
Ox tongue, Chicken liver patties
Garden peas Mushroom sauce
Lemon sorbet

Roast Surrey capon
New parsley potatoes, French salad
Asparagus vinaigrette
Praline wonder ice gâteaux
Fruit salad
Black coffee and Petits fours
Fresh fruit in season

Later in the evening—4 hours—pastries and tea would be offered, and sometimes fruit salad and ice cream. Later still about 12.00-1.00 a.m. frankfurters and mustard would be served.

On each table where a meal is to be served a card must be displayed stating all food served is under supervision of the *Beth Din* and *Kashrus* committee. Certain wines are Kosher wines and this would be shown on the label. If this is the case at a certain function then it would be necessary to have a Jew on the staff to handle and serve these wines, otherwise the host would have to do it.

Anyone contemplating Kosher catering must realise that he must double up on all equipment, which may prove very costly. This form of catering has been made a little easier, with the advent of fat free foodstuffs, vegetarian margarines, cooking oils and so on. The *Beth Din* and the *Kashrus* committee issue licences to caterers to show that they are eligible to cater for Jewish functions, and great care has to be taken to adhere to all the dietary laws and traditions. Obviously to understand and appreciate completely the reasons for these dietary laws one has to be aware of the principles involved in the Jewish faith.

AUTOMATIC VENDING

Defined briefly this means the supply of food and beverages, both hot and cold, and of a wide variety, through coin-operated machines. Where do we find these machines in use at the present time? Two spheres of the catering industry benefit most at the present time from automatic vending: industrial and transport catering. These machines are found sited in canteens, factories, industrial concerns, offices, railway stations, garages including motorways, swimming pools and hotels, to name but a few.

The growth of the automatic vending machine in catering may be noted from the fact that in 1960 there were less than 500 British factories with vending machines. By 1968 this figure had risen to over 7,000. Although this

growth figure may seem good, automatic vending has penetrated the catering industry very little in comparison with its advances in America. As an approximate comparison it may be said that we have one vending machine to each 600 workers as against one vending machine to every 20 workers in America.

The machines themselves are normally used in conjunction with the conventional kitchen approach to catering. At the same time they relieve some of the pressure of work on the counter-hands and cashier by taking some of the customers away from the counter and to the machine. This is especially true where only hot or cold beverages are required together with a limited range of snacks for a certain percentage of those being catered for.

This is one of the many advantages of automatic vending. Other advantages are that:

2. The automatic vending machines provide a round the clock—24 hour—service, and at a lower cost to operate than by conventional

methods of service.

3. It is generally recognised that good staff facilities mean an increase in productivity, and to this end the correct siting of automatic vending machines can give a boost to the employees morale by providing for his needs 24 hours a day. This is done without him having to move any great distance from his place of work, or waste time in queuing.

4. Automatic vending allows for standardised portion control.

5. Standard quality of product at a set price.

6. Food cost control is an advantage because this type of service allows for strict portion control.

7. There is economy of labour resulting in a reduction in wages bills.

8. With the advent of these machines the fixed tea break has given way to the natural tea-break with the result that less working time is lost due to workers slowing down in anticipation of a break and being back a few minutes late from their break. This also means that productivity is increased.

9. A main meal may be served but if beverages are available by machine then they are fresh and piping hot, and taken as and when required. This means the beverage does not go cold whilst the main meal is being consumed.

10. Automatic vending machines offer at the present time a wide variety of hot and cold snacks and beverages and contained within a space considerably smaller than necessary for the conventional forms of large equipment, another important saving as space is so costly.

11. Automatic vending machines are also being used in conjunction with the microwave oven. Here all snacks and meals are kept in refrigerated compartments. The customer chooses his meal, takes it from the machine, and then places it in a micro-wave oven to reheat.

12. A further advantage is that wastage may be cut to the minimum as long as the customer demand has been correctly gauged and the *right machines* providing the *right items* at the *right price* have been sited in the *right place*.

13. Maintenance is easy and a member of the permanent staff can be trained to do the replenishing daily.

The numbers and types of machines required will depend on their location, the type and numbers of people they are providing a service for, the cost factor and the variety of food and beverage items they may require. The machines required may be installed either individually or in small groups to supplement the conventional catering establishment, or to cover a small sales demand that does not warrant the expense of employing the extra labour and plant. The opposite to this would be the installation of a complete coin-operated service where demand is highly seasonal space is limited, and the use of unskilled labour would be uneconomical. Many garages have now sited a single beverage machine in a prominent position in their forecourts providing motorists with a welcome hot or cold beverage. The more popular machine here is the one which offers coffee black or white, with or without sugar, or with extra sugar. Also tea with the same combinations as coffee, and, what has proved to be a great favourite, hot chocolate. The same machine may also provide a range of cold drinks.

A further advancement in the development of microwave oven techniques in conjunction with vending is the Micro-vend Buffet. This is a complete refreshment unit for hot/cold meals and hot/cold drinks. Here complete meals are prepared to standard recipes and retained in refrigerated conditions. With each meal the customer receives a small token which enables him to operate a micro-wave oven incorporated in the automatic vending unit. This system has been found ideal for hospitals and factories where a 24 hour shift system is in operation. It would also be useful to the small establishment where the usual form of cafeteria service would be uneconomical. It must be borne in mind here that packaging of the meal is most important in order to make it acceptable to the customer. The companies supplying disposables have produced an attractive range of plates and dishes which are suitable for such heat.

It is suggested that automatic vending cuts running costs by approximately one third. Where these modern techniques are applied to industrial catering, and in the right situation, a great saving can be made and many of the old problems of lack of staff and profit or loss on subsidised meals may be solved. As an instance: a new staff restaurant recently opened in Kent with automatic vending machines to dispense all its food. The staff may now obtain an inexpensive, freshly cooked and good quality meal by simply placing a coin in a slot.

Food is prepared in a conventional kitchen sited immediately behind a bank of vending machines. The food is all carefully portioned and pleasantly presented in foil containers wrapped in cellophane before being loaded into the rear of the hot or cold vending machines direct from the kitchen. A suggested range of machines for this type of operation would be as follows, hot food vendors, refrigerated food vendor, confectionery machine, snack machine, hot drink machine and a refrigerated soft drink machine. From this range hot or cold snacks may be obtained, or a full-three course meal. Ancillary requirements such as gravy, custard, sauces etc. would come from a self help bain-marie unit. When siting these machines in a 'bank' if more than one hot vendor is in operation they should be spaced apart to avoid crowding in one section of the unit, and to help a smooth even flow of customers at all times. In this form of operation a 'money-change' machine is always necessary. By using the bank of machines as one wall of the kitchen they can be loaded easily and if there is a run on one particular item then the kitchen staff are able to cope easily. The kitchen staff requirements are reduced by this system of food service operation. If a night-shift is in operation then the food can be prepared by the day-shift and placed in the heated and refrigerated machines ready for consumption by the night-shift workers. The food will keep hot in these machines for up to 16 hours, thus reducing the need of night canteen staff. A suggested menu for this type of operation may be as follows:

Menu

First course	Fruit juice.	2½ p
	Soup of the day.	2½ p
	Grapefruit.	4 p
Main courses	Roast pork, stuffiing, Roast potato and Broad beans.	10 p
	Cold meat and salad.	10 p
	Liver, bacon, fried onions Creamed potato and peas.	10 p
	Buck rarebit.	6 p
Sweets	Plum tart and custard.	2½ p
	Creme caramel.	2½ p
	Fruit salad.	2½ p
	Cheese and biscuits.	5 p
Beverages	Tea/coffee/chocolate.	2½ p

A suggested variation on this form of menu may be as follows:

First Course	Soup	1 p
Main Course	Roast lamb, roast potato, peas.	12½ p
	Roast pork, stuffing, roast potato and peas.	12½ p

	Steak pudding, boiled potato and cabbage	10 p
	Ham salad.	9 p
	Egg salad.	7½ p
	Cheese salad.	7½ p
Snacks	Mixed pack of sandwiches, ham and cheese.	5 p
	Ham sandwich, half round.	2½ p
	Cheese sandwich, half round	2½ p
	Pork pie.	5 p
	Meat pie.	5 p
Sweets	Choice of hot and cold sweets.	2½ p
Beverages	Tea/coffee/hot Chocolate.	2½ p
	Variety of soft drinks.	2½ p

The advantages of being able to operate this type of food service system allows the food service unit serving a typical staff canteen to break even, or even make a slight profit. At the same time the caterer is able to keep the price of a meal well within the national average for a conventionally operated staff canteen. This therefore is one of the great advantages and good prospects for the future, that automatic vending can offer industrial catering.

Motorway catering is becoming increasingly important. This can be seen from the fact that service areas are being built on an average every 64-72 kilometres (40-45 miles) of motorway, and there are 18 major motorways planned by the Ministry of Transport. The majority of travellers need only a snack and a drink, and the fact that it is obtainable quickly will pull them into the food and beverage service area. Here there are problems of providing various forms of service to meet everyones needs. This has shown the necessity for a first-class waitress service restaurant with a table d'hôte and limited à la carte menu. Here business men can eat and entertain whilst on the move from one business meeting to another; the family can eat when out on a long journey, and the late night traveller returning from the theatre can round off his evening with a pleasant meal, attractively served in comfortable surroundings. The restaurant would be fully licensed.

A cafeteria is also a necessity to provide the hot or cold snacks and beverage required by the multitude of travellers now using the motorway, and who only wish to stop for 10-15 minutes.

An incentive here to the early morning traveller is the 'Commuter Breakfast' consisting of two rashers of bacon, a fried egg, slice of toast, a pre-portioned and wrapped pat of butter, an individual pot of marmalade and a cup of tea or coffee for an all in price of 25 p.

Provision also has to be made in a separate food service area for all the heavy transport drivers who now use the motorway. One of the main problems of the motorway catering unit is labour. It is necessary to operate a three shift system of eight hours each over a 24 hour period. At the same time staff have generally got to be transported to and from their place of work because access is not easy except for the motorway traveller. This is therefore bound to increase the overall cost of overheads.

Automatic vending is now just beginning to enter motorway catering, and this will cut out the staffing problem and the worry over extra cost of transport for staff. It will be a slow and gradual changeover if it is to be accepted by the public at large. However two 'Pick-a-Platter' restaurants have been opened on the M1 motorway. They are the first restaurants to offer a fully automatic service of cold meals on any United Kingdom motorway, and have been specially designed for high density catering. This I feel is a major step towards the catering of the future. It overcomes many of the present day caterers problems of staffing, wage costs, food cost, portion control, wastage, variation of menu within a limited cost, unskilled staff and so on.

Sufficient has been said to show that automatic vending is now beginning to establish itself as a service industry and has a lot to offer the catering industry as a whole. Developments during the 1970's will move forward even more rapidly than they have in the past. This development must be helped by those in catering who are directly or partially involved in providing an efficient food service. Namely those in industrial establishments, canteens, factories, hospitals, transport catering and so on. They must acknowledge that automatic vending will become a neccessity as part of the food service set up, and will help to keep up the standard required today. One of the big problems at the present time is that technically improved machines are coming on the market so rapidly that a 5 year old machine may be said to be obselete. The Micro-vend Buffet in which complete meals are kept in a frozen state and reheated as required in a micro-wave oven is accepted as the ideal method of dispensing meals, rather than putting hot foods in a machine and keeping them hot over a period of time. The wastage ratio here is higher as one cannot always calculate the likely turnover, and after a certain period of time the hot meals have to be replaced. What will the next breakthrough be? All that can be said at this stage is that the automatic vending machine will be an accepted part of the food and beverage service area in the 1970's, being used to provide the best possible and most economic service.

SCHOOL MEAL SERVICE

This is a most important aspect of Welfare Catering. All school meals served should reach the required nutritional standard. The aim of all local authorities is to provide a certain heat energy value of dietary components for a child in his mid-day meal. The energy value of food is measured in joules The average school meal should aim at the following energy contents:
1. Under 7 years—min of 2090 joules (500 cal)
2. 7 - 11 years—   ,, of 2720 joules (650 cal)
3. Over 11 years—   ,, of 3350 joules (800 cal)

The aim of the menu is to provide as much variety as possible. No main course meat dish should appear more than once in a two week period. Salad and raw vegetable appear as often as possible and either the 1st or 2nd course is always a hot dish. In infant schools small concentrated meals are required containing plenty of protein and less carbohydrates.

The problems of providing a meal according to the standard briefly outlined above are many and varied. It is sufficient to say that the school meals service is subsidized and has been growing steadily over the last quarter of a century until at the present time we have a growth rate of somewhere in the region of 25 million meals per year, involving the School Meals service in a net annual expenditure of over £100 million at the end of the financial year 1967/1968. To this has to be added a yearly estimated increase in costs of five and a half million pounds. There is a need therefore to have a new look at and approach to the school meals service.

There are many problems to overcome if the School Meal service is to pay its way more than it has done in the past. These may be listed briefly as follows:

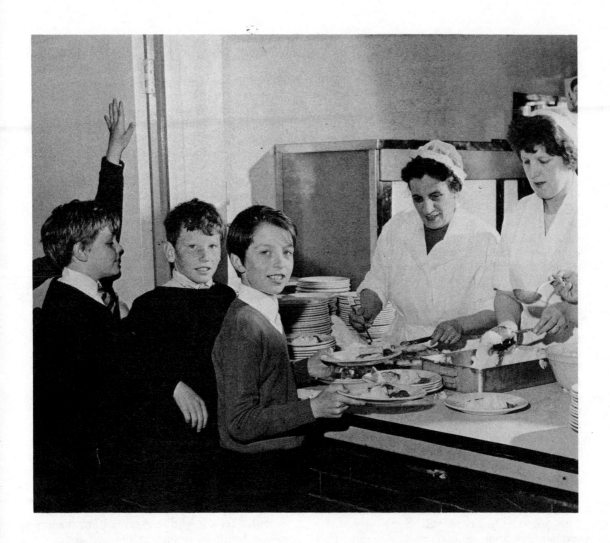

1. Labour problems—shortage of trained and unskilled staff.—labour costs which are certain to rise.
2. Many of the large items of cooking equipment are used far less than a quarter of the time available and the rest of the time stand idle. They are under used, therefore and are not giving full value for money.
3. Staff spend a greater percentage of their time involved in the menial tasks of washing up clearing up and preparation as opposed to actual cooking. This takes time and therefore money.
4. A fantastic amount of capital is invested in kitchens and their equipment to provide one meal a day from Monday to Friday.
5. For approximately 12 weeks each year—school holidays—the kitchen does not func-

tion. Might not this staff and the kitchens and equipment be utilised in some other way to cut down much wastage of labour, materials and space.
6. Costs of transport to deliver meals from a centralised kitchen to schools in the area. This cost alone can amount to thousands of pounds per annum. Where this is the case it is generally not feasible to build a kitchen in each of the schools concerned. Therefore alternative methods for the provision and service of school meals will have to be found.
7. Washing up in many schools is a problem as it has to be done by hand. This again involves cost and time and causing great difficulties in the kitchen if for some reason the washer-up does not arrive. Is the answer here the use of disposables? This is now being looked into as

a thought for the future. It would also do away with the problems of storage and breakages.

How can these problems, or most of them, be overcome in the future. One answer would be to have centralised food production with a working unit working to full capacity for 8 hours a day. All meals produced would be immediately blast frozen sealing in both nutritive value and flavour with no loss of colour. The meals on distribution would be reheated by placing in a forced air circulation oven. This oven takes the same length of time to reheat all forms of food from custard to chips. This then means that the meals would be transported from a centralised kitchen to the various schools in their frozen state in insulated containers. The only item of equipment then needed is the forced air circulation oven to reheat the meals ready for service. Washing up would virtually be eliminated by the use of disposables and beverages to be served could possibly come from an automatic vending machine. If this system came into operation nationally it would mean a complete reversal of old ideas of a new kitchen with every new school, and would be a great saving in space. This system is already in operation in some hospitals. The other main advantage is that meal production could be carried on for 8 hours per day, 5 days per week and right throughout the school vacations, thus utilising the food production unit, both staff and equipment, to the full. The deep freeze store holding the frozen meals acts as the link between preparation and service. On average no food would be held in a frozen state for more than 8-10 weeks. Quality of all meals would be standardised from the food production unit. This is looking to the future but these are the possible developments.

We have mentioned briefly that there is the possibility of using disposables in the schools meal service of the future. The 'Top Tray' or Meal-on-a-tray system where the tray is discarded after consumption of the meal is the first possibility. Here there is a space and labour saving advantage because frozen food is being used. Also a competent hand can more than double the meals she is able to serve when the meal-on-a-tray system is used as against the conventional kitchen catering and service methods. Other savings are in labour for washing up, water heating, cost of detergents and capital expenditure on equipment and breakages. A further major consideration is hygiene. Young children are very vulnerable to illness and the spread of all forms of infection. The use of disposable plates, cutlery, place-mats and cups would cut out the possibility of cross-infection from handler to consumer. The use of disposables in schools is the fastest growing sector of the vending industry in the U.S.A.

The meals-on-wheels service, another aspect of Welfare Catering is also very slowly turning over to this method of producing and serving meals.

The likely changes in the School Meals Service are great but it will be a slow and gradual process as development must be accepted by parents and children alike. It is possible that by the 1980's we will be looking back on the present conventional kitchen production and service set up as history and accepting frozen foods, blast freezing, forced air circulation ovens, meals-on-trays, micro-wave ovens, disposables and may be even a refined 'micro-vending automatic meal service' as common place in all our schools.

PUBLIC HOUSE CATERING

Public house catering is something which has developed suddenly and rapidly over the past few years. Now many of the large breweries are planning rapid expansion programmes to give training to all grades of staff in their houses with particular emphasis on the catering services to be provided.

The 'pub' or 'house' may be managed in two ways.

1. By the tenant who buys himself in, the sum involved being according to the size and contents of the establishment concerned. The tenant then buys the breweries beer, sells it and retains a certain percentage of the profit.

2. A brewery can employ a manager to take care of all operations both food and drink, and pay him a salary. The number of pubs or houses incorporating restaurants providing a full meal, rather than the accepted snacks and sandwiches has more than trebled over the past few years. Here equal thought is given to the catering service and the drink service. The reasons for this sudden developement is that the public are eating out as a habit rather than a luxury and they do not mind spending that little extra for quality, quantity and service in the right price range. The luncheon voucher trade is something not to be overlooked and if menu's are within this range then the houses will benefit

by attracting this market. In most cases food as food is not provided to help increase drink sales, but often no drink would be sold if food service was not provided. Food and drink naturally go together.

One of the major problems is staff. To retain staff you must show interest in them and get them interested in the job. This is done by providing training both on and off the job. Two main factors are taken into account here:

1. The standard which the trainee has already attained, and
2. His specific training requirements according to the job.

Three types of courses are offered and cover each area of the licensed trade from cellar management, bar service to catering. They are as follows:
a) A basic training for new entrants to the licensed trade
b) An upgrading course for those with limited experience.
c) A refresher course for the more experienced in order that they may attain certain standards.

The general approach in all pubs and houses seems to be a standard menu with only a variation in dishes according to locality or the speciality of the tenant or manager. Other features such as décor, tableware, and furnishing vary from house to house, to give each its own atmosphere. Great emphasis is put on the use of convenience foods and pre-prepared foods. A number of pubs have installed micro-wave ovens, which are used to heat, in seconds, pre-prepared and plated dishes which come straight from the refrigerator as ordered. The meals themselves can be served in the plastic ovenware that they are stored and heated in. Perhaps a disadvantage of the microwave is that the 'through-put' or 'turnover' of dishes is not very fast, especially at peak periods. Secondly the micro-wave does not colour and therefore it has to be used in conjunction with a high speed grill.

The following is a guide to the range of dishes which might be found on various pubs or house menus:

1. English beef with yorkshire pudding Horseradish Sauce
2. Gammon steak poached in cider
3. Beef casserole flavoured with ale
4. Galway oysters
5. Irish stew
9. Shepherds pie
7. Faggots
8. Sausages
9. Hot dog
10. Hamburger
11. Steak & kidney pie
12. Steak and mushroom pie
13. Apple pie
14. Braised steak
15. Salad Counter: Assorted. Have as much as you wish within price of the meal.
16. Egg and bacon pie
17. Curried beef and rice
18. Home made paté
19. Grills
20. Lobster
21. Salmon
22. Jugged hare pie
23. Cheese board
24. Gaelic coffee

There are obviously problems in production, not so much in the newly built houses where proper catering facilities are incorporated, but in the old established public houses which were not originally equipped to cope with food production. What sells the food is presentation over the counter, together with ample portions at competitive prices. Today's manager or tenant has at his command a wide range of equipment and specially prepared food dishes which are all aimed at use in public house catering. He must make use of these facilities in order to progress. At the same time speed of service and turnover of custom is very important in order to fully utilise all equipment and space provided for catering. The types of equipment used vary from pub to pub and house to house. Some of that used is listed below:

1. Deep freeze
2. Refrigerator
3. Bain Marie
4. Grill
5. Gas oven
6. Heated display unit
7. Deep fat frying
8. Mini-chef unit
9. Salamander
10. Micro-wave
11. Infra-red grill
12. Cona coffee machine

Undoubtedly Public House catering, is here to stay. The method of service however is bound to change over the years. Automatic vending machines for the dispensing of beers, spirits, and minerals will soon be coming on the market. Can this take over the present day methods of drink service and perhaps form a unit with the Micro-vend Buffet thus giving us the complete service through coin operated machines of alcoholic beverages and hot and cold snacks? This may be a thought for the future especially if we bear in mind the problems of staffing for 7 days a week, of the range of hours that a house is open, split shift, and the fact that wages are bound to rise. This of course is not the complete answer but could be part of it. The house of the future will also provide much more entertainment in the form of dancing, music, coin operated machines, and will be the meeting place for the house wife over coffee and a snack.

This could mean a pub or house would be virtually open from morning till late at night, with a larger team of staff being required on a two shift system.

AIRLINE CATERING

This is a branch of catering which has increased rapidly over the past 25 years. Its growth and development are mainly the result of introducing tourist and economy class fares and the vast number of passengers who now travel by air. It has expanded the horizons of the business world and it has given the ordinary man a hunger and thirst to see parts of the world which 50 years ago would have been out of his reach.

First class service on a Quantas V jet.

Initially in Great Britain there was one large airline of repute, namely the 'Imperial Airways'. In 1944 three airlines were formed into a national corporation, these being B.O.A.C., B.S.A.A., and B.E.A. In 1968 approx. 12 million passengers flew in or out of London airport. B.O.A.C. is one of the largest airlines, and they carry approximately 1 million passengers a year all over the world over a network of routes of nearly 113 000 kilometres.

The International Air Transport Association (I.A.T.A.) thought it necessary to lay down maximum standards of meals in both the tourist and economy classes, because of the vast increase in the number of customers. The standard of meals was obviously lowered in ratio with the smaller fare paid, and the sudden vast increase in numbers created demands the

kitchens could not meet. The cabin crews had to serve more meals in the same time, and their numbers proved inadequate. The first catering seen on planes was virtually a packed lunch of assorted sandwiches and a thermos of tea, and it was a case of take it or leave it. Within five years a completely new B.E.A. catering kitchen, was inadequate to meet the demand put on it. B.E.A. now have a new *catering commissary* which is fully automated with a conveyor system to cope with all demands. A commissary is a term used to cover the catering, cabin requirements, bonded stores, cleaning and other passenger requirements, which are all stored under one roof.

The International Air Transport Association lays down standards, for the scope of a meal rather than the price, since costs would obviously vary in two different countries thousands of kilometres apart. It is now recognised that where only short distances and flight times are involved then only snack type meals, open sandwiches and beverages are offered. Where longer distances are involved then the cabin staff and stewardesses have time to give a first class service of food and beverages, be it silver or gueridon service.

Apart from the two or three main airlines many other smaller airlines have built up catering units, as have many private companies to cater for the various airlines flying into London airport. Some of these are Fortes Flight Catering, and the Gatwick based flight catering firm, NAS Airport Services.

For the economy and tourist flights all meals must be of the same size and with all portions identical. The meals are arranged in silver foil individual trays, sealed, frozen and then stored until required. At times 4 tonnes of frozen food may be in cold storage waiting to be used. For the first class passenger, who would receive a food and beverage service equivalent to that of a first class hotel or restaurant, there would be no portion control. The service would be such that joints may be carved from a carving trolly as it moves up the central aisle, and served with the appropriate garnish and vegetables. This combined with the fine bone china, silver plate, fine glassware and cutlery used creates an atmosphere of content and well-being whilst the meal is being served. The economy or tourist class meal would be served on a plastic or melamine tray using disposable place mats, cutlery and serviettes and disposable glasses for any drinks required. Great use is made here of pre-portioned foods such as salt, peppers, mustards, sugars, cream, cheeses, dry biscuits, preserves, etc. This aids portion control, cuts down on wastage and reduces washing up and breakages.

When all the food has been cooked the required quantities of each portion are placed in the dish by the 'servers'. Garnish would be added where appropriate. This dish may then be placed into hot cupboards and kept hot until being transported into the plane where they would be plugged into the aircrafts supply. An alternative to this would be that the meal is frozen, stored in the catering unit until required and when necessary re-heated on board the aircraft.

Conveyor belts are used for cold dishes made up of a variety of cold items, and the dishes pass down a slow moving belt and 'servers' add the necessary items in their correct order. To help this process a colour photograph of the dish concerned is used as a visual reminder to the 'servers' as to what the end product should look like. The completed trays have to be stored in air-larders on shelves very close together because of the shortage of space. Therefore there has to be a height limit for the contents of a dish—usually 5 centimetres (2 inches). We now have the hot food stored in hot cupboards and the cold food in air larders.

We have said that under the one roof of the commissary we find everything needed for a flight. To complete the service to the passenger other items have to be provided apart from hot and cold food and beverages. These would include—newspapers, brochures, toys, crayons, playing cards, first aid kits, slipperettes, toilet requisites, pens, magazines, etc.

Over 500 catering staff work to provide the meals and snacks for the passengers carried by B.O.A.C. As an example of the quantities of food used in such an exercise.

Annually: 50000 Roasting chickens
20000 Boiling chickens
Weekly: 78 Bottles of liqueurs
650 Magnums of Champagne
1200 Bottles of wine
1500 Cans of beer
350000 Cigarettes
Daily: 355 kg (7 cwt) Potatoes
360 Lettuce
68 kg (150 lbs) Strawberries (Seasonal)
60 Bundles Asparagus
108 kg (240 lbs) Tomatoes
45 kg (100 lbs) Fresh Salmon
34 kg (75 lb) Smoked Salmon
200 Soles

These quantities go towards producing an average of 5000 meals and 2000 snacks per day. It is worth mentioning at this stage that the commissaries are regulary inspected by Public Health Inspectors and the airlines' own health authorities.

Fortes Flight Catering Company caters for numerous airlines, including *Alitalia* (Italian Airlines), *Trans World Airlines* and *Aer Lingus* (Irish International Airlines). Because of the variety of airlines catered for there are many special requirements. *Alitalia* want hot meals taken on board on hot trollies and kept at a constant temperature on the plane. This is because the trip is short and the meals therefore need to be ready for immediate service. *Trans World Airlines* on the other hand need the meals to be loaded in a chilled or frozen state so that they may be re-heated as and when required on the longer trip to America.

To cope with the demand for meals and beverages and the various requirements of the different airlines as much labour saving equipment as possible is used. This includes:

Washing machine: cleans, sterilizes and dries 12,000 pieces of equipment per hour.

Bread and butter machine: Producing 55 slices of buttered bread per minute.

Coffee stills: Producing 54 litres (12 gallons) every 20 minutes.

Auto Ice Units: Making 1.5 kg (3 lb) of ice cubes every minute.

Each airline will supply its own equipment such as cutlery, china, glassware and so on. They will also provide certain foods from their own countries for the catering unit to incorporate in their particular menu's. *Alitalia* would provide salami, sausages, etc.

All alcoholic beverages and cigarettes will be drawn from the bonded stores on the catering premises under the watchful eye of a representative of Customs and Excise.

When the aircraft is in the air it is the well trained cabin crew who provide the service to the passengers. Their job at times is very difficult especially when the time for a trip is very short, i.e., 45-60 minutes in which a meal has to be served. No cooking is done on a flight apart from some ancillary items such as toast, making beverages and so on. High speed circulation ovens heat 48 meals in 20 minutes. The tray with the meal on it sits on a pull-out table. In between meals tea, coffee, biscuits and cakes are served together with cold drinks. If special dishes are required for vegetarians, children or invalids this will be done. The menus and wine lists are presented in a colourful and decorative fashion. An example of these menu's and wine lists would be as follows:

Tourist Class
Smoked salmon
Roast saddle of English lamb
Broccoli spears   New potatoes
Fruit gâteaux
Cheese and biscuits
Coffee

First Class
Dinner   Cream of new carrots
Consommé yvette
Fillet of Dover sole bréval
Roast loin of English lamb; mint sauce
Buttered French beans   Château potatoes
Cold buffet; Tossed green salad
Vinaigrette or Rôquefort dressing
Gâteau milles feuilles with dairy cream
English and continental cheeses
Cream crackers
Fresh fruit;
Café

Bar—Wine list
Apéritifs
Cocktails, Campari, Manhattan, Martini, Champagne
Highballs
Whiskey, Brandy, Gin, Rum
Sherry
Dry, Medium dry, Sweet
Gin
Gordons and Booths
Whisky
Scotch, Bourbon, Rye
Rum
West Indian
Beer
Soft Drinks

Wines
Selected Australian wines
Sydney, Singapore
Hock
Oppenheimer Krötenbrunnen 1963
Weingut Louis Guntrum
Burgundy
Chablis 1966
Collin and Bourisset
Nuits St. Georges 1964
Maison Groffier-Leger
Bordeaux
Château Haut-Marbuzet 1964
H. Duboscq
Champagne
Mumm
Cordon Rouge
Möet & Chandon
Première Cuvée
Liqueurs
Drambuie, Cointreau
VSOP brandy
Cockburns fine old tawny port

Bar service and beverages

Cocktails: Champagne, Manhattan
Old Fashioned, Martini (Sweet or Dry)
Vodka
Highballs: Bourbon, Scotch, Brandy, Gin, Rum
Sherries: Dry and Medium Dry
Whiskies: Scotch, Canadian, American
Beers: English, Lager
Juice: Orange, Tomato
Mineral Waters, Coca Cola, Squashes
Wines from the vineyards of Bordeaux and the
Côte d'Or
Champagne Cordon Rouge Brut
Drambuie, Cointreau
Bisquit Dubouché V.S.O.P.
Hot Beverages:
Tea, Coffe, Bovril
with sweet or dry biscuits
With your Coffee:
English or American cigarettes

As an investment for the future Fortes Flight Catering Division have extended their premises to cope with the '747 Jumbo Jets'. Seven a day, each carrying an average of 375 passengers. The Fortes Flight meal production area is claimed to be one of the finest in Europe.

N.A.S. Airport Services, who are already producing 5000 fresh and blast frozen meals per day at Gatwick are opening a second £ 50,000 kitchen at Crawley which will double its output to 2¼ million meals per year. Some of this range of frozen meals produced will be for banqueting, conferences—a new field N.A.S. have just entered. The new kitchen however is mainly built for the 'Jumbo Jets' and has a conveyor belt assembly and high capacity storage for frozen meals.

SHIP CATERING

Catering on board ship is vastly different to shore catering. It will be appreciated that conditions are entirely different. Most lines appoint what is termed a 'catering superintendent' or Superintendent Purser to be in charge of all catering afloat. He has an assistant and an agent ashore who will represent him. This agent is known as a Victualling Agent. The other chief members of staff aboard are the Purser, Chief Steward and Head Chef. These all work together to ensure the smooth and efficient running of the catering services on board ship. The type of catering varies between passenger service, cargo vessels and ships carrying mainly cargo and a small number of passengers. The service on a large passenger ship may be compared to that of a first class hotel ashore, and that on a cargo vessel to an industrial type of establishment. In the same way the Catering Superintendent may be compared with the Director of a hotel ashore; the Purser with the Hotel Manager; the Chief Steward with the Restaurant Manager and with the Head Chef in overall charge of the kitchens. Two main factors are aimed for by all steamship lines in competition with one another: service and speed. The passenger liners vary considerably in size from a tonnage of 1,500 up to 70-80,000. The type of catering service offered depends to a large extent on the following:

1. Length of trip
2. Type of passenger (first class, cabin, or tourist)
3. Cost
4. Facilities available

A stores department is responsible for all purchasing and the duties here may be sufficient to occupy two or three officers full-time, depending on the size of the passenger liner concerned. The majority of stores required are taken aboard at the home port, but every advantage would be taken by the ships officers concerned to buy at reasonable prices at any ports of call. All alcoholic drink is purchased in bond from bonded warehouses at the ports. The keys for the warehouses are held by both the Customs and Excise Officer and the Victualling Agent. Outside the '3 mile' limit drinks are sold at duty free prices. As many fresh foods as possible, of all varieties, are stored on board and these would be supplemented by a wide variety of frozen foods.

The ocean going passenger liners are like floating hotels with great consideration being given to heating, lighting, ventilation, space allocation, equipment furnishing and the general comfort of the passenger. Many amenities are provided, such as, libraries, ballroom, swimming pool, laundries, and shops. In the case of large steamship lines with ocean going passenger liners the Catering Superintendent remains ashore and controls and directs from his office desk, deciding on policy and issuing directives.

The kitchen on board ship is known as the Galley. The kitchen equipment used is normally oil or electricity fired. The menu's offered in large passenger liners are equivalent to, if not

The grill room on the quarter deck of **Queen Elizabeth 2** which is decorated with life-size statues representing the four elements.

better than, those found in first class establishments ashore. Because of this highly skilled staff are needed to work in the kitchens, which are organised into the recognised parties. In the same way the food service areas have restaurant managers, head waiters, chef and commis de rang and wine butlers. The service given is full silver service and may involve the use of a carving trolly, sweet trollies, a central cold buffet and so on. Apart from this main food service offered in the restaurants there are supplementary food services offered in smoke rooms, saloons, lounges and private cabins.

The cost the passenger pays for food on board ship is generally inclusive with the fare, and according to 'class' an allowance per head, per day is made for catering purposes. It is generally accepted that all drinks and other purchases are paid for at the time of 'sale'. To give one an appreciation of the food stores that need to be

taken on, the following are approximate quantities required for a ship taking 650 passengers and 450 crew on a six week voyage:

17 tonnes of meat
 6 tonnes of poultry
10 tonnes of fish
18 tonnes of dairy produce
75 thousand eggs
33 tonnes of groceries
48 tonnes of fresh and root vegetables, salads and fruit.

The following are quantities of wines, spirits and tobacco sold during the voyage of a 45 000 tonne ship carrying 600 first class and 1 700 tourist class passengers.

250 dozen bottles of wine
230 dozen bottles of spirit
29 550 litres (6 500 gallons) of beer
 3 500 bottles of minerals
790 000 cigarettes

3600 cigars
115 kg (250 lb) tobacco

It will be realised from the examples given how important it is for proper use to be made of all available space for storage, and for great care to be exercised in ordering of foods for the type of passenger one is carrying in relation to the length of voyage.

All stores taken on board are placed in storerooms or cold rooms which are maintained by refrigeration machinery. The foods stored in the latter must be kept at certain temperatures to ensure that when it is required for use it is in perfect condition. Great care is taken over hygiene as this can very quickly affect both crew and passengers and regular inspections are carried out by the Purser who is in overall charge, whilst afloat, of all the catering services.

For the food service the area used for 1st class service is usually large enough to seat all first class passengers at one sitting but for Cabin and Tourist class it is usual to operate two sittings. The waiter ratio to passengers according to the type of menu offered, would be as follows:

1st class   2 waiters to 11 passengers
Tourist class   1   ,,   ,, 10   ,,
Cabin class   1   ,,   ,, 8   ,,

It was originally the custom for all meal service to be given by male waiters. Fairly recently however experiments have been carried out using waitresses or as they are termed aboard: Stewardettes. A great deal of attention and thought is given to the service to the individual on the occasion of a special anniversary or birthday. This creates an atmosphere of goodwill which is passed on to the rest of the passengers and is a means of advertising the facilities and services on board the ship and thus eventually creating more demand for passages abroad.

From this brief examination of Ship Catering it can be seen that it demands the same qualities of initiative, organisation and administration, and an ability to control staff from the Catering superintendent, Purser, Chief steward and Head Chef as from their equals in a 1st class hotel ashore. There are obviously great differences between the large ocean going passenger liner and those smaller passenger liners which only travel short distances and with a limited number of passengers. But the difference is no greater than that between catering ashore in a 1st class establishment or in an institution.

The essence should still be to provide every facility possible to create efficient service for the passenger.

A tourist class breakfast menu

BREAKFAST
Iced tea   Iced coffee
Juices: orange   pineapple
Stewed prunes   Preserved damsons
Quaker oats Sugar frosted flakes Puffed rice
Grape-nuts   Shredded wheat
Cream   Yoghourt
Kippered herring
Eggs: fried   scrambled
Omelets: plain   Ox tongue
Bacon   Dry hash cakes with   Tomatoes
fried onions
Sauté potatoes
Cold: Roast sirloin of beef Breakfast sausage
Rolls   Toast
Jams   Honey   Marmalade   Golden syrup
Coffee   Ceylon and Indian tea   Cocoa
American coffee: Chase and Sanborn

A tourist class luncheon menu

LUNCHEON
Lentil soup
Salmon salad mayonnaise
Spaghetti and tomato sauce
Steak and kidney pudding
Grill to Order:
Lamb cutlets, réforme
Cold: Leicester pie   Brisket of beef
Lettuce, celery and red cabbage salad
Lemon dressing
Buttered carrots   Boiled potatoes
Sweets
Assorted jellies   Fruit salad
Pistachio ice cream
Cheese
New Zealand cheddar   Danish blue
Biscuits
Dessert
Ceylon and Indian tea   Coffee
American coffee: Chase and Sanborn

Tea and Coffee are also served in all Public Rooms

A tourist class dinner menu

DINNER
Tomato juice
Consommé lorette
Boiled salmon, mousseline sauce
Devilled breast of lamb with mushrooms
Fried chicken, sweet corn cakes,   Horseradish
cream
Cold: Melton Mowbray pie   Terrine of game
Lettuce and salad russe
Chantilly dressing
Green peas   Allumette potatoes
Sweets
Fruit sponge trifle   Meringue glacé
Sardines on toast
Cheese
New Zealand cheddar   Gorgonzola
Biscuits
Dessert   Ceylon and Indian tea   Coffee
American coffee: Chase and Sanborn

**Tea and Coffee are also served in all Public
Rooms**

A first class breakfast menu

BREAKFAST
Iced tea   Iced coffee
Juices: orange, tomato, pineapple, liquid apple
Stewed prunes, Chilled raspberries, Preserved
pears,
Scotts porage oats
Rice krispies, Sugar frosted flakes, Grape-nuts
Puffed wheat   Weetabix
Cream   Yoghourt
Smoked haddock, Fried scallops, tomato sauce
Eggs: fried   poached   buttered
Omelets: plain   princess   celery
Bacon   Gammon slice   Tomatoes
Minute steak   Chipolata sausages
Sauté potatoes
Cold: ham   roast lamb
White and brown rolls   Danish pastries   Toast
Melba toast   Caraway seed   Vienna bread
Waffles
Hovis and procea bread
Jams   Honey   Marmalade   Golden syrup
Ceylon, Indian and China Tea Coffee Nescafé
Cocoa
American coffee: Sanka

A first class luncheon menu

LUNCHEON
Tomato juice   Hors d'oeuvre variés
Mulligatawny soup
Fillet of plaice, tartare sauce
Avocado pear and shrimp salad
Chicken liver omelet
Khandahar curry with rice
Vol-au-vent of beef and mushrooms
Pork and baked beans en casserole
Mixed Grill to Order:
Cold: Ham corned silverside of Beef
Potato salad
Tossed green salad, Roquefort dressing
Buttered cabbage   Broad beans, parsley sauce
Potatoes: baked jacket   bataille   boiled
Sweets
Chocolate layer cake   Orange pancakes
Lemon ice cream
Cheese
Specially matured   Gouda   Gruyère   Port du
English cheddar   Salut
Double Gloucester   Assorted biscuits
Dessert
Coffee Ceylon, Indian and China tea Nescafé
American coffee: Sanka   Chase and Sanborn

**Tea and Coffee will be served in the Res-
taurant only**

A first class dinner menu

DINNER
Swiss pâté truffé   Fruit cocktail
Consommé lorette   Potage andalouse
Iced consommé
Dover sole niçoise
Dover sole veronique
Lamb pilau
Green peppers piemontaise
Venison with cucumber tartlets, Cumberland
sauce
Roast duck with baked apple, liver and sage
stuffing
Grill to Order:
Fillet steak, continental
Cold: ham   Ox tongue   Lettuce and
artichoke salad
Tossed green salad, tarragon dressing
Green peas Française   Buttered parsnips
Potatoes: château   boiled

A familiar scene under canvas for those involved with outdoor catering. Quantities of strawberries being plated-up under the eagle eye of the cook in charge of the function.

Sweets

Strawberry gâteau   Meringue glacé
Petits-Fours   Assorted pastries
Olive talmousse
New Zealand cheddar   Gruyère
Assorted biscuits
Dessert   Crystallised ginger
Coffee   Ceylon, Indian and China tea   Nescafé
American coffee: Sanka   Chase and Sanborn
Tea and Coffee are also served in all Public Rooms

OUTDOOR CATERING (O.D.C.)

Outdoor Catering is a specialist aspect of the catering industry and deserves special consideration. Many catering establishments whether large or small do a limited amount of Outdoor Catering—i.e. away from ones own private premises or catering establishment. Some firms specialise entirely in Outdoor Catering, providing all the equipment, tentage, staff, foodstuffs and alcoholic liquor necessary for a particular function, where this is the case one requires expert administration and planned organisation down to the last detail. REMEMBER that once a unit has left the firms Outdoor Catering depot there is no time for them to return for anything forgotten. If Outdoor Catering is ones first contact with the catering industry as a whole then very often the problems experienced may be sufficient to discourage entry into the profession. Some of these problems are due to working conditions; staff problems; lack of equipment or proper facilities for the job in hand. Staff must be adaptable; of an even temperament and at the same time be willing and hard workers. Outdoor Catering may cover many different types of function apart from those mentioned under 'Banqueting'. Some of these are:

a) Exhibitions
b) Garden parties
c) Agricultural shows
d) Sales shows
e) Regattas
f) Air shows
g) Weddings
h) Rallies

The business of an Outdoor Catering firm should as far as possible continue throughout the year to ensure that the **plant** (equipment provided for a particular function) and staff are used to the full. At each function carried out the organiser should aim to give a fully comprehensive sales service, covering not only meals and drinks but such things as confectionery, cigarette, hot-dog kiosks etc. We have already said the organisation must be planned to the last detail and an initial survey must be exact and thorough. The following points should be included in the initial survey:

a) Type of function
b) Date
c) Site and distance from depot
d) Local transport
e) Local commodity purchase
f) Staff recruitment
g) Lay-out of site
h) Number of people expected to attend
i) Availability of water, gas, electricity, drainage, refrigeration
j) Spending power of people attending
k) Kiosk and stand details
l) Time allowance for setting up catering units and dismantling
m) Type of license: if required
n) Mobile units adaptable to hot/cold food
o) Lines of communication to ensure control of staff and continuous supplies.
p) Photographers
q) Press
r) Changing room and toilets
s) Insurance against weather/fire
t) First aid
u) Cost of overheads on a particular site
v) Type of service: find the one most suited to each particular catering operation
   1. Buffet style service may be preferred to restaurant service.
   2. Provision of the take-away meal service in disposable containers.
   3. Supply of some simple hot dishes: soup, fish, and chips etc.
   4. Flexibility of drink service: hot or cold—according to weather.
w) Washing-up facilities.
x) Containers supplied for litter and disposable items.

Each outdoor catering operation is different and varies to some extent in the main points that have to be noted during the initial survey.

From the basic list shown above one appreciates the organisation needed beforehand and some of the problems that may arise at the outset or during an operation. The person in charge needs to be decisive, quick-thinking, able to command, adaptable to varying situations and circumstances and above all have the respect of the staff working under him. Always **remember** that it is very easy for the inexperienced caterer to run at a loss, but to run at a profit demands certain standards and qualities of both the caterer, his staff and the service he provides.

DISPOSABLES

We have mentioned briefly the term 'Disposables'.

In outdoor catering particularly this and all the other aspects have to be considered very carefully from the point of view of cost. If the *cost* goes too high our profit becomes less and less, or we even make a loss. It is the trend in many establishments today to use *disposables* to help cut costs. At the same time the disposables must be both attractive, presentable and acceptable to the client and help to attract customers. When it is noted that the national expenditure on food in 1967 was only 4/4d (21½p) in every £, it will be realised that it is not only the food that attracts the customer into a food and beverage service establishment but how it is presented—the type of equipment used—the furnishings and fittings—staff and many other things which combine as a whole to attract the potential client.

The growth in the market of *Disposables* or *Throw-aways* as they are sometimes termed is due to a number of factors, namely:
a) The need to reduce costs
b) The difficulty of obtaining labour for washing-up.
c) The cutting of the high cost of laundering.
d) Improved standards of hygiene
e) Breakage costs are minimised
f) Less storage space is required.

The types of disposables that may be used to replace the normal restaurant linen would be serviettes, place mats, traycloths, tablecloths, coasters etc. When considering hygiene, it is in the use of the conventional glass cloth for drying up that cross infection is more likely to occur. This risk is eliminated when disposables are used. The caterer must always bear in mind that his is an industry where eye-appeal and the creation of the right atmosphere are particularly important, and therefore disposables must be made to fit into all levels of catering establishment.

Most forms of disposables can today be of various colours, patterned or have the house style motto or crest reproduced on them. A disposable serviette is not so inclined to slip off the knee as a linen serviette. Then again with the vast range of colours available one can ring the changes in a food and beverage service area with different colours for each meal, provided that it blends with the surroundings. Throw away packs of knives, forks and spoons are both more convenient and hygienic where the turnover of custom is very high over very short periods of time. This might apply in industrial canteens and transport catering. It will eliminate delays at service points where the speed of washing-up is inadequate.

In hospitals where any form of cross infection should be avoided a great variety of disposables are used. This gives a substantial saving in staff time and costs.

A considerable advance in the range of disposables available has been the introduction into this country in 1968 of the CHI-NET range.

The approximation to china-tableware is very close. It has a high quality, overall finish and a smooth hard white surface. The plates themselves are strong and rigid with no tendency to bend or buckle, and a plasticising ingredient ensures that they are grease and moisture proof, even against hot fat and gravy. Through this range there is an oval luncheon plate, snack tray and compartment plate all of which are quite new to this market.

A selection of disposables'

24 banqueting

Introduction

Banqueting is the term used to cover the service of special functions in an establishment which is separate from the normal service found in the various restaurants, grill rooms and on the floors and in the lounge. It would include functions such as luncheon parties, conferences, cocktail parties, weddings, dinner-dances and so on. In the large first class establishments all functions would take place within the banqueting suites and be under the administrative control of the Banqueting manager.

In the smaller hotel these functions would normally take place in a room set aside for the purpose and come under the jurisdiction of the Hotel manager or Asst. manager. Most of the staff available for functions are employed on a casual basis. At busy periods there may be two or more functions running at the same time.

Types of function:

There are two main types of function which come under the heading banqueting, and these may be called:
1. *Formal Meals*
   Luncheons
   Dinners
   Wedding breakfasts
2. *Buffet Reception*
   Wedding reception
   Cocktail parties
   Buffet teas
   Running buffets for dances etc.
   Anniversary parties
   Hunt balls
   Conferences

A *further* breakdown of the *types of function* may be as follows:

Social
Dinners (Old Boys)
Luncheons (Rotarians)
Receptions
Cocktail parties
Charity performance
Fashion parades

Conferences (Most profitable type of function)
National and international sales
Industrial Training Boards

Public relations
Press party to launch a new product
Fashion parade
Exhibitions
Dealers meetings
Seminars

Season

The banqueting season runs approximately from October to May.

Banqueting staff
In large first class establishments there is generally a small nucleus of permanent staff dealing with banqueting alone. These would include Banqueting manager, one or two Asst. banqueting managers, one or two Banqueting head waiters, a Dispense barman and a secretary to the Banqueting manager. In smaller establishments where there are fewer functions the necessary administrative and organisational work would be undertaken by the Manager, Asst. manager and Head waiter.

The Sales Administration Manager of a Group or Company of Hotels.

The main object of the Sales administration manager is to sell the banqueting facilities of a hotel to a client, and where necessary make the initial approach and contact. After this he refers the client to the Banqueting manager concerned. Because of the varied make-up of each banqueting suite in the various hotels the Sales administration manager must have an extensive knowledge of room specifications, size, light switches, electric points, heights of doorways, maximum floor loads etc. This enables him to give positive and negative answers to any requests at his initial meeting with a client without causing any delay to either party. A certain approach is required when meeting a client, who must immediately be made to feel at ease. The first thing to determine is how much cash the client has available per head, and to decide whether his requests come within that particular price range. If not this must be made clear right from the start. The client must also be given by the Sales administration manager a booklet of menus to study. These must be well presented and therefore act as a good selling point for the hotel concerned. The menus should be variable with a choice for each season of the year and to include such seasonable foods as game. The price range should be variable as well. The Sales administration manager must at the same time be a man of ideas. For very special occasions he should be able to make suggestions for that function. For instance a theme might be introduced to be carried throughout the meal i.e. Flowers, a popular colour, James Bond Dinner: soup with 007 pasta, speciality menu's and so on.

Banqueting Manager

He has the entire administrative responsibility. He meets the prospective clients, and discusses arrangements with them concerning menus, table plan, costs, wines, bands, toastmaster etc. He must send, to all the departments concerned, a memo, telling them the date of a function, numbers, and any further details that might be applicable to a certain department.

Secretary

Must work with the Banqueting manager and is reponsible for handling all incoming and outgoing mail, for seeing any memos dictated

are sent to the appropriate departments and for the correct filing of any correspondence. The secretary should handle all telephone calls, and in the absence of the Banqueting manager may take *Provisional Bookings* for functions ensuring the details are entered on the correct form *(Banqueting Memorandum* see page 168*)*. Bookings are generally made in one of three ways—by telephone, by letter, or by interview. All enquiries, however made, should be confirmed by letter.

Banqueting Head waiter

He is in charge of the banqueting suites and their organisation in getting them ready for various forms of functions. He may also be responsible for the engaging of staff, on a casual basis, to cover the various duties at a function. The Banqueting head waiter would normally have a list of names and addresses and telephone numbers of the best casual staff, and he will ensure that they are well employed. This shows results in that staff work well together as a team producing a good all round end result which benefits both the client and management. Casual staff are normally paid by the hour and also given a meal as part of their contract.

Dispense Barman

If he is a member of the permanent banqueting staff, he will be responsible for the allocation of bar stock for various functions, the setting up of the bars, the organisation of the bar staff, control of stock and cash during service and for stocktaking when a function is completed. He would also be responsible for the restocking of the banqueting dispense bar.

Banqueting Head Wine waiter

May work in conjunction with the Dispense barman, or if there is no permanent Dispense barman he may take over the latter's duties together with those of organising the banqueting wine waiter's and alloting them stations, giving them floats if there are cash wines and discussing the service with them.

Permanent waiting staff

These are usually experienced Chefs de rang who can turn their hand to any job concerning banqueting and who generally do most of the mise-en-place before the function, that is the laying of tables. Their job during service is mainly wine-waiting. They may also help to clear after service is completed.

Casual staff
Care is taken here as to the type of staff employed. They normally report approximately 1 hour before a function commences. They would be allocated stations and given a brief talk with regard to the procedure for the service of a particular function. After service they would be paid and then dismissed.

Porters
There are generally two or three porters on the permanent banqueting staff. They are essential members of staff as there is a great deal of heavy work to be carried out.

Points to note concerning the work of Banqueting waiters and Wine waiters

A *waiter* at a banquet is generally expected to serve between 8-10 covers on a station. Establishments vary on their service of guests at banquets. Generally the waiter commences at one end of his station and works along to the other end. He may however commence at the left of his station for one course and from the right for the next course, or for smaller parties he may serve from the right of the host and then right round the table. Apart from the top table no precedence is given to rank or sex at banquets. The waiters should all be numbered, once the stations are allocated, so that the waiter with a station furthest from the service entrance will be nearer the head of the queue at the hotplate. The waiters on the top table are always at the head of the queue and enter the room first with each successive course. No waiter commences service on his station until those on the top table have commenced their service.

A banqueting Wine Waiter
will serve approximately 25 covers, but this depends on the type of function, the amount of wines on offer, and whether any wine is inclusive in the price of the menu or if cash drinks are being served. The wine waiters will normally aid the food waiters with the service of vegetables and sauces for the main course. When cash drinks are served the wine waiters are normally given a float with which they will pay the cashier or barman as drinks are ordered and collected from the bar. The

responsibility then rests with the wine waiter to collect the cash for any drinks he has served. This should be done immediately the liqueurs are served and before the toasts commence. If any guests sign their bills or wish to pay by cheque this must first of all be confirmed by someone in authority. The wine waiters may also be required to serve aperitifs at a reception before the meal and if so they will be required to do the necessary mise-en-place to ensure the reception area is ready. i.e. ashtrays, cocktail snacks, setting-up of portable bar, polishing glasses, etc. They must ensure there are plenty of small tables available.

Booking a function
At the initial meeting of the Banqueting manager and the client a file must be opened recording all points mentioned concerning this particular function and to hold all correspondence received. If the enquiry is not immediately a firm booking then the provisional details are only pencilled in until the booking is confirmed. It would then be inked in. The Banqueting manager should have available specimen luncheon and dinner menus with the costs per head and photographs of the various table lay-outs for different numbers. This gives the client a clear picture of the facilities available in the price range he can afford.

After the initial meeting and the booking having been confirmed the following basic points should have been noted:

1. Type of function
2. Date
3. Time
4. No. of covers (final numbers 24 hours beforehand).
5. Price per head
6. Menu: method of service
7. Wines: inclusive or cash
8. Type of organisation
9. Table plan

After this the finer points should be decided upon:
1. Toastmaster
2. Band, cabaret, dancing
3. Place cards
4. Seating plan
5. Type of menu for printing: humerous, books, etc.
6. Specialist information: vegetarians, etc.

BANQUETING MEMORANDUM

Function	
Date of Function	
Name and Address of Organiser	**Information to:**
	Restaurant
Tele. No.	Kitchen
	Office
Number of Covers	Linen Room
	Cellar
Accommodation	Hall Porter

MENU	
	Time of Arrival _____
	Time of Departure _____
	Toast Master _____
	Sound Relays_____
	Commissionaires _____
	Car Park _____
	Cloak Rooms_____
WINES and BAR	Artistes_____
	Changing Rooms_____
	Flowers_____
	Table Plan and Place cards _____
	Menus_____

Cash or Credit _____	**Notes:**
Cigars and Cigarettes _____	
Occasional Licence and No. _____	

Specimen Banqueting menu's

Luncheon

a) Pâté maison
   Entrecôte steak chasseur
   Pommes parmentier
   Céleri braisé
   Iced meringue chantilly
   Café

b) Turtle soup, cheese straws
   Truite de rivière Normandie
   Selle d'agneau rôti
   Pommes fondantes
   Petit pois au beurre
   Pêche Melba
   Café

Dinner

a) Consommé au Xerès
   Filet de sole mornay
   Poulet sauté chez soi
   Pommes nouvelles à la menthe
   Haricots verts au beurre
   Bombe pralinée
   Café

b) Melon rafraiché
   Suprême de turbot waleska
   Filet de boeuf forestière
   Pommes parisienne
   Brocoli au beurre
   Savarin au fruits
   Café

Menus

There should be a varied choice of menu within a wide price range, with special menus available for occasions such as weddings; 21st birthday parties; New Year's Eve and so on. As functions are booked up months in advance special care is called for with regard to foods in season. The minimum number of courses is usually four plus coffee. These are made up by:

Hors d'oeuvre or a substitute	This is more popular today, but extra courses such as entrées, and savouries may be added. A combination of these courses can be made to suit the guests requirements.
Fish	
Meat	
Sweet	
Coffee	

Wines

The banqueting wine list should be small, but contain good wines from the main wine list and all these wines should be in good supply. Use a shipper of good repute who can ensure replacement supplies quickly. Wines may be inclusive with the meal or on a cash basis, the money, being payable to the sommeliers who work on a float system. Very often the aperitif served before a function is also inclusive with the meal, but if not there is generally a 'cash bar' set up in the reception area.

Tabling

The type of table plan put into operation for a particular function depends upon a number of major factors, these being:

1. Organisers wishes
2. Nature of the function
3. Size and shape of room where the function is to be held

4. Number of covers

For the smaller type of function a 'U' or 'T' shaped table may be used, or where the luncheon or dinner party is more informal there may be a top table and separate tables, round or rectangular for the various parties of guests. Where the function to be held has a very large number of covers then the generally accepted form of table plan is a top table and sprigs. However, before these various table plans can be shown to the organiser when a function is being booked, a great amount of consideration must be given to **spacing,** i.e. widths of covers, gangways, size of chairs and so on. This is to allow a reasonably comfortable seating space to each guest and at the same time giving the waiter sufficient room for the service of the meal. Also the gangway space must be such that two waiters may pass one another during the service without fear of any accident occurring. *Remember* that these factors must always be borne in mind to ensure that you seat the *maximum* number of covers in a limited area thus gaining maximum income from the particular room being used.

It is generally recognized that the minimum space between sprigs is 2 metres (6 ft). This is made up of 2 chair widths: from edge of table to back of chair (46 cm or 18 ins) plus a gangway of 1 metre (3 ft); allowing each waiter passing space.

A total of 2 metres. (6 ft)

Table widths are approximately 75 cm (2 ft + 6 in).

The length along the table per cover should be 50-60 cm (20-24 in).

The space from the wall to edge of the table should be a minimum of 1.4 metres (4' 6'') This is made up of a 1 metre (3 ft) gangway plus 1 chair width of 46 cm (18 in).

The height of the chair from the ground will vary according to the style and design but is approximately 46-50 cm (18-20 in).

The length of the table used is generally 2 metres (6 ft) but 1.2 and 1.5 metre lengths (4 and 5 ft) may be used to make up a sprig.

Round tables would be 1, 1.5 or 2 metres (3,5, or 6 ft) diameter with the appropriate extensions.

Suggested area allowance for sit-down functions per person is approximately 1/1.4 square metres (12-15 sq ft), for buffets the allowance is 0.9/1 square metres (10-12 sq ft).

Laying of cloths

The size of banqueting cloths is from 2 metres (6 ft) wide by 4 metres (12 ft) in length and then running upwards in length. i.e. 5½ metres (18 ft) and so on. These cloths would be used on top tables and sprigs and therefore very often avoid the necessity of overlapping when smaller size table cloths are used. When laid the centre crease should run straight down the centre of the table, and the overlap must be the same all round the table. All cloths should be in the same fold and have the same pattern. Any overlap of cloths should face away from the main entrance, so that the join is not visible to the guests as they look down the room on arrival. When laying the cloth it may require depending on its size, three or four waiters to manipulate it thus ensuring that it is laid correctly without creasing or becoming dirty.

Seating arrangements and plans

Of the total number of people attending a function it must be determined how many will be seated on the top table, and how many on the 'sprigs', round or oblong tables making up the full table plan. Ensure that you know whether the number on the top table includes the ends, and always avoid seating thirteen on the top table. All tables, with the exception of the top table, should be numbered, but again avoid using the number thirteen. In its place it would be permissable to use 12A. The table numbers themselves should be on stands of such a height that they may all be seen from the entrance of the banqueting room. The approximate height of the stands would be 75 cm (30 ins). After the guests are seated and before the service commences these stands are sometimes removed. If left they are an aid to the Sommelier when checking for cash wines. As far as possible when formulating your table plan, you should avoid seating guests with their backs to the top table. Normally there are three copies of the seating plan. These go to:

1. The organiser: so that he may check all necessary arrangements.
2. The guests: This seating plan would be placed in a prominent position in the entrance of the banqueting suite so that all guests may see where they have been seated and who else is sitting at their table, and the position of their table in the room.
3. The Banqueting manager: for reference purposes.

Examples of banquet organisation

Dinner of 110 guests: 15 guests on top table; 3 sprigs required
Method of work
1. Length of table required for top = 15 guests × 60 cm (2 ft) = 9 m (30 ft) or 5 × 2 m (6 ft) tables.
2. No. of covers on each sprig = 110—15 = 95:3 = 32, 32, 31.
   Therefore each side of a sprig will have 16 covers, except one of 15 covers.
3. Length of sprig = 16 covers × 60 cm (2 ft) = 9.7 m (32 ft) or 6 × 2 m (6 ft) tables.
4. To check if three sprigs may be fitted to the top table =
   3 Sprigs × 75 cm (2 ft 6 in) wide = 2.25 m (7 ft 6 in) ⎫
   2 Gangways × 1 m (3 ft) wide = 2 m (6 ft) ⎬ 6 m (19 ft 6 in)
   4 Chair widths × 46 cm (18 in) = 2 m (6 ft) ⎭
   Thus there is plenty of room.

An alternative method of seating at the same table plan
1. Use 5 × 2 m (6 ft) tables per sprig instead of 6 × 2 m (6 ft) giving a length of 9 m (30 ft).
2. This will then accommodate 15 covers on each side allowing 60 cm (2 ft) per person.
3. Total number of covers down the sides of the sprigs is 6 × 15 = 90 covers.
4. This leaves 5 covers to be accommodated.
5. This may be done as follows:
   1 either end of the top table = 2
   1 either end of the sprigs = 3
   Total = 5

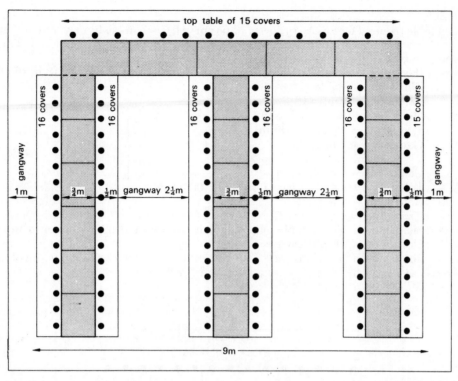

Table and seating plan
General

Plan 1 allows for 5 extra covers in case of emergency.

Plan 2 is very close and allows for no extra covers.

This plan may be effective in a smaller size room.

If the Host had wished could a similar plan have been evolved making the table plan more compact compact and therefore fitting into a slightly smaller sized room.

i.e. Can we get four sprigs on a 9 m (30 ft) long top table?

4 Sprigs × 75 cm (2 ft 6 in)	= 3 m (10 ft)	
3 Gangways × 1 m (3 ft)	= 3 m (9 ft)	9 m (28 ft) *total*
6 Chair widths × 46 cm (1 ft 6 in)	= 3 m (9 ft)	

Therefore four sprigs will give a more compact layout and bring everyone closer to the speakers on the top table.

THE USE OF A TOP TABLE AND ROUND TABLES:

110 covers. 15 on the top. 95 covers on round tables.

Dimension of Room = 18 m (60 ft) long by 11 m (36 ft) wide.

How many covers can sit at a round table?

To find the circumference of a round table we say: diameter × π

If π = 22/7 then it is diameter × 22/7.

Therefore a round table 1 m (3 ft) in diameter will seat =

$$1 \text{ m} \times 22/7 = 22/7 = 3\,^1/_7 \text{ or } 3 \text{ m.}$$
$$3 \times 3^1/_7 = 66/7 = 9\,^3/_7 \text{ or } 9 \text{ ft.}$$

Allowing 60 cm (2 ft) per person = *4 covers*

Round table 1.5 m in diameter	=	1.5 × 22/7 =	33/7 = 4.7 m or 470 cm.	*Allows 8 covers.*
– or – (5 ft)	=	5 × 22/7 =	110/7 = 15 $^5/_7$ or 16 ft.	*Allows 8 covers.*
2 m	=	2 × 22/7 =	44/7 = 6.3 m or 630 cm.	*Allows 11 covers.*
– or – (7 ft)	=	7 × 22/7 =	154/7 = 22 ft.	*Allows 11 covers.*

Method of work

1. Length of table required for top = 15 guests × 60 cm (2 ft) = 9 m (30 ft) or 5 × 2 m (6 ft) tables.
2. Number of covers on each round table = 110 — 15 = 95:8 = 11 × 8 and 1 × 7. This will be using round tables all the same size = 1.5 m (5 ft) *diameter*.
3. To check if the tables as per the table plan will fit in length of the room i.e. 18 m (60 ft).
   From wall behind the top table:

Top table	Gangway = 1 m (3 ft) Chair = 46 cm (1 ft 6 in) Top table = 75 cm (2 ft 6 in) Gangway = 1 m (3 ft)	} 3 m (10 ft)
Rounds	Chairs = 1 m (3 ft) Table = 1.5 m (5 ft) Gangway = 1 m (3 ft) *Times* × 4 = 3.5 m (11 ft)	} 14 m (44 ft)

   } 17 m (54 ft)

4. To check if the tables as per the table plan will fit in the width of the room i.e. 11 m (36 ft).
   3 Round tables 1.5 m (5 ft) in diameter = 4.5 m (15 ft)
   6 Chair widths at 46 cm (1 ft 6 in) each = 3 m (9 ft)   11 m (36 ft) = width of the room.
   4 Gangways at 1 m (3 ft) = 3.5 m (12 ft)

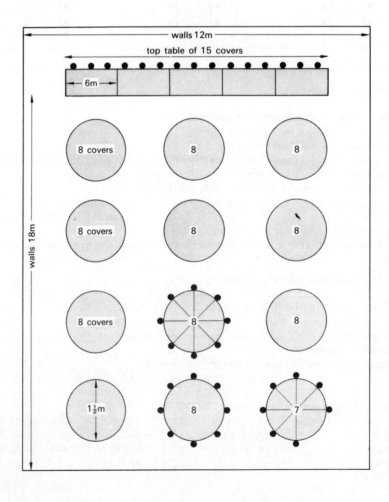

walls 12m

top table of 15 covers

6m

walls 18m

8 covers — 8 — 8

8 covers — 8 — 8

8 covers — 8 — 8

1½m — 8 — 7

172

Table and seating plan

The following plan also shows 110 covers. This time allowing 15 covers on the top and then separate rectangular tables to seat the remaining 95 covers (7 × 12 and 1 × 11). The advantage of this plan is that no guest has his back directly to the top table.

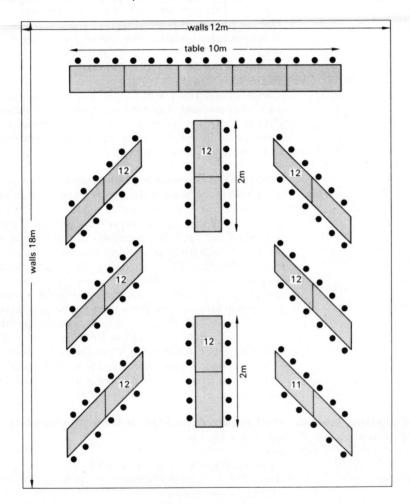

Instructions to staff

The purpose of the staff instruction sheet is to ensure that all duties are covered and that a particular function is laid up and everything is in order in the shortest possible time. The following is a simple example:

A function of 150 Covers

Staff	15 food waiters allowing 10 covers each. 7 sommeliers allowing 20/25 covers each. 1 banqueting head waiter or assistant manager. 3 washers-up
Table Plan	Top table and rounds

Mise-en-Place

Nos. 1-5		Laying-up
6-7		Cruets
8-9	food waiters	Linen and clothing-up
10-11		Polishing plates and stocking hot-plate
12-13		Service tables or sideboards (Service silver etc).
14-15		Dusting and general cleaning

Sommeliers   Polishing glasses/ashtrays/ice buckets/set up cash bar for reception.

General Points   1 soup station to every two waiters.

Plenty of ashtrays

1 set of cruets and 1 ashtray per 3 covers on top

1 set of cruets and 1 ashtray per 5 covers on sprigs

Toastmaster   Generally arrives 30 minutes before reception is due to commence. Checks with organiser on necessary details with reference to the function. Provided with a meal and drink.

Allotting Stations

When all the necessary mise-en-place has been completed, and all the staff are assembled together the stations are alloted to the waiters and wine waiters. Care must be taken in the allocation of the top table and usually one of the more experienced and proficient members of the brigade will be given this job. One must bear in mind the age and agility of the staff when allocating stations, giving the older members of the brigade the stations nearest the service doors. When the waiters queue up at the hotplate for each course this should be done in an orderly fashion with the waiter for the top table at the head of the queue and then the various waiters in order according to the distance of their station from the service hotplate. This order must be maintained throughout the service. After the service of each course the brigade should remain outside the banqueting room and in readiness to clear and serve the next course.

Examples of allotting stations, staff required, and the order at the hotplate

1) *Dinner* of 84 Covers: 12 on the top table

and

24 on each sprig (12 on each side)

Table requirements: Top: 4 × 2 m (6 ft) tables = 7.296 m (24 ft) = 60 cm (2 ft)
(plan opposite)   allowance per person.

Sprigs: 4 × 2 m (6 ft) tables = 7.296 m (24 ft) = 60 cm (2 ft) allowance per person.

A total of 3 sprigs in all: 12 on each side.

Stations Top: 12 covers   = 12 } 84 covers.
        Sprig: 6 × 12 covers = 72 }

Order at Hotplate 1.

2.

3.

4.

5.

6.

7.

Stations 7 × 12 = 84 covers.

(Service Doors)

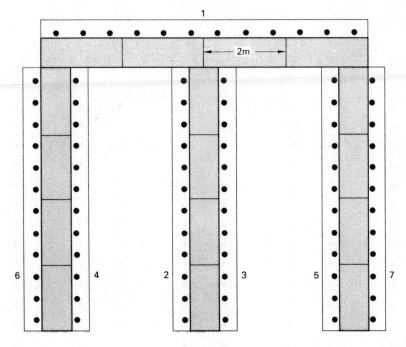

2) *Total covers* 193   18 on top table.   5 sprigs of 35 covers each.

Top table = 11 m (36 ft) or 6 × 2 m (6 ft) tables = 18 covers

Sprig   = 11 m (36 ft) or 6 × 2 m (6 ft) tables = 17 covers each side and one on each end

with 5 sprigs = 10 sides = 10 × 17 = 170 covers $\left.\right\}$ 175 covers.

1 on each end   +   =   5 covers

Can 5 Sprigs be fitted to a top table 11 m (36 ft) in length?

8 Chair widths at 46 cm (1 ft 6 in)   = 3.68 m (12 ft)

5 Tables at 75 cm (2 ft 6 in) wide   = 3.75 m (12 ft 6 in) $\left.\right\}$ 11 m (36 ft)

4 Gangways at 1 m (3 ft) wide   = 3.648 m (12 ft)

With a minor adjustment of gangways or table width and 5 sprigs may be acommodated.

It should be noted that this table plan will seat an extra 10 covers if required. i.e. Two (2) on each sprig—as the sprigs are 11 m (36 ft) in length and there are only 17 covers to be seated on each side of a sprig.

Staff Allocation

1 Banqueting head waiter

16 Waiters: stations of 10 covers = 160 $\left.\right\}$ 193 covers

 3 Waiters: stations of 11 covers = 33

1 Dispense barman

10 Wine waiters (1 on top and the rest will have 2 stations each).

175

Suggested order of queue at hotplate: 1. 19. 2. 12. 9. 13. 8. 11. 10. 14. 7. 16. 5. 15. 6. 17. 4. 3. 18.

Table and seating plan

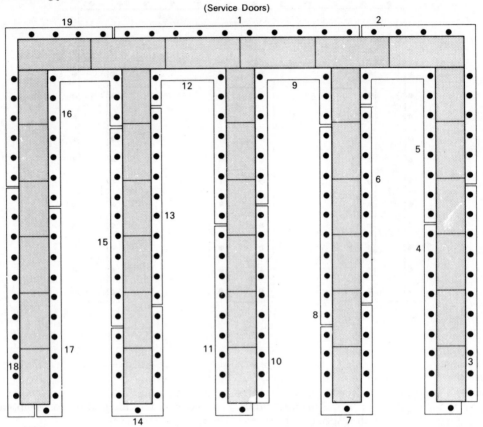

Sequence of Service

1. Dinner announced by the Toastmaster.
2. Grace.
3. Guests seated. Chairs pulled out by waiters. Serviettes across laps.
4. If first course is not already on the table proceed to hotplate to collect first course.
5. Line up as previously mentioned. Top table first.
6. Serve first course—top table waiter to commence service first.
7. All waiters (food) to leave room after each course is served.
8. Take in fish course plates.
9. Clear first course and lay fish plates.
10. Take out dirties and collect fish course.
11. Serve fish course. Leave room taking dirty silver.
12. Take in meat plates.
13. Clear fish course and lay meat plates.
14. Take out dirties and collect potato and vegetable dishes.
15. Deposit on sideboard or sidetable.
16. Return to hotplate and collect main meat dish.
17. Present on each table and serve.
18. Serve accompanying potatoes and vegetables.
19. Leave room taking dirty silver.
20. And so on until the end of the meal.

N.B. The Head waiter will control all the food waiters at the hotplate, and variations on this service may be adopted according to the situation. The Head waiter also controls the exit from hotplate into the banqueting room.

The Reception and Ordering of Wines

If required a bar must be set up in the reception

area away from the main entrance, so as to avoid overcrowding in one area as the guests are arriving and being announced by the Toast-master. The bar should be clothed up as for a buffet, with the cloth within 1.27 cm ($\frac{1}{2}$ in) of the ground in the front and both ends boxed in. Remember to keep the drawing pins you use hidden when boxing a corner. Keep the rear of the bar open so that you may use it for storing extra supplies of drink, glasses and any necessary equipment such as glass jugs, soda syphons, extra ice, etc. Always allow ample working space behind the bar. The latter is generally higher from the ground than the average table and if no shelves are available for storage purposes then sometimes smaller tables may be incorporated under the bar to fulfil that particular function.

There should always be a good stock of drink, which is generally brought from the cellar approximately 45 minutes before the reception is due to commence. Once the drink is at the bar there should always be one barman on duty at all times. Depending on the function drinks may be served either 'cash' or 'inclusive' which-ever may be the case a stocktake should be made when service is completed. Where necessary do not forget to have on hand—*price lists—till—floats—notices regarding size of measures—occasional licence* (if required).

When the drinks are to be served on a 'cash' basis, this very often can be a lengthy process. To speed this up there should be a wine waiter on duty near the table plan in the reception area together with a commis. They will have a:
1. Wine list
2. Menu
3. Check pads
4. Wine waiters names and
5. Stations
6. Table plan

The order will be written in duplicate, one copy going to the cellar or dispense bar and the duplicate to the correct wine waiter. The order would be prepared by the dispense barman or cellarman and when the wine waiter shows the duplicate he will be given the required order. Do not open until the guests arrive at the table—red wine at room temperature and white wine chilled. At a cash reception the wine waiters very often act as lounge waiters and therefore are always to hand to receive any orders in readiness for the service.

As for food service the top table is always served first with drink. The toasts very often commence immediately the coffee is served. By this stage the wine waiters should have taken all the liqueur orders, served them and collected all the *cash outstanding* in the case of cash drinks. Whilst the speeches are going on all the food waiters should be out of the room. The wine waiters may circulate if necessary. On comple-tion of the function and when the food and wine waiters have cleared their stations and the latter returned any floats, they will be paid off after returning service cloths, jackets, etc.

WEDDINGS

Wedding functions are usually of two main types a) Wedding Breakfast
b) Wedding Reception (Buffet)
At the initial meeting of the client and Banquet-ing manager when a wedding function is being arranged similar points should be borne in mind as those for 'booking a function' already mentioned. The requirements of the client depend on the type of wedding function, the number of guests attending and the cost per head to be paid. Some main points to bear in mind which require discussion with the client are his requirements concerning a wedding cake stand and knife and whether a room should be available for the Bride and Bridegroom to change prior to leaving the function to go on their honeymoon. Also it should be noted whether the wedding presents will be displayed and if so how much space will be needed, and whether the services of a photographer will be required.

Menu

The type of menu offered will depend on the cost per head to be paid. For a wedding the menu is often printed in 'silver', together with the names of the couple and the date as they are usually kept as souvenirs. If the wedding is a 'sit-down' affair then the same points should be noted as previously mentioned with reference to spacing of tables, covers, gangways, etc., and also for the service. In this instance the cake will be cut at the end of the meal—after the coffee and this will be followed by any necessary toasts. A seating plan should be available for a wedding breakfast and the table plan may be either 'U' shaped, top table and sprigs or top and rounds. Room allowance i.e. sit down function 1/1.4 square metre (12/15 square ft) per person, and 0.9/1 square metre (10/12 square ft) per person for buffets.

Wedding reception (Buffet)

The buffet itself should be placed in such a position that it is on view to all guests as they enter the room, but within easy access of the service doors for ease of clearing and re-stocking the buffet. The buffet should be clothed up correctly in that the buffet cloth should reach to within 1.27 cm ($\frac{1}{2}$ in) of the floor and both ends should be boxed neatly. The creases along the top and front of the buffet should all be lined up. Adequate room should be left between the buffet and wall to allow two people to pass and for any extra supplies and equipment required. If the function is being carried out in a marquee in private grounds then the ground should be covered with canvas or a form of corded matting. Behind the buffet and in the service area's duck-boards may be used on canvas to avoid walking on wet ground or in mud and carrying it into the main part of the marquee.

The buffet itself may be split into three sections for ease of service of food, tea and coffee, and wines and spirits. The food should be presented appetisingly and attractively on the buffet and the cutlery and china required placed conveniently near the service points and in a decorative manner. Food for replenishing the buffet should be close to hand. The centre of the buffet may be raised in order to show off the dishes to greater effect.

The section set up for the service of beverages, tea and coffee, should have all the relevant equipment close to hand. This will include teacups and saucers, teaspoons, sugar basins, cold milk jugs, tea and coffee urns, and hot-plates for the pots of hot milk. The service of beverages does not normally take place until after all the toasts have been completed. It is advisable to allow a little more in quantity than is actually required.

The section of the buffet required for drinks will have all the correct size glasses for the drinks to be served, i.e. spirits, cocktails, wines and champagne, plus ice-buckets for the white and rosé wines to be chilled, service salvers, waiters cloths, and all the ancillary equipment required for mixing drinks and cocktails to give the correct form of service. Any champagne or other sparkling wine used for the toasts must be well chilled to approx. 7°C (45°F). A surplus of glasses would be kept under the buffet in their appropriate boxes. Soft drinks should be on hand if required.

The floral arrangements are an important aspect of the decoration of the room, and help show off the room to best effect. A large vase of flowers would normally be placed near the entrance to be noted on arrival by all the guests. A further large centrepiece of flowers may be placed in the centre of the buffet and other smaller arrangements of flowers placed at intervals around the room on the occasional tables. The final floral arrangements will depend on the cost involved. The front of the buffet cloth may be decorated with some greenery (smilac) of some sort, or some coloured velvet may be draped along in order to take away the plainness of the white buffet cloth.

The wedding cake may be used as a separate focal point away from the buffet and would be placed upon its stand with a knife on a special table clothed-up for the purpose. This is a very important aspect of the dressing of the room, as the main formalities of the function take place, at a certain stage of the proceedings, around the wedding cake. It must therefore, be in full view to everyone in the room. The bride's and bridesmaids bouquets are often placed on the table around the base of the wedding cake, together with any telegrams of congratulations that are to be read out by the best man or toastmaster.

Occasional tables should be placed at regular intervals around the room and clothed up in a suitable manner. Groups of chairs should be placed around each table ensuring there is still space left for people to walk around and meet one another. All the ancillary items required for the efficient service of the meal will be placed upon the occasional tables. This means that the majority of the brigade on duty will be either serving drinks or clearing away used items, and will not be involved in the service of food which will be done from the buffet by other members of the brigade or one or two chefs if there is any carving involved. Items on the occasional tables will include butter, rolls/ french bread, sideplates, sideknives and serviettes, sugar basins and tongs, accompaniments for cold meats and salads, and ashtrays. Where possible some large standing ashtrays should be used as well.

It should be noted that the buffet itself may be used entirely for displaying the food and separate service points may be set up for the service of beverages, both alcoholic and non-alcoholic. This depends upon the exact nature of the function, the room available, number of guests, requirements of the client and the type and amount of drinks to be served. Cigars and cigarettes would be supplied at additional cost and again placed around the occasional tables. The client may also request that you arrange for a photographer to be present and this then is a further charge that has to be made. The photographer will probably take photos of the bride and bridegroom on arrival at the reception together with a group photo of those in the 'receiving line' and also one of the Bride and Bridegroom cutting the cake and maybe one or two of the buffet while it is complete. At this stage the photographer will go to develop all the photographs and return the proofs for everyone to see before the function is over.

Fully attended cloakrooms must be available for all guests on arrival.

Staff: The number of staff required will depend on the nature and requirements of a particular function. As a guide, at a buffet type reception, which is the more popular type of wedding function, one would need:

Brigade: 1 Head waiter/banqueting head waiter
1 Waiter   25/30 Covers
1 Wine waiter   40   ,,
1 Barman   every 3 wine waiters
1/2 Commis for fetching and carrying and clearing
1 Chef to every 35/40 guests for service.

Procedure at a wedding buffet reception

1. Any casual staff required would report approximately an hour beforehand to complete the necessary mise-en-place, be allocated duties and briefed on the procedure to be carried out.
2. If a toastmaster is to be on duty he will arrive approximately 30 minutes before the arrival of the bride and bridegroom to acquaint himself with the room where the function is being held and to enquire what his duties will be with regard to announcing guests on arrival. He must liaise with the best man to discuss the timing of cutting the cake, the toasts, and who is to give them. If there is to be a social evening afterwards then the toastmaster may act as M.C. for the duration of the function.
3. Bride and bridegroom will arrive first from the church. Some photographs may be taken at this stage and an aperitif offered or a glass of champagne.
4. Immediately following the bride and bridegroom will be the parents of the bride and bridegroom and bridesmaids and/or pages. These people will generally make up the 'receiving line' to greet the guests as they are announced by the toastmaster.
5. All guests will generally arrive together. Cloakrooms at this stage must be fully manned. Guests announced by toastmaster then pass down the receiving line and enter room.
6. Toastmaster will 'count' guests entering room. This is a help to management for costing purposes.
7. The wine waiters will be placed at strategic points in the reception area for the service of aperitifs or champagne to the guests as they move on from the 'receiving line'. These trays will be replenished with full, fresh glasses. No bottles handled. The wine waiters, at the initial briefing, will be allocated different sections of the room for service after the reception so as to ensure efficient service for all guests in the room.
8. After the reception the buffet will be open for service. The turnover on the buffet should be quick and efficient so as to avoid any major delays which may cause congestion at the buffet. The wine waiter at this stage will be going round serving drinks and topping up glasses. An important factor to note during the service of the food and drink is to ensure that at all times some members are always going round keeping the tables clear of any dirty equipment. Ashtrays should be changed as and when necessary.
9. At a time agreed upon the toastmaster will announce the cutting of the cake by the bride and bridegroom. Portions of the cake will then be passed around to all guests and champagne will be taken round by the wine waiters. When this has been done the toasts will commence, being announced by the toastmaster, who will have all the principal people concerned in a group by the wedding cake, or in a central position so they can be seen and heard by everyone present.

10. After the toasts any remaining cake and tiers are packed ready to be taken away by the host. The top tier is sometimes kept for a christening.

11. Bride and bridegroom will then change. If required food and champagne should be placed in the changing rooms. Here liason is demanded between Floor service and Banqueting staff to ensure that timing is correct as far as the movements of the bride and bridegroom are concerned.

12. When the bride and bridegroom have left the reception the flowers should be packed up for the host to take away.

Family line-up to greet guests at reception

Toastmaster

Entrance

1. Brides father	or	Brides father
2. Brides mother		Brides mother
3. Bridegrooms father		Bride
4. Bridegrooms mother		Bridegroom
		Bridegrooms father
5. Bride		
6. Bridegroom		Bridegrooms mother
7. Best man		
8. Bridesmaid/ Matron of honour		Bridesmaid/ Matron of honour

N.B. Best man sees everyone gets away from church and no one is left. Therefore does not always arrive in time for beginning of reception.

Procedure of toasts (two alternatives)

a) Cutting of cake
b) Whilst it is being cut telegrams may be read out by best man.
c) Pass cake and champagne for toasts
d) Toastmaster announces toast to bride and bridegroom proposed by brides father or near relation.
e) Response of bridegroom. Proposes health of bridesmaids.
f) Best man replies on behalf of bridesmaids
g) Any other toasts: Close relative of bride or bridegroom. – or –
a) Pass champagne for toasts
b) Toastmaster announces toast to bride and bridegroom proposed by brides father or near relation.
c) Response by bridegroom. Proposes health of bridesmaids.
d) Best man replies on behalf of bridesmaids

e) Any other toasts: Close relative of bride or bridegroom.
f) Cutting of cake: Reading of telegrams of congratulations by Best man. Pass cake and more champagne.

Suggested wedding menu

The menu for a wedding breakfast is rather lighter and shorter than for Dinner.

1st Course: Cocktails, smoked salmon, fruit, hors d'oeuvre or soup.

2nd Course: Cold salmon, roast poultry, grilled butchers meats, cold suprême of chicken, aspics etc.

With Vegetables and potatoes, or salad and potatoes.

3rd Course: A very good sweet course—fruit sundaes, coupes, flans, trifles etc.

and Sometimes with petit fours or French pastries, Coffee.

The menu for a buffet wedding reception would be chosen from the following:

Shellfish: Oysters, prawns etc.
Fruit: Melon cocktail, florida cocktail.
Smoked: Salmon, ham, trout.
Canapés: Fingers of toast covered with savoury items.
Savouries: Chicken, lobster, salmon and mushroom bouchées.
Fish: Cold salmon, lobster, crab fillets of sole etc.
Meats: Chicken suprêmes, cold roast turkey, cold decorated ham, cutlets in apsic, cold ribs of beef etc.
Salads: Lettuce, russian, tomato and all other kinds mixed and plain.
Sandwiches: Ham, chicken, smoked salmon etc.,
Cold Sweets: Bavarois, jelly, trifle, creme caramel etc.
Beverages: Tea or coffee

The menu for a finger buffet wedding reception would be chosen from the following:
Fingers of toast covered with savoury items.
Chipolatas: on sticks, wrapped in bacon etc.
Celery branches: piped with cheese spread.
Game chips or gaufrette: very dry and seasoned.
Sausage rolls and other puff pastry savoury items.
Sandwiches: brown or white: smoked salmon, egg and cress, tomato etc.,
Sweets (cold): jellies, bavarois, ice cream, coupes, fruit salads etc.,
Beverage: tea or coffee.

25   gueridon service

History

Flambée dishes and subsequently gueridon service first became popular in the Edwardian era. The first claimed flambée dish was Crêpes Suzette which was supposedly invented by Henri Charpentier when working as a Commis at the Café de Paris in Monte Carlo. (1894). The origin of gueridon service itself is hard to trace. It includes carving, salad preparation, filleting, preparation of fresh fruit etc. This form of service is normally found in higher class establishments with an à la carte menu and service, the cost of the dishes being priced individually and the average cost of the meal being therefore higher than a table d'hôte meal. Another reason for the higher cost with an à la carte type of meal is that it demands a skilled service, and this form of labour cost in itself is much higher, and is included within the cost that the guest must pay. Also a more expensive and elaborate form of equipment must be used for the service to be carried out efficiently, and this necessitates more room area for the movement of trollies etc.

Definition

The definition of the term *gueridon* is a movable service table or trolly from which food may be carved, filleted, flambéed, or prepared, then reheated and served. It is in other words a movable sideboard carrying sufficient equipment for the immediate operation in hand, whatever it may be, together with a surplus of certain equipment in case of emergency. It should also carry any special equipment that may be necessary. The gueridon itself may come in various forms, i.e. Calor gas trolly specially made for the purpose; plain trolly or even a small table.

Mise-en-place for gueridon

Where necessary the top and undershelf of the gueridon should be covered with a folded tablecloth. This of course depends on the nature of the gueridon itself and its general appearance. For convenience of working the cutlery lay-out should be similar to that of the sideboard. This saves time and speeds up the service. From right to left

1. Service spoons and forks (joint).
2. Dessert spoons and forks.
3. Soup, tea and coffee spoons.
4. Fish knives and forks. Special equipment including a soup and sauce ladle.
5. Joint and side knives.

The hotplates or table heaters are generally placed on the left-hand side on the top of the gueridon. These heaters may be gas, electric, or methylated spirit. If the latter then coffee saucers should be placed under the burners.

Also on the top will be found a carving board, knives for carving and filleting and a selection of basic accompaniments such as oil and vinegar, Worcestershire sauce, English and French mustard and castor sugar.

Underneath will be found a service plate and service salver, sideplates, and some joint plates for dirty cutlery when an operation is being carried out. There should also be some silver underflats of assorted sizes for the service of vegetables and sauces. A selection of doilies etc. are useful for the presentation of sauces and other accompaniments.

A Gueridon trolly is heated by a gas lamp connected to a Calor gas cylinder. The service top is flat as the gas lamp has been lowered into the upper casing. This makes it much safer when cooking dishes or carrying out any form of flambée work at the table. The top of the trolly is stainless steel which allows for easy cleaning. Note the control switch for the gas lamp; the drawer for surplus service cutlery; the cutting board for use when cooking dishes at the table. The bracket on the lower tray used for holding bottles of spirit and liqueurs, and the indentation on top of the trolly for holding accompaniaments.

Any other mise-en-place required, such as coffee saucers, accompaniments, check pads, etc., will be on the waiters sideboard together with a surplus of all the gueridon equipment in case of emergency.

SPECIAL EQUIPMENT

Flare lamps

These are an essential item of equipment for gueridon service, and are used in reheating, cooking and flambéeing dishes. The maintenance of the flare lamp is very important and should be carried out very carefully, ensuring each part is fitted together correctly, that it is filled to the correct level with methylated spirits and that the wick is of sufficient length to give adequate heat when in use. The flare lamp should be cleaned regularly with the aid of platepowder. Regular trimming of the wick is essential to avoid methylated spirit fumes leaking out and spoiling the aroma of the food. The lamps are usually 20-25 cm (8-10 in) high with a grid diameter of 15-20 cm (6-8 in). In a specially made gueridon trolly the lamp is incorporated in the trolly, thus giving the same working height all along the trolly top. This is much safer for the waiter as he works since there is less chance of accidents. Care over its use is essential as it is a costly item, a silver plated one costing anything from £40.

Chafing dish or Suzette pans

The true chafing dish is rarely seen nowadays. This was deeper, had a lid and made to fit into its own individual heating unit. The shallower pans which are used today are called suzette pans. They resemble frying pans in shape and size and have a diameter of 23-30 cm (9-12 in) with or without a lip. The lip is usually found on the left hand side. The pans are generally made of silver plated copper as this gives an even distribution of heat.

Hotplates

Are always positioned on the sideboard, but may often be found on both the sideboard and the gueridon. There is a vast range in sizes, and they may be heated by gas, electricity, methylated spirits, and there are even infra-red ones available. The majority of hotplates in present day use are heated by methylated spirits and therefore, as with the flare lamps, care should be taken in cleaning, filling and trimming the wicks. The hotplates main function is to keep food hot before it is served to the guest. The wicks in both hotplates and flare lamps should be long enough and adequate for the service.

GENERAL POINTS

To note

a) Gueridon service is essentially a chef and commis service. Therefore there must be complete liason and teamwork between them and every member of the brigade.
b) Always push the gueridon and never pull it. This helps to avoid accidents, as one is able to see more easily where one is going.
c) When the service is finished at one table move the gueridon on to the next immediately. It will then be ready for the commis coming from the kitchen with his loaded tray. Where possible avoid wheeling a loaded gueridon around the room, this is another factor to remember in avoiding accidents.
d) The gueridon should be kept in one position for the service of a complete course and not moved from guest to guest.
e) Where more than two covers are being served from the gueridon, only the main dish of each course should be served from the gueridon, and vegetables, sauces and accompaniments passed in the normal manner. This speeds up the service as generally there

is not sufficient room on the gueridon for the service of the complete meal.
f) The service spoon and fork is not used as in silver service, but by holding the spoon in one hand and the fork in another. This gives more control when handling the food for service.
g) When transferring foods and liquids from the silver to the plate always run the fork along the underside of the spoon to avoid drips marking the plate.
h) Never fillet or carve on a silver dish. Use either a carving board or a hot joint plate. When using a fork in carving always work with the curved side downwards otherwise the prongs will puncture the meat.
i) The Commis must always keep the gueridon clear of dirties.

Sequence of service

Presentation of all dishes for all courses is very important both before the actual service commences and in placing the meal upon the plate, especially when filleting and carving.

Hors d'oeuvre or substitutes
These are served in the normal way except for speciality dishes such as pâté de foie gras, which may have to be cut into slices. Accompaniments passed in the normal manner.
Soup. Always served from the gueridon whether in individual soup bowls or in soup tureens with a ladle. All accompaniments passed.
Fish. Filleted when necessary and served from the gueridon.
Meat. Carved where necessary and served from the gueridon.
Vegetables, sauces and accompaniments served as previously mentioned.
Sweet. Served from gueridon if a flambé type dish or from the cold sweet trolly. All accompaniments passed.
Savoury. Served from the gueridon.
Coffee. Normal silver service.

CARVING

The carving of a joint is a skilled art only perfected by continual practice. The following points should be noted:

1. Always use a very sharp knife, making sure it is sharpened beforehand and not in front of the customer. Remember you are going to *carve* a joint and not cut it to pieces.
2. You must cut economically and correctly, and at the same time be quick.
3. Meat is carved across or with the grain, with the exception of saddle of mutton or lamb which is sometimes cut at right angles to the ribs.
4. The carving fork must hold the joint firmly. This is the only time the fork pierces the meat.
5. *Practise* as much as possible to become perfect.

Selection of tools

For most joints a knife with a blade, 25-30 cm (10-12 in) long and about 2.5 cm (1 in) wide is required.

For poultry or game a knife with a blade 20 cm (8 in) long is more suitable.

For ham a long thin flexible carving knife is preferred.

A carving fork is needed to hold the joint.

Preparation of joints

The correct preparation of joints before cooking is very important, and any bones which make carving difficult should be removed in the preparation of the joint for cooking. One should ensure that the larder chef has a knowledge of your requirements to ensure maximum economy, and a saving in food cost and waste. At the same time the person carving must have a knowledge of the bone structure of a joint in order to carve correctly and thus acquire the maximum number of portions.

Methods of carving

Beef and Ham are always cut very thinly.

Lamb, Mutton, Pork, Tongue and Veal are carved at double this thickness.

Boiled Beef and Pressed Meats are cut a shade thicker than roasts and each portion of the former will include some fat.

Saddle of Lamb is carved along the loin in long thickish slices.

Shoulder of Lamb has an awkward bone formation. Start from the top, cut down to the bone, then work from top to bottom. Then turn the piece over and work gradually round.

Cold Ham is carved onto the bone from top to bottom in very thin slices.

Whole Chicken of medium size is dissected into six portions.

Broilers are generally dissected into four portions.

Poussin may be either offered whole or split into two portions.

Duckling may be carved into four/six portions, two legs, two wings and the breasts cut into long strips.

Turkey slice down the breast into nice even portions and give each guest a slice of brown meat off the leg as well as a share of the stuffing.

Salmon is first skinned whether it be hot or cold. It is then served in fillets one from each side of the bone. Cut slices up to 10 cm (4 inches) long and 2.5 cm (1 inch) thick.

Lobster or Crayfish. Hold firmly. Pierce vertically with a strong knife and cut with a levering motion towards tail and head. Hold shell down with a spoon on a dish, slowly lifting out the meat with a fork. Slice the meat diagonally.

Sole. First the bones along either edge are removed. Then the fillets are drawn apart with the aid of two large forks. Serve a top and bottom fillet per portion.

The carving of all hot food must be performed quickly so that no heat is allowed to escape.

Carving trolley

This may be a very expensive item of equipment costing anything from £ 250/300 upwards depending on style and design. Because of this great care must always be taken with the maintenance and use of the carving trolley to ensure that it functions correctly.

Maintenance. The carving trolly should be cleaned at regular intervals with the aid of plate powder, ensuring that all the plate powder is finally polished off so that none comes into contact with any foodstuffs. A toothbrush may be used for cleaning any intricate design work.

Function. The function of the carving trolly is that it is an aid to *selling*. At all times the waiting brigade must be *salesmen* and *sell* the dishes on the menu by brief and accurate description. The carving trolly supplements

The Carving trolly is heated by two methylated spirit lamps. The container on which the carving board is resting contains hot water. This container has a steam outlet, which for safety reasons, should not be covered at any time.

Note the plate rest of hot joint plates and the two containers for gravy and sauces. When making up the carving trolly ready for service these two containers should always be placed at the end nearest the plate rest. This is for ease of service.

Nothing should be placed on the upper shelf of the trolly.
The reason for this is that when the cover of the carving trolly is in the lowered position it would come into contact with anything placed on the upper shelf, knocking them over and thus causing delays and maybe accidents during the service. The lower shelf should be used for carrying the service place; spare service cutlery and clean joint plate.

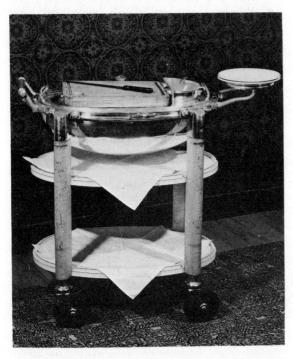

2. Ensure the base is filled with hot water before the lamps are lit.
3. Make sure the safety valve is set on correctly and screwed down tight. There is a small hole set in the safety valve which allows the surplus steam to escape. This must never be covered over. If it is, the pressure builds up within the base which can buckle the trolly and may cause an accident.

Presentation of trolley. In use the carving trolly must be presented at the table in the correct manner. It should be placed next to the table, in between the customer and yourself. This ensures that the customer can see every operation performed by the waiter and appreciate the skills involved. It should be positioned in such a way that the lid is drawn back from the trolley towards the waiter and the safety valve is positioned on the side away from the waiter. The latter makes sure that the waiter will not be scalded in performing his duties.

this by being a *visual aid* to *selling* and should be at the table as orders are taken by the waiter so that he may suggest and show off particular items to the guest. Always remember to *push* the trolly and not *pull* it.

Safety factors. There are certain safety factors to observe in the handling of the carving trolly and these must be carefully adhered to. Points to note:
1. Ensure the lamps are functioning properly, with trimmed wicks and holders filled with methylated spirits. They must be sufficient to last over the service period.

Mise-en-place. For its satisfactory operation in the restaurant the correct mise-en-place must be placed on the carving trolley:
1. Carving board
2. Carving knives
3. Sauce ladles
4. Service spoons and forks
5. Joint plate for dirty cutlery
6. Spare serviette and service cloth
The waiter must always ensure that the carving trolly is correctly laid up before it is taken to the table.

THE GUERIDON WAITER

Certain qualities and attributes are expected of a waiter in carrying out this form of service. It will be as well to bear the following points in mind at this stage:

Taking the order

Remember first and foremost that you are a *salesman*. You must sell the dishes which will involve you in work at the table. *Suggest* to the customer items on the menu, thus focusing his attention on dishes *you* may wish to sell. Use the *carving trolly* and *sweet trolly* as visual aids. You must always have a good *knowledge* of the *menu* so as to give good descriptions to the guests of the dishes available. *Recognition* of the *host* is an important factor.

a) Stand to left of the host. Each guest should have a menu including the host. Have one yourself for reference purposes.
b) Do not position yourself too close to guests as this may cause embarrassment.
c) Size up your host and his guests according to age, dress and nature of the party, i.e. Business lunch/Eating out/Celebration etc. This should then give you some indication as to the type of dishes one may suggest.
d) Take all orders through the host. Try to ascertain the *length of time available* for the meal as this could determine the type of dishes sold, i.e. *à la carte.*—Warn customers of waiting times.
e) Take note as to whether the party is all *male* or *male/female*.
f) Always take the order as soon as possible i.e. if possible in the *bar*.

Suggested cooking times of à la carte dishes

Hors d'oeuvre	10 mins.
Soups	10 mins.
Egg dishes	10 mins.
Fish (fried or grilled)	15 mins.
Macaroni or spaghetti	15 mins.
Omelettes	10 mins.
Liver or veal	15 mins.
Roast chicken	30 mins.
Chicken en cocotte	40 mins.
Lamb cutlets	10 mins.
Lamb chops	15 mins.
Grilled salmon	20 mins.
Lobster, mornay, thermidor	10 mins.
Fried potatoes	10 mins.
Soufflés	25/30 mins.

Order of service of guests

a) The host is always last except at dinners and banquets where he is served first.
b) If there are ladies in the party, serve the lady on the host's right, and then follow round the table. Then serve the males round the table starting from the first male on the host's right and go round the table. Host last.
c) Where the party is all female, the eldest lady is served first and the hostess is served last.
d) Where the party is all male the same principle applies.
e) When there is a family party, serve *mother* first, then *daughter*, then *son*, and *father* last.

Correct mode of address in the restaurant

On entering the restaurant the reception of the guest by the Head waiter should always take into account the *rank* or *title*, i.e. 'Milord', 'Your Grace', or Service Ranks such as 'Captain' or 'Major'.

After the original reception all adults, regardless of official titles or ranks, should be addressed as 'sir' or 'madam', except female members of the Royal Family who should be addressed as 'maam'.

Young people should be addressed as 'sir' or 'miss'. With the very young no mode of address is required.

Uniform

This at all times should be immaculate. Remember first impressions are usually those which are retained by the guest. A pleasant manner plus a good appearance help create this good initial impression. The uniform must be complete and correct. All buttons on the jackets, black socks worn, etc. Do not forget the waiters equipment that he should always carry: *waiters friend, (wine knife), matches, etc.*

General points to note

Time factor
Speed is essential in the service of the meal to ensure maximum turnover in shortest time available. Also to give customer satisfaction.

Labour Force

The work of the labour force must be efficient. Staff must work together, each knowing their own job so that there is complete unison in producing the end result, i.e. satisfactory service to the guest. Full use must be made of the skills necessary in the food and beverage service operation.

Expensive Equipment

Great care must be taken of all equipment used. Correct handling/cleaning/and storage.

Method of serving a dish at the table

First *present* the dish to the customer, then return to the gueridon. Place the hot plates on the side of the trolley, with the food for service standing on the hotplate. The food for service is then carved or filleted if necessary, and is placed onto the plate of the guest. Unlike silver service, when the spoon and fork are used together in one hand, gueridon service requires that the spoon and fork are used one in each hand. The vegetables are then placed onto the plate by the waiter while the plates are still on the gueridon. The sauces are also placed onto the plates by the waiters and the plates are then placed in front of the guests. It should be noted that when there are more than two people at one table the main dish is served as described but the vegetables are served as for normal silver service, and will be kept hot and in readiness for service on the hotplate on the waiters sideboard. During this operation it will be the Commis' or Debarrasseurs' function to keep the gueridon clear of dirty dishes and equipment.

26 dishes involving work on the gueridon

1. HORS D'ŒUVRE OR SUBSTITUTES

a) **Smoked Eel (Anguille fumé)**

Cover	Fish knife and fork—cold fish plate.
Accompaniments	Horseradish sauce / Cayenne pepper / Peppermill / Segment of lemon. Brown bread and butter.
Equipment for Gueridon	Smoked eel on a board. Small sharp knife and a joint fork. Spare plate for skin and bone. Spare plate for dirty cutlery. Service spoon and fork.
Service	1. Commence at the tail end. 2. Cut a section about 10 cm (4 inches) long. 3. Insert the knife between skin and flesh on one side and loosen the skin. 4. Insert the skin between the prongs of the fork and roll up on the fork towards the backbone. 5. Cut round the backbone. 6. Roll skin off the other side and cut free with the knife. 7. Filet each side removing the backbone. 8. Place onto a cold fish plate and serve.

Note This is a dish which is very often carved on the buffet rather than on the gueridon because of the length of the whole eel and the room needed in order to have it on a flat surface for carving.

b) **Smoked Trout (Truite fumé)**

Cover	Fish knife and fork and cold fish plate.
Accompaniments	Horseradish sauce / Cayenne pepper / Peppermill / Segment of lemon. Brown bread and butter.

Equipment for Gueridon	Smoked trout dressed on a silver flat. Service spoon and fork. Spare plate for dirty cutlery. Service spoon and fork.
Service	1. Present dish to customer—return to gueridon. 2. Place little crisp lettuce leaves and tomato on the fish plate. 3. Place the smoked trout onto a cold joint plate before removing the head and tail. 4. With the aid of the service spoon and fork remove both the head and tail. 5. Set the smoked trout neatly onto the cold fish plate and serve.

c) Smoked Salmon (Saumon fumé)

Cover	Fish knife and fork and cold fish plate.
Accompaniments	Cayenne pepper / Peppermill / Segment of lemon / Brown bread and butter.
Equipment for Gueridon	Smoked salmon on a board. Carving knife and a joint fork. Service spoon and fork. Spare plate for dirty cutlery.
Service	1. Remove the black line in the middle of each slice by making a small 'V' shaped incision in the side of smoked salmon before carving. 2. Carve each slice wafer thin, giving 2/3 slices per portion. 3. Insert the edge of the slice of smoked slamon between the prongs of the joint fork and roll up. 4. Lift over to the cold fish plate and unroll neatly. Serve.

Note For the same reasons as with Smoked Eel the Smoked Salmon is more often than not carved on the buffet.

d) Caviare: This is the roe of the sturgeon.

Cover	Caviare knife on the right hand side of the cover. Cold fish plate. If a caviare knife is not available then a fish knife is an adequate substitute.
Accompaniments	Hot breakfast toast/Butter/Segments of lemon/Sieved hard-boiled white and yolk of egg/Chopped shallots.
Equipment for Gueridon	Caviare pot in a dish of crushed ice on an underflat. Sweet spoon—or—two teaspoons for service. Spare plate for dirty cutlery.
Service	If a sweet or dessert spoon is used then generally one spoonful, which will weigh approximately 30 grammes (1 oz), is recognised as being a portion. If two teaspoons are used, the caviare is moulded in the two spoons, 3/4 teaspoonfuls per portion. When served direct from the pot in this fashion the caviare is

usually weighed before and after service and charged according to the amount served.

Note It should be noted that the caviare may be served already pre-plated by the larder or already pre-portioned by the larder and silver served onto the cold fish plate using a spoon.

e) **Whole Melon (Melon frappé)**

Main Varieties	Cantaloupe/Honeydew/Charentais.
Cover	Dessert spoon and fork or dessert spoon and fork plus a small (side) knife; this is in case the melon is a little unripe. Cold hors d'oeuvre or fish plate.
Accompaniments	Ground ginger and Castor sugar.
Equipment for Gueridon	Melon in small container of crushed ice. Cutting board. Sharp knife. Clean serviette. Spare plate for debris of melon. Spare plate for dirty cutlery. Soup plate for pips from melon. Service spoons and forks. Cocktail cherries in small silver or glass dish. Cocktail sticks in a holder.
Service	1. The melon should be in a small container of ice. Ensure all mise-en-place required is to hand before commencing the service. 2. Lift the melon with the aid of a clean serviette onto a board. Trim both ends. 3. Stand on end and cut out the required portion or portions. Use your judgement as to the size of a portion, but as a guide there would be approximately six portions to one whole melon. 4. Place the cut portion on your clean serviette and hold firmly in your left hand. Scoop out any pips with the aid of a service spoon into remainder of the whole melon. If there is less than half the melon left then scoop the pips straight onto a soup plate. 5. Trim base of each portion so it stands squarely on the cold fish plate and will not roll or slide about. 6. If required the waiter may cut the flesh of the melon from the rind and slice. 7. Decorate with a cocktail cherry on a stick. Serve.

Note The Charentais melon which is usually served half to a portion has a teaspoon which is placed on the plate or on the right hand side of the cover.

f) **Globe Artichoke (Artichaut)**

A globe artichoke can be served either hot or cold, and either as an hors d'oeuvre substitute or as a separate vegetable course.

Cover	Hot or cold fish plate as appropriate.

Large (joint) fork on the right hand side of the cover; used to consume the base of the artichoke.

Fingerbowl containing lukewarm water and a slice of lemon, placed on a doily on an underplate, and positioned at top left hand corner of the cover.

Spare serviette placed at the head of the cover.

Accompaniments	If served *hot:* Sauce hollandaise or Beurre fondue *cold:* Sauce vinaigrette (See section on Salads and Salad dressings).
Equipment for Gueridon	Lamp if served hot. Globe artichoke on a silver flat Service spoons and forks Spare plate for dirty cutlery Sauce-boat of sauce on an underflat, with a sauce ladle.

Service

1. Present dish to customer—return to gueridon.
2. With the service spoon and fork transfer the globe artichoke from the silver flat to the hot or cold fish plate.
3. Lift out the center leaves and arrange neatly on the edge of the hot or cold fish plate
4. Pour the appropriate sauce into the resultant space.
5. Serve, ensuring the correct cover and accompaniments are already on the table.

g) **Pâté de foie gras**

The true pâté is made from the goose's liver, and the geese are specially bred and fattened for this purpose. However the more commonly known is 'Pâté Maison'—Pâté of the House or establishment —where each recipe may vary slightly according to the individual who prepares this particular dish.

Cover	Small/side knife and a dessert fork. Cold fish plate.
Accompaniments	Hot breakfast toast, with crusts removed, cut into triangles and served in a serviette on a sideplate.
Equipment for Gueridon	Terrine (pot) of foie gras. Two teaspoons. Silver jug of *very* hot water. If pâté maison is being offered then a side knife will be required. Service spoons and forks. Spare plate for dirty cutlery.

Service

1. Present dish to guest—return to the gueridon.
2. If terrine de foie gras is being offered, place the two teaspoons in the silver jug of *very* hot water.
3. Using each in turn, drawing the teaspoon across surface of the foie gras, 'curls' of foie gras may be formed.
4. Give 4 or 5 per portion and as they are formed place them on the cold fish plate.
5. Decorate with little crisp lettuce leaves and some segments of tomato. Serve.

6. If pâté maison is being offered then the waiter must use the side knife frequently dipped in hot water to cut 2 or 3 slices per portion. Decorate as in 5 above and serve.

Note It should be noted that in some instances the 'Pâté' will come already sliced from the larder and dressed onto a silver flat. In this case serve as for silver service.

h) **Shellfish Cocktail (Cocktail de crevettes)**

Cover	Teaspoon / Oyster fork / Shellfish cocktail holder on a doily on a sideplate.
	The oyster fork and teaspoon may be placed to the right and left of the cover, or on the doyley on the sideplate on either side of the shellfish cocktail holder.
Accompaniments	Brown bread and butter.
Equipment for Gueridon	Small glass dishes with teaspoons, to hold the ingredients, all placed on a silver salver.
	Soup plate for mixing the sauce.
	Service spoons and forks.
	Spare plate for dirty cutlery.
Ingredients	Shellfish / shredded lettuce / tomato concassé / mayonnaise / sieved hard boiled white and yolk of egg / chopped parsley / tomato ketchup / Worchestershire sauce / lemon juice / slice of lemon.

Service

1. Ensure there is some crushed ice around the base of the shellfish cocktail holder and that it is well chilled.
2. Place tomato concassé in the base of the shellfish cocktail holder.
3. On top of this place some shredded (chiffonade) lettuce followed by the shellfish which may be prawns or shrimps. Keep one or two shellfish by for decorating the finished dish.
4. Make up the sauce by mixing the mayonnaise, tomato ketchup, Worcestershire sauce and a little lemon juice together in the soup plate.
5. Coat the shellfish with the tomato flavoured mayonnaise. Be careful not to put too much mayonnaise in as this then overpowers the rest of the ingredients.
6. Now decorate the top with the sieved hardboiled yolk and white of egg, and chopped parsely.
7. Place the remaining shellfish and slice of lemon over the edge of the holder and serve.

2. SOUP

Real Turtle Soup (La tortue vraie)

Cover	Sweet/Dessert spoon. Hot consommé cup on consommé saucer on an underplate.

Accompaniments	Brown bread and butter (offered to the guests). Segments of lemon in a lemon press, placed on a sideplate at the head of the cover. Cheese straws (offered to the guests). Measure of warm Sherry: added by the waiter at the gueridon.
Equipment required for the Gueridon	Portion of soup in a soup tureen, measure of Sherry, sauce ladle, lamp.
Service	1. Served from the gueridon. 2. Reheat on the lamp and then pour into the consomme cup, which will be sitting on the consomme saucer on an under-plate. 3. The measure of Sherry may be warmed and added to the soup at the last moment in the kitchen, or it may be heated in a sauce ladle over the lamp, flambée, and then poured over the soup. 4. Serve immediately.

3. FISH

a) **Sole grillée ou meunière**

Cover	Fish knife and fork and a hot fish plate.
Equipment for the Gueridon	Silver flat with the sole, service spoons and forks, hot joint plate for filleting, spare plate for dirty cutlery, spare plate for debris, lamp.
Service: Method (a)	1. Present dish to the customer. Return to the hot plate or lamp 2. Remove from the silver flat onto the hot joint plate. 3. With the aid of a service spoon and fork remove the side bones. 4. Run the tip of the spoon down the backbone. 5. Place two large forks back to back at the head of the fish and on the backbone. Press the forks down, so that the tips of the forks pierce the flesh on either side of the backbone. Now ease the fillets slowly away from the backbone. 6. Continue to do this working the forks gradually down the backbone towards the tail. 7. Lift out the bone. 8. Place the fillets back together in their original shape on the silver flat. Reheat as necessary. 9. Coat with beurre fondue, or replace garnish and serve.
Method (b)	1. 1, 2, 3, 4 as above. (a) 2. Start at head of fish and with the aid of a service spoon and fork loosen the two top fillets. 3. Hold the fish firmly with the spoon and run the fork down from head to tail between the two top fillets and the backbone. 4. Repeat this with the other two fillets, placing fork between the bottom fillets and the backbone. 5. Lift out backbone. 6. 8-9 as above.

Note An 227 gramme (8 oz) sole may generally be served as a complete portion, if it is any larger one usually offers a top and bottom fillet per portion.

b) **Sole poché (with sauce over it)** i.e. Bonne Femme / Véronique

Cover	Fish knife and fork. Hot fish plate.
Accompaniments	According to garnish.
Equipment required for Gueridon	Sole on silver flat, hot joint plate for fileting, service spoon and fork, two joint forks, lamp.
Service	1. Present dish to guest. Return to gueridon.
	2. Remove sole from silver flat onto hot joint plate.
	3. Remove side bones with the aid of the joint fork.
	4. Run the tip of the service spoon down backbone of the sole.
	5. With aid of two joint forks, fillet sole as in Sole grillé ou meunière, disturbing the glazed sauce coating the fillets as little as possible.
	6. Replace fillets together in the shape of fish on the silver flat.
	7. Recoat with sauce and serve.

Note Poached sole is normally filleted in the kitchen, but where whole soles are poached and then coated with a sauce and glazed ready for service it should be filleted in the room, as above.

c) **Sole frite** (Deep fried: flour, egg and breadcrumbed)

Cover	Fish knife and fork and a hot fish plate.
Accompaniments	Sauce tartare and segments of lemon.
Equipment required for Gueridon	Service spoon and fork, hot joint plate for filleting, spare plate for debris, spare plate for dirty cultery, lamp.
Service	1. Ensure gueridon is laid up fully with all required mise-en-place.
	2. Present dish to guest.
	3. Lift sole onto hot joint plate.
	4. Remove side bones as for Sole grillé.
	5. Run the point of spoon down centre of the sole, from head to tail, making a slight incision.
	6. Cut off tail approx. 2.5 cm (1 in) from end.
	7. Hold the spoon curved side upwards and insert the point between the fillet and the bone at the tail end of the fish.
	8. Hold the sole firmly with the fork and push the spoon up towards the head, lifting off one top fillet.
	9. Repeat for other top fillet, and then lift the two loosened top filets off the backbone.
	10. Lift out the backbone.
	11. Replace top fillets on the bottom ones on the silver flat and reheat and then place onto a hot fish plate for service.
	12. Add garnish of lemon and serve.

d) **Saumon poché ou grillé** (cutlet or 'darne' de saumon)

This type of dish is generally served in an earthenware dish, and therefore it is not necessary to remove it to a hot joint plate for skinning and filleting.

Cover	fish knife and fork and a hot fish plate.
Accompaniments	According to the garnish i.e. Hollandaise, Doria.
Equipment required for Gueridon	Service spoon and fork, lamp, spare plate for debris, spare plate for dirty cutlery.

Service
1. Present to the customer. Return to lamp on the gueridon.
2. Hold the salmon firmly in place with the fork.
3. With the point of the spoon, curved side outwards, run round the edge of the cutlet removing the skin.
4. As an alternative to this method of removing the outer black skin one may use a joint fork, inserting the skin between the prongs of the fork. Now twist the fork around the outer edge of the 'darne' rolling the skin up on the fork as you proceed.
5. Insert the point of the spoon between the flesh and the centre bone and push the fillets away from the bone.
6. Remove the bone.
7. Lift the two fillets onto the hot fish plate, being careful not to break the flesh, and add the garnish. Serve.

e) **Blue Trout (Truite au bleu)**

Cover	Fish knife and fork and hot fish plate.
Equipment required for Gueridon	Fish knife and fork, Service spoon and fork, lamp, spare plate for dirty cutlery, spare plate for debris.
Accompaniments	Hollandaise sauce or Beurre fondu.

Service
1. Ensure gueridon is correctly laid up.
2. Present dish to customer and return to gueridon. This dish should come from the kitchen in an individual copper fish kettle.
3. Lift out on draining tray.
4. Remove garnish of sliced carrots and onions.
5. With the point of the fish knife make an incision from head to tail on the thin line showing on the side of the trout. Only cut the skin and not the flesh.
6. Lift off the skin below that line with the knife and also above the line to the backbone.
7. Turn fish over and repeat process of removing the skin on the second side, remembering to remove the fins.
8. Lift trout carefully onto a hot fish plate and decorate with a few slices of carrot and onion. Moisten with a little stock.
9. Serve and then offer the appropriate accompaniment.

4. STEAKS

a) **Entrecôte double** (Double entrecôte steak; coming from the boned sirloin.)

Cover	Steak knife and a joint fork. Hot joint plate.
Accompaniments	English and French mustard.
Equipment required for the gueridon	Silver flat with the double entrecôte steak on it. A board for portioning the entrecôte steak. Sharp knife for carving. Service spoons and forks. Two sideplates, for pressing the trimmed ends to extract all juices. Spare plate for dirty cutlery. Lamp.
Service	1. Present dish to the customer—return to gueridon.
	2. Lift the double entrecôte steak from the silver flat onto the board.
	3. Trim the ends.
	4. Cut on the slant into two portions. Place back on the silver flat on the lamp.
	5. Press the trimmed ends between two hot sideplates allowing the juices extracted to fall over the two portions of steak.
	6. Place the portions of steak onto the hot joint plates and add the garnish. Set it out attractively. Serve.

Note It must always be remembered that this is a dish that must be ordered by a party of two guests. When taking the order the waiter should ask how the guests wish the steak to be cooked. If one guest wants his steak to be 'rare' and the other guest 'medium', then the steak will come in from the kitchen 'rare' and once carved one portion will be cooked a little longer in a pan on the lamp at the table.

b) **Châteaubriand** (Double fillet steak)

Although the Châteaubriand is commonly termed a double fillet steak it may be large enough to serve a party of 2, 3, 4 or 5 guests as required.

The cover, accompaniments, equipment required for gueridon and service are as for Entrecôte Double; with the following exception:
When the Châteaubriand is being carved each portion will be carved into approximately 2 or 3 slices, each 13 mm thick ($\frac{1}{4}$ in), rather than being left in one whole piece as is the case with an Entrecôte Double.

c) **Porterhouse Steak or 'T' Bone Steak**

This is a steak made up of part sirloin and part fillet, the whole being held together by the backbone and with a rib separating the sirloin from the fillet.

Cover	Steak knife and joint fork. Hot joint plate.
Accompaniment	English and French mustard.
Equipment required for Gueridon	Silver flat containing the Porterhouse steak Board for carving

Sharp knife
Spare plate for dirty cutlery
Spare plate for debris
Service spoons and forks
Lamp.

Service

1. Present dish to customer—return to gueridon.
2. Remove from the silver flat onto the carving board.
3. Cut out the 'T' bone to give two separate pieces of meat: one of sirloin and one of fillet.
4. Return the two pieces of meat to the silver flat: reheat quickly.
5. Dress attractively onto the hot joint plate with the garnish.
6. If the porterhouse steak is for more than one person then carve the fillets as for a Châteaubriand.

d) **Steak tartare**

Cover

Joint knife and fork and a cold joint plate.

Accompaniments

Cayenne pepper and peppermill.

Equipment required for Gueridon

Soup plate
Service spoons and forks.
Spare plate for debris
Spare plate for dirty cutlery
Containers for the various ingredients.

Ingredients

Portion of chopped raw fillet steak, moulded into a cake shape and presented on a round silver flat. The portion of raw fillet steak will be welled in the center to hold a whole egg. Only the yolk of the egg will be used. Chopped gherkins, capers, parsely and shallots.
Oil and vinegar
Peppermill.
Salt
French mustard
Worcestershire sauce.

Service

1. Ensure your gueridon has all the necessary mise-en-place before proceeding to make the sauce.
2. Add the seasoning of salt, peppermill and French mustard together in the soup plate. Mix well.
3. Separate the yolk from the white of egg, placing the yolk into the soup plate and the white into a spare container.
4. Beat the yolk and seasoning together using a service (joint) fork.
5. Add vinegar and mix in and then add a little oil and mix in, according to the amount of sauce you wish to make.
6. Be careful of the quantity of sauce you make as the finished product should be moist but not runny or too liquid.
7. Add the chopped gherkins, capers, parsley and shallots and bind the whole well together.
8. Now place in the raw chopped filet steak together with a

dash of Worcestershire sauce, incorporating the sauce and fillet steak well together.

9. Shape into a round flat cake and place on the cold joint plate. Serve.

e) Steak Diane

Cover	Steak knife and joint fork. Hot joint plate.
Accompaniments	English and French mustard.
Equipment for the Gueridon	Lamp, Pan on an underplate, Service spoons and forks, Tea spoons, Plate for dirty cutlery.

Ingredients

Minute steak on a plate	Cayenne pepper and peppermill
Chopped shallots	Cruet
Chopped parsley	Oil and butter
Fines herbes	Worcestershire sauce
Jug of double cream	Measure of brandy.

Service

1. Ensure the gueridon is correctly laid up with all the mise-en-place.
2. Enquire of customer how he would like his steak cooked.
3. Place some butter and a little oil in the pan and allow to melt. The oil will prevent the butter from burning.
4. Season the steak with cruet, cayenne pepper and peppermill.
5. Place the chopped shallots in the pan and sweat without colouring until cooked.
6. Place steak in the pan and cook as required.
7. Add a dash of Worcestershire sauce, and then sprinkle with some chopped parsley and fines herbes.
8. Add a measure of brandy and flambé.
9. Serve immediately from the pan onto a hot joint plate at the table.
10. Before serving, if requested, a thickened sauce may be made by the addition of a little double cream. Bring up to simmering point but do not boil.
11. If a sauce is made the steak must be kept on a hot joint plate on the hotplate, and covered whilst the sauce is being prepared.
12. Coat the steak with the sauce and serve ensuring it is piping hot.

Note There are many variations in the making of Steak Diane, each done to an establishments traditional recipe or being a speciality of the waiter carrying out the operation according to his own particular techniques.

5. SALADS (LA SALADE VERTE)

A *green* or *fruit* (orange) salad is generally offered as an accompaniment with a main course dish such as chicken, duck, or grilled steak.

The *cover* for a salad when offered with a main course dish will be a salad crescent shaped dish, or a small round wooden bowl with a small or dessert fork, or a small wooden spoon and fork. The prongs of the small or dessert fork should be pointing downwards to avoid tarnishing the silver with the acids in the dressing.

There are a variety of both *salads* and *dressings* which may be offered to the guest according to choice.

Dressings The three main types of dressing are as follows:

Sauce vinaigrette
This would be mixed by the waiter in a soup plate from the gueridon.

The ingredients used would be placed in the soup plate in the following order, and all mixed together   1 teaspoonful of French, or English mustard.
Seasoning to taste (salt, pepper, peppermill)
1 Tablespoon of vinegar
Then add   2 Tablespoons of oil, mixing slowly.

The proportions of vinegar and oil used are according to individual taste. Once the Vinaigrette is made to the guests liking the salad will be tossed with the dressing in a salad bowl.

Roquefort dressing
This form of dressing is again made according to taste, and in a soup plate.
The main ingredients used are: Roquefort cheese
Vinegar
Olive oil
Seasoning *(salt)*
There are two main methods of making this form of dressing:
i) Break down the Roquefort cheese into small lumps or cream it right down by mixing in a soup plate with a little vinegar. Add the olive oil and season with salt. This will help to bring out the full flavour of the cheese.
ii) Break down the Roquefort cheese into small pieces in a soup plate and with the aid of a large fork, fold the pieces of Roquefort into some Sauce mayonnaise. Season with salt, again to help bring out the flavour.

The main ingredients used are: Roquefort cheese
Sauce mayonnaise
Seasoning (salt)
The Salad should be tossed with the dressing in a salad bowl.

Acidulated cream dressing
This form of dressing is mainly offered with salads containing fruit, i.e. Orange salad. The ingredients required are:

Lemon juice
Seasoning (salt)
Single cream
Paprika

The method of making is as follows: mix the lemon juice with seasoning, then add the single cream. Toss the fruit from the salad with the dressing. Place on a bed of lettuce leaves on the salad crescent and sprinkle with Paprika pepper.

Other forms of dressings are:

Mustard cream: $\frac{1}{5}$ litre ($\frac{1}{3}$ pt.) cream
Tablespoon of mustard
Juice of a lemon
Seasoning.

Lemon dressing :	Oil
	Lemon juice
	Seasoning

Equipment required on the Gueridon when preparing a Salad Dressing	1. The ingredients depending on the type of Dressing required.
	2. Soup plate.
	3. Service cloth.
	4. Service spoon and fork.
	5. Salad crescent or wooden salad bowl.
	6. Dessert or small fork or a small wooden spoon and fork.
	7. Glass bowl for tossing the salad.
	8. Teaspoon: for tasting the dressing.

Service	The dressing required will be prepared by the waiter on the gueridon at the table. The dressing and salad are tossed together in the glass bowl. The salad or fruit will then be dressed on to the salad crescent which is then placed at the top left hand corner of the cover before serving the dish which it accompanies.

A presentable method of serving raw vegetables and fruit is in the form of a salad. All salads should be served chilled, crisp and attractive. Remember a salad is not complete without a well made salad dressing or sauce, such as Vinaigrette or Mayonnaise. Basically there are two main types of salad. Firstly 'a plain salad' which consists entirely of vegetables and secondly a 'compound salad' which is a plain salad plus other ingredients such as meat, fish, mushroom, etc.

Varieties of salad

Française	Lettuce hearts, sections skinned tomato, hardboiled egg, vinaigrette separate.
Verte	Lettuce hearts, vinaigrette separate.
Saison	Lettuce hearts, plus salad, vegetables in season, vinaigrette separate.
d'Orange	Lettuce hearts, in sections. Filletted orange, fresh cream separate.
Mimosa	Lettuce hearts, filletted orange, grapes skinned and stoned, sliced banana, sprinkle with egg yolk, acidulated cream, dressing separate.
Japonaise	Lettuce, bananas, apple, tomatoes all in dice, shelled walnuts, fresh cream separate.
Lorette	Corn salad, Julienne of beetroot, raw celery heart, vinaigrette separate.
Russian	Vegetable salad decorated with tomatoes, eggs, anchovies, lobster, ham, tongue, Mayonnaise sauce.
Niçoise	French beans, tomato quarters, sliced potatoes, anchovies, capers, olives, sauce vinaigrette.
d'Endive	Hearts of lettuce, endive, sauce vinaigrette.

6. POULTRY

a) **Chicken (Poulet rôti)**

Cover	Joint knife and fork. Hot joint plate.
Accompaniments	Bread sauce, roast gravy.
Equipment required for Gueridon	Carving board Sharp carving knife Service spoons and forks Spare plate for dirty cutlery Spare plate for debris Lamp Chicken on a silver flat.

Service

1. Present the whole chicken to host at the table—return to lamp on gueridon.
2. With the service spoon and fork lift the chicken from the silver flat onto the carving board, draining off any liquid that may be inside of it.
3. Lie the chicken on its side on the board from right to left in front of you and with a leg uppermost.
4. Holding the bird firmly on the board with the flat of the knife insert the service fork beneath the leg joint and raise the leg until the skin surrounding it is taut.
5. Cut round the taut skin surrounding the leg with the tip of the knife at the same time pulling the leg away fron the joint and cutting the flesh where necessary.
6. Cut the leg into two pieces through the joint and also remove the claw end.
7. Place the two pieces of leg onto the silver flat.
8. Proceed in the same manner with the other leg.
9. Turn the chicken onto its back. Insert the joint fork into the base of the carcass to hold it firmly.
10. Carve part of the breast and down through the wing joint, giving one piece made up of the wing and a little breast.
11. If necessary turn the chicken on its side and with the aid of the service fork lever the wing away fron the carcass, at the same time holding the chicken firmly with the flat of the knife.
12. Proceed in the same manner with the other wing.
13. Position the bird on its back. Cut down one side of the breastbone and lever off half the breast.
14. Proceed in the same manner with the other side of the breast.
15. An alternative method of removing the breast is by turning the chicken on to its side and cutting through the wish bone joints.
16. Turn the chicken on to its breast, holding it firmly in place with the service fork.
17. Insert the knife between the flesh and the wishbone and holding the whole breast on the board with the knife lever the carcass away with the aid of the service fork.

18. Cut the whole breast into two portions lengthways.
19. Reheat the carved chicken on the lamp. If nesessary whilst the carving operation is being carried out add a little liquid (gravy) to the silver flat to prevent the carved chicken from burning.
20. Serve the chicken giving some brown and some white meat per portion. Remember to add some game chips and watercress if these make up the garnish.

b) **Poussin:** (Young Chicken: 6 weeks old)

Cover Joint knife and fork. Hot joint plate.

Accompaniments As per menu garnish.

Equipment required for Gueridon Poussin on silver flat
Lamp
Board
Knife
Service spoons and forks
Plate for dirty cutlery
Plate for debris.

Service
1. Present to customer—return to the gueridon.
2. Lift the poussin from the silver flat onto the carving board with the aid of the service spoon and fork.
3. Insert the service fork into the base of the carcass and hold firmly on the board with the breast uppermost.
4. With the tip of the knife cut the poussin in half down through the breast.
5. Take the half poussin attached to the backbone and remove the backbone.
6. Place the two portions of poussin on the silver flat and reheat if necessary.
7. Present attractively on to the hot joint plate. Add garnish and/or sauce. Serve.

c) **Duck (Canard rôti)**

Cover Joint knife and fork. Hot joint plate.

Accompaniments Apple sauce, sage and onion stuffing, roast gravy.

Equipment required for Gueridon Duck on a silver flat
Lamp
Carving board
Sharp carving knife
Service spoons and forks
Spare plate for dirty cutlery
Spare plate for debris.

Service Before commencing to carve a duck the waiter should remember that the joints are much tighter and more compact than those on a chicken, and therefore more difficult to find and cut through when carving. Also the wing joints lie a little further under the base of the carcasse than those on a chicken.

The initial stages in carving a duck are the same as for a chicken until the legs and wings have been removed.

1. Hold the duck firmly on the carving board with the aid of a joint fork in the base of the carcasse.
2. The breast bone on a duck is wide and flat in comparison with that of the chicken. It is therefore easier to remove the complete half-breast from the breastbone.
3. Now cut into long thin slices (aiguillettes) on the carving board.
4. Repeat with the other half breast.
5. Dress back onto the silver flat. Reheat if necessary. Serve with the appropriate accompaniments.

Note In the case of a duckling, very often when carving, the wing and breast are carved all in one portion.

7. GAME

a) **Grouse (Grouse)** Season 12th August—12th December.
Grouse is regarded as a particularly choice dish. If small it is generally served whole. Otherwise it would be split into two portions by carving down through the middle of the breast-bone.

b) **Partridge (Perdeau)** Season 1st September—1st February.
Depending on its size the partridge may be carved into two or three portions. If large the three portions would consist of (a) One leg and one wing with a little of the breast attached. (b) As far (a). (c) The breast left on the bone. If small it would be split into two portions by carving down through the breast-bone.

c) **Woodcock (Bécasse)** Season August—1st March.
Split into two portions as for Grouse or Partridge. Generally served on a croûte spread with a pâté made from the giblets of the Woodcock.

d) **Snipe (Bécassine)** Season August—1st March.
Served whole as Snipe are too small for carving into portions.

e) **Pheasant (Faisan)** Season 1st October—1st February.
The flesh of the pheasant is very dry and the waiter should use a very sharp knife. Remove the legs as for chicken or duck. These are normally not served. Carve in thin slices on either side of the breast down to the wing joint. One does not normally remove the wing as a separate portion.

f) **Wood Pigeon (Pigeon)** Season 1st August—15th March.
Carved in half through the breast to give two portions.

g) **Saddle of Hare (Selle de lièvre)** Season 1st August—28th February.
Carved in slices lengthwise as in a Saddle of Lamb. Flesh is dark in colour.

8. JOINTS

These would be carved on the carving trolley at the table. Mise-en-place as previously mentioned.

a) **Contrefilet de boeuf (Boned Sirloin of Beef)**

Carved in thin slices giving mainly lean meat and a little fat per portion. The beef itself should be a little underdone. The *accompaniments* offered would be roast gravy and Yorkshire pudding from the trolley and English and French mustard and Horseradish sauce placed on the table by the waiter.

b) **Aloyau de boeuf (Sirloin of beef on the bone)**

The portions here should be carved in thin slices down towards the ribs. On reaching a rib bone the waiter must release the meat attached to the rib bone by running the knife along the rib bone and between the rib bone and the sirloin. This then allows the slices of meat carved to fall free. The *accompaniments* offered would be as for a Contrefilet.

c) **Carré d'agneau (Best-End of Lamb)**

Carve two cutlets per portion. Hold the Carré firmly on the board by inserting a service fork into the base at one end of the Carré. Hold the Carré upright. Carve into cutlets using the exposed end of the ribs to guide you as to the correct amount per portion.

An alternative method is to lay the Carré flat on the board with the exposed end of the ribs pointing downward. Holding the carré firmly with a service fork and using the exposed ends of the ribs as a guide carve into cutlets. Give two per portion.

The *accompaniments* offered would be roast gravy and mint sauce.

d) **Selle d'agneau (Saddle of Lamb)**

There are two alternative methods of carving the saddle.

1. By removing the whole side loin from the saddle and then carving into slices parallel with the ribs and approximately 6 mm ($\frac{1}{4}$ in) thick, giving some lean meat and some fat per portion.
2. The alternative method is to cut down one side of the backbone reaching approximately halfway along the length of the saddle. Cut right down the side of the backbone to the short ribs. Where you have finished cutting half way along the backbone turn the knife at right-angles and cut down through the meat and fat. Now cut out lengths of meat from the saddle commencing at the backbone and paralell to the backbone where you made your intial incision. Work outwards to the edge of the saddle. Each wedge of meat that you cut out will then be carved into thin slices lengthwise.

Accompaniments offered would be mint sauce and roast gravy.

Note   With method
1. each customer is given a portion of some lean meat and a little fat, whereas, with method
2. if the waiter is not careful it is possible for one customer to have a portion of all lean meat and another customer receives nearly all fat and very little lean meat.

e) **Gigot d'agneau (Leg of Lamb)**

The waiter should remember here that initially he should carve onto the bone. Take a small 'V' shape portion of meat out just above the knuckle. Now proceed to carve your portions of meat by carving onto the bone from the 'V' shaped cut. This part of the joint is known as the 'nut' and is the most choice part. After the initial portions have been carved from the 'nut' of meat the suceeding portions should be carved, a slice from the 'nut' and a slice from the underside.

The accompaniments offered are roast gravy and mint sauce.
When carving a leg of lamb, to hold it steady on the board the waiter should hold the knuckle in a clean serviette.

f) **Cuissot de porc (Leg of Pork)**

Carved in a similar fashion to a leg of lamb.

The accompaniments offered are roast gravy, apple sauce and sage and onion stuffing.

9. SERVICE OF FLAMBÉ SWEET DISHES AND DESSERT AT THE TABLE

a) **Pêche flambée**

Cover	Dessert spoon and fork and a hot sweet plate.
Accompaniments	Castor sugar.
Equipment for Gueridon	Lamp, pan on an underplate, sauce ladle, matches, spare plate for dirty cutlery, Service spoons and forks on a service plate, one measure of brandy, castor sugar, portions of warmed peaches in peach syrup in a timbale.
Service	1. Place peach syrup in pan and heat.
	2. Add the portion of peaches.
	3. Pierce peaches with a fork to allow the heat to penetrate more quickly.
	4. Baste the peaches occasionally, allowing the peach syrup to reduce right down until it is almost caramelising.
	5. At this stage sprinkle with castor sugar. This speeds up the caramelising effect and aids flambéeing.
	6. Ensure the hot sweet plate is now placed in front of the guest.
	7. Pour over brandy and flambée.
	8. Serve from the pan on to hot sweet plates at the table, or serve on to hot sweet plates at the gueridon.

b) **Poire flambée**

As for above using pears and pear syrup instead of peaches and peach syrup.

c) **Banana flambée**

Cover	Dessert spoon and fork and a hot sweet plate.
Accompaniments	Castor sugar.

Equipment for Gueridon	Lamp, pan on an underplate, butter in a butter dish on a doyley on a sideplate, butter knife, matches, portion of banana, castor sugar, measure of rum or brandy, service spoons and forks on a service plate, Spare plate for dirty equipment, board, small carving knife (20 cm) (8 in).
Service	1. Place a banana on a board. Trim both ends of the banana.
	2. Slit the skin down the length of the banana, through to the flesh.
	3. Remove the skin.
	4. Cut the banana in two lengthways.
	5. Place the butter in the pan and melt.
	6. Pierce both halves of the banana with a fork, to allow the heat to penetrate more quickly.
	7. Place the banana in the pan and heat. Baste with the butter occasionally.
	8. At this stage place the hot sweet plate on the table in front of the guest.
	9. When heated sufficiently, flambée with the rum or brandy.
	10. Serve at the table from the pan on to the hot sweet plates, or serve on to hot sweet plates on the gueridon.

Note   Be careful not to overheat the banana at any stage.

d) **Cerises flambée au kirsch**

Cover	Dessert spoon and fork and a hot sweet plate.
Accompaniments	Castor sugar.
Equipment for Gueridon	Pan, lamp, matches, spare plate for dirty cutlery, portion of cherries in syrup in a timballe, sauce ladle, service spoons and forks on a service plate, castor sugar, measure of kirsch.
Service	1. Place the cherries and cherry syrup into the pan and heat.
	2. Reduce the cherry syrup to a minimum.
	3. Sprinkle with castor sugar to help caramelise the remaining syrup and to aid flambeeing.
	4. Place the hot sweet plates on the table in front of the guests.
	5. Add the kirsch and flambée.
	6. Serve at the table from the pan on to hot sweet plates, or serve on to hot sweet plates on the gueridon.

e) **Cerises flambée au glace vanille**

As above with the vanilla ice-cream being served immediately before the Cerises flambée.

f) **Cerises jubilées: Omelette soufflé aux cerises jubilées**

Cover	Dessert spoon and fork and a cold sweet plate.
Accompaniments	Castor sugar.
Equipment for Gueridon	Lamp, pan on an underplate, measure of brandy, silver dish containing portion of cherries in syrup, service spoons and forks, spare plate for dirty cutlery.

Service	1. As exact timing is required to serve this dish correctly ensure that your gueridon is correctly laid up with all your mise-en-place before commencing.
	2. Light lamp. Place portion of cherries in syrup in the pan and heat up to simmering point.
	3. Allow the syrup to reduce quickly until almost caramelised.
	4. When the syrup is reduced to a minimum sprinkle with castor sugar. This is an aid to flambéeing and speeds up caramelisation.
	5. At this stage the 'omelette soufflé' should be brought from the kitchen and served by the commis on to the cold sweet plate in front of the guest.
	6. The measure of brandy is now added to the cherries and they are flambéed.
	7. Serve immediately from the pan over the omelette soufflé.

g) Omelette au rhum

Cover	Dessert spoon and fork and a hot sweet plate.
Accompaniments	Castor sugar.
Equipment for Gueridon	Lamp, pan on an underplate, matches, spare plate for dirty equipment, service spoons and forks on a service plate, measure of rum, castor sugar, omelette: received from the kitchen on a silver flat, at the last moment. It should be cooked; baveuse.
Service	1. Present omelette—return to lamp.
	2. Trim the ends of the omelette with the aid of a service spoon and fork.
	3. Sprinkle with castor sugar.
	4. Pour the measure of rum round the edge of the flat.
	5. Heat quickly. Light with a match.
	6. Serve immediately onto hot sweet plates at the table or onto hot sweet plates on the gueridon.

h) Fraises romanoff

Cover	Dessert spoon and fork and a cold sweet plate.
Accompaniments	Castor sugar.
Equipment for Gueridon	Spare plate for dirty cutlery, service spoons and forks on a service plate, portion of strawberries in a silver dish, portion of double cream in a silver jug, one measure of orange curaçao or grand marnier, glass bowl.
Service	1. Pour the liqueur to be used over the strawberries and allow to macerate for a few minutes.
	2. Stir the double cream until it thickens.
	3. Remove two thirds of the strawberries plus the liquid into a glass bowl and cream together with the aid of a service fork.
	4. Add the thickened double cream a little at a time until the mixture is firm.

5. Set onto a cold sweet plate and decorate the top with the remaining strawberries. Sprinkle with a little castor sugar.
6. Serve.

Alternative method

1. Stir the double cream until it starts to thicken.
2. Place two thirds of the strawberries in the glass bowl with the portion of thickened cream.
3. Cream together with the aid of a service fork, blending the strawberries and double cream well together.
4. Allow to macerate for a few minutes: this mixture should now be firm.
5. Add the measure of liqueur. (orange curaçao or grand marnier)
6. Blend well together.
7. Set neatly onto the cold sweet plate.
8. Decorate the top with the remaining strawberries.
9. Sprinkle with a little castor sugar and serve.

i) Ananas rafraîche au kirsche flambée

Cover

Hot fruit plate or sweet plate and a fruit knife and fork or a dessert spoon and fork.

Accompaniments

Castor sugar.

Equipment for Gueridon

Lamp, pan on an underplate, matches, knife, fresh whole pineapple, spare serviette, small knife and fork, measure of kirsch, sauce boat of sugar syrup on an underflat, sauce ladle, Service spoons and forks, spare plate for dirty cutlery.

Service

1. Place the sugar syrup in the pan and heat.
2. Place the whole pineapple on its side on the board and hold firmly with the aid of a clean serviette.
3. Trim the leaf end.
4. Cut the required number of slices per portion: approximately 6 mm ($\frac{1}{4}$ in) thick.
5. Remove the whole pineapple and the leaf end. Place the leaf end back on the cut end of the pineapple to keep moist.
6. With the aid of the small knife and fork remove the outer skin and then the core.
7. Pierce with a fork to allow the heat to penetrate more quickly.
8. Place the portion of prepared pineapple into the heated sugar syrup.
9. Allow to heat quickly reducing the liquid to the stage where it is almost caramelising.
10. At this point sprinkle well with castor sugar. This helps caramelise the sugar syrup and aids flambéeing.
11. Place the hot fruit or sweet plate in front of the guest on the table.
12. Pour over the kirsch, allow to heat, then flambée.
13. Serve onto the hot fruit or sweet plate from the pan, at the table.

j) Crêpes suzette

Cover
Dessert spoon and fork and a hot sweet plate.

Accompaniments
None.

Ingredients Two portions
85.05 grammes (3 oz) castor sugar | 85.05 grammes (3 oz) butter
2 Satzumas | Zest of 2 satzumas
½ Lemon | 1 measure of curaçao
4 Pancakes | 1 measure of brandy

Equipment for Gueridon
Lamp, pan on an underplate, service spoons and forks on a service plate, two teaspoons on a sideplate, two halves of lemon with the bases trimmed, two dessert forks on a sideplate, oval flat with a doyley for the portion of pancakes, oval flat with a doyley plus three small sauce-boats for the creamed mixture—orange juice—and lemon juice, brandy and liqueur glass on an underplate, one bottle of orange curaçao and one of brandy, two hot sweet plates.

Service
1. Pour out the required measure of liqueur.
2. Place the creamed mixture of castor sugar, butter and zest into the pan and melt.
3. Add the juice of half a lemon if required; according to taste.
4. Add one measure of curaçao.
5. Mix well stirring with a spoon: taste.
6. Place in the pancakes, one at a time, heat well, turn over and then fold.
7. During this process the sauce should be reducing all the time and thickening.
8. When the sauce is reduced sufficiently add the measure of brandy and flambée.
9. Serve onto the hot sweet plates from the pan, at the table.

10. DESSERT (FRESH FRUIT AND NUTS)

Cover
Fruit knife and fork, fruit plate, one finger bowl on a doyley on an underplate with cold water, or a small glass bowl if more than two portions of grapes are to be served, a second finger bowl on a doyley on an underplate containing warm water and a slice of lemon, spare sideplates for shells and skins etc., spare serviette, nutcrackers, grape scissors.

Accompaniments
Castor sugar and salt.

Service
Present the fruit basket to the guest allowing him to make his choice. If the guest chooses grapes the required portion will be cut from the main bunch, and held in the grape scissors, will be rinsed in the finger bowl or glass bowl containing the cold water before being placed onto the fruit plate. If the pineapple, oranges, pears or bananas are chosen then these may be prepared on the gueridon by the waiter.

a) **Salade d'Orange**—See also Salads, p. 200

Equipment required for the Gueridon Small very sharp knife, dessert fork, two oranges on plate, spare plate for dirty cutlery, small glass dish, fruit plate, board.

Accompaniments Castor sugar.

Service

1. Cut slice from one end of the orange with the aid of the sharp knife.
2. Pierce the cut slice with the fork to act as a guard when sectioning the whole orange.
3. Now pierce the whole orange with the fork from the uncut end, so that it is firmly held on the fork.
4. Make an incision around the uncut end of the whole orange through the skin to the flesh. (through the rind and pith).
5. Remove the peel and pith by cutting strips from the cut end to the incision made around the orange.
6. At this stage you should now have a whole orange on your fork with the peel and pith removed.
7. Holding the orange over the glass bowl cut out each section of the orange leaving the pith on the fork. Let the sections of orange fall into the glass bowl.
8. With the aid of a second fork squeeze the pith over the glass bowl to remove all the juice.
9. Sprinkle with castor sugar.
10. Dress onto the fruit plate and serve.

b) **Poire**

Service

1. Pierce the base of the pear with a small fork so that it is held firmly.
2. Remove the skin by cutting in strips from the stalk end to the base.
3. Cut the whole pear into quarters.
4. Remove the core.
5. Dress onto the fruit plate.

Note The pear may be left whole after removing the skin, if the customer so wishes. If this is the case do not remove the stalk.

27 revision exercises

A great deal depends on the individual teaching a subject as to whether it is interesting to his students. A student can only absorb a certain amount of information over the limited period of one lesson. This lesson must therefore be broken down into a series of steps, each one leading to the next and at the same time holding the students interest to such an extent that when the time comes he will ask questions concerning the subject under discussion. The steps may be listed as follows:

1. Introduction
2. Impart new knowledge
3. Conclusion
4. Questions

Depending on the time available it is always a great help to commence a lesson by recapping on the previous lesson, and this should act as a stepping stone for new information. Where possible a lecture should incorporate a demonstration of some sort as it is much easier to talk about something which can be seen.

Having introduced the new subject material to the student it must be endorsed and revised. How will you go about it? The obvious resort is—question and answer. This however is very often time-wasting and boring to the student as only one student is participating in the lesson at any one time. Other, less time wasting and out of the ordinary methods are required to capture the imagination of the class.

The following are a number of suggestions which, although initially causing the teacher some extra work, will I feel benefit the student by holding his interest rather than losing it:

Revision is achieved by

1. Finding the correct accompaniment
2. Crosswords
3. Objective revision tests
4. Distractors
5. 10 question tests
6. 'Right' or 'Wrong'
7. 'True' or 'False'
8. Individual tests

For example:

1. Find the correct accompaniment

DISH		ACCOMPANIMENT
1	Roast pork		Sause hollandaise
2	Curry		Castor sugar
3	Smoked eel		Chilli vinegar
4	Tomato juice		Sauce tartare
5	Turtle soup		Grated parmesan cheese
6	Spaghetti		Worcestershire sauce
7	Oysters	5	Sherry
8	Deep fried fish		Mango chutney
9	Asparagus	1	Apple sauce
10	Grapefruit cocktail		Horseradish sauce

The student is required to put the correct dish number in the centre column against the correct accompaniment, i.e.

The number 1 against roast pork would be placed in the centre column against apple sauce, as shown above.

Number 5 against turtle soup would be placed in the centre column against sherry, and so on. Can you complete it?

2. Crosswords

The crossword should be made up on subject matter already covered. The students working in pairs and given a limited time to complete the crossword. As well as encouraging teamwork, the competitive spirit prevails and enthusiasm grows. Can you complete them?

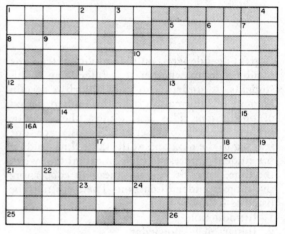

ACROSS

1. Double fillet steak (13)
2. A smoked one may be served as an Hors d'oeuvre (3)
3. A sweet dish ... Creole (6)
4. A 'BAD' one of these may cause complaints (3) (Anagram)
5. Qualification of a good waiter (10)
6. A cutlet—but not of meat (7)
7. A commodity made from sugar cane (5)
8. Type of restaurant service (8)
9. Serviette fold (4)
10. Term for a dry sherry (4)
11. Restaurant staff are split into these (7)
12. This together with 32 Down and 9 Down form a type of menu (1.2.5.)
13. French goose (3)
14. Wine butler (9)
15. Not the 'out' door (2)
16. A boned sirloin steak (9)
17. The necessary china, glass and cutlery needed for one person for a specific meal is known as a ... (5)

DOWN

1. Floor waiter (10)
18. Used as a flavouring agent (3)
19. A Dutch cheese (4)
20. Card used in cellar control (3)
21. 4½ gallons backwards (3)
22. Preparation beforehand (4.2.5.)
23. Used in buffet work (5)
24. 30 Down plus this may be served as an Hors d'oeuvre (4.4)
25. A complete dish in itself—served as received from kitchen (6)
26. A commodity made from milk (6)
27. Method of cleaning silver (7)
28. Term applied to sweet sherry (7)
9. See 12 Across (5)
29. Made from hops (3)
30. Offal (4)
31. Type of catering establishment (3)
32. See 9. Down (1)
33. A cutlet of salmon (5).

ACROSS

1. Accompaniment served with a class of soup (8)
6. Chump ...? (4)
8. Tropical fruit from the West Indies (5)
10. Part of an oyster cruet (7)
11. Served in a demi-tasse (4)
12. Made from Fuggles and Goldings (4)
13. ... sauté turbigo (6)
14. Second copy (9)
15. An abbreviation of Overproof (2)
16. Fish used in the making of Hors d'oeuvres (4)
17. Hunting sauce (8)
20. French goose (3)
21. Used in risotto (4)
23. Natural mineral water (7)
25. Spanish town famous for sherry (5)
26. This soup is served with the following accompaniments,—cheese straws, brown bread and butter, half lemon, warm sherry (6)

DOWN

1. French cheese from Normandy (9)
2. System of collecting waiter's gratuities (5)
3. 4½ gallons backwards (3)

4. All spirits are this (2)
5. French term for a 'clearing' waiter (12)
6. A long leaf lettuce (3)
7. Type of sweet sherry (7)
9. Root vegetable in French (5)
10. Mexican spirit obtained from cactus plant (7)
14. A cut from a round fish (5)
16a.Cross between a grapefruit and tangerine (4)

17. 'Fillers' and 'Binders' are parts of one of these (5)
18. Half-glaze sauce finished with mustard (6)
19. The floor waiter (6)
21. All the basic sauces are built up from this (4)
22. Best End without the 'é' (1)
24. ... ordinaire (3).

---

3. Objective revision test

This is a test which may be given as revision or taken in and marked as a form of classwork. Each student completes his own paper in the time allowed. This type of revision test covers a lot of information and therefore it is often better to mark the papers in class immediately the time allowance has expired and when any queries will be fresh in the students mind.

Can you complete the test correctly in 10 minutes?

Objective Revision Test

Instructions
Put your name (in BLOCK LETTERS) in this space
This part of the paper consists of a number of short exercises. In each exercise you are given three words or phrases, two of which are related and the third is an odd man out. You are required to underline the one that does not fit with the other two.
Some examples are shown below.

Example 1
Smoked salmon   *Petite marmite*   Melon
Here Petite Marmite is the odd one out, this is a soup and the other two are Hors d'Oeuvres substitutes.
Example 2
Benedictine   *Château Climens*   Chartreuse
Here Château Climens is the odd one out, it being a white wine from the Bordeaux area, whilst the other two are liqueurs.

Do NOT turn over until you are told to do so. You will be given 10 minutes to do as many as you can. You are not expected to do all, but you are advised to work steadily through the exercises omitting those which you cannot answer.

1. Chef de rang	Sommelier	Sous chef
2. O.K.	Mousseline	H.P.
3. A la carte	À l'Anglaise	Table d'hôte
4. Demi-tasse	Petit marmite	Consommé cup
5. Malvern	Ginger ale	Vichy
6. Carré	Suprême	Aloyau
7. Angels on horseback	Scotch woodcock	Buck rarebit
8. Melon	Petite marmite	Smoked salmon
9. Béarnaise	Choron	Vin blanc
10. Mango chutney	Brown bread and butter	Poppadum
11. Savarin	Baba	Genoise
12. Ginger beer	Tonic water	Perrier water
13. Grenadine	Raspberry syrup	Orange cordial
14. Benedictine	Chartreuse	Château Climens

15. Croissant	Danish pastry	Brioche
16. Gruyère	Camembert	Emmentaler
17. Clam chowder	Bisque des crevettes	Consommé celestine
18. Cona	Sautée	Filtre
19. Bronx	White lady	Mèdoc
20. Pommes duchesse	Pommes parmentier	Pommes croquette

4. Distractors

This is a method of revision whereby a question is asked and a number of suggested answers given, only one of which is correct. The number of suggested answers to each question is four, this being thought most suitable. The student has to tick or underline the answer he believes to be correct. This method of revision may again cover a wide area of subject matter and therefore it is in the students interest to correct the papers immediately they have been completed in a class.

After reading carefully each question, tick the answer 1/2/3/4 which you believe to be correct.

1. Worcester Sauce is an accompaniment with . . . .
   1. Tomato juice
   2. Orange juice
   3. Grapefruit juice
   4. Pineapple juice

2. Cassis is a fruit syrup with a flavour of . . . .
   1. Pomegranite
   2. Strawberries
   3. Blackcurrent
   4. Lemon

3. Parmesan is a hard, continental cheese from . . . .
   1. Belgium
   2. Italy
   3. France
   4. Switzerland

4. Carré d'agneau denotes. . . . .
   1. Saddle of lamb
   2. Leg of lamb
   3. Shoulder of lamb
   4. Best end of lamb

5. The amount of ground coffee required to make 1 gallon of black coffee . . . .
   1. 10 oz
   2. 8 oz
   3. 1 lb
   4. 14 oz

5. 'Ten' question test

Although we have said that the question-answer revision test is not very satisfactory it does not hurt to have one used now and again, especially if, after completion, the students can exchange papers with one another for marking. This is very often a challenge to the student who will endeavour to produce his best possible result knowing that a fellow student is going to see how well he gets on. As wide a variety of question as is possible should be asked.

REVISION TEST

Explain the meaning of the following menu terms:
   1. Entrecôte grillé
   2. Foie de veau

State the accompaniments to be served with:
   3. Saumon fumé
   4. Longe de porc rôti

What is the 'cover' a waiter should lay for the following dishes:
   5. Consommé royale
   6. Kari de boeuf madras

Miscellaneous:
   7. What are the two main types of menu?
   8. State 3 different sizes of tablecloth
   9. Where does the top copy of the wine check go?
   10. List 3 different ways in which coffee may be served.

6. 'Right' or 'wrong'

This is a variation on the straight forward

214

question and answer method of revision. A statement of fact is put before the student who has to make the decision. This form of question is not suitable for examination purposes but as a variation on a theme for revision purposes it may be used.

Read each statement carefully and then answer it by putting the word RIGHT or WRONG in the space provided.

1. Oil and vinegar are the accompaniments for hors d'oeuvres. . . . .
2. A waiter should position himself between the legs of a table in order to lay a tablecloth correctly. . . . .
3. A dessert spoon and fork and a hot fish plate is the cover required for spaghetti. . . . .
4. Gaelic coffee has rum added to it . . . .
5. The team of staff working together in a dining room is called a brigade. . . . .

7. 'True' or 'False'

This is a further variation on the question-answer theme above, the student having to answer each statement of fact by writing in the space provided.

Read each statement carefully and then answer it by putting the words TRUE or FALSE in the space provided.

1. Castor sugar is an accompaniment with cream cheese. . . . .
2. The waiter in charge of a station is the debarrasseur . . . .
3. A soup spoon is laid as part of the cover when a consommé is to be served. . . . .
4. Lager is a beer which should be served chilled. . . . .
5. Burnishing is a method of cleaning silver. . . . .

8. Practical individual tests

Wherever it is possible practical work should be carried out in conjunction with theory work in order that certain subject matter may be more easily retained by the students. The practical work may take the form of demonstrations or class/group participation. Where the students themselves participate it is best to give each one a selected task and a minimum amount of time to complete that task. When the time allowed has expired the class should study each task whilst the student concerned explains what he has done and gives his reasons. There are too many possible practical exercises to mention them all here, but the following are some examples.

1. Lay the cover for Oeuf en cocotte à la creme.
2. Lay a service salver in readiness for the service of orange squash in the lounge.
3. Cloth up a buffet and box the ends using two different methods.
4. Lay the cover for, and show how you would serve oysters to one guest.
5. In which glasses would you serve the following—
a) Tomato juice
b) Bass
c) Pimms
d) Draught beer
e) Whisky and ginger ale

Index